WHEN THE

SAINTS CAME

MARCHING IN

A History of
The Church of Jesus Christ
of Latter-day Saints
In Denton, Texas
1958 to 2008

GEORGE U. HUBBARD

Printed in the United States of America

Cover and Book Design by Crystal Wood

ISBN 978-0-9679779-3-9
Library of Congress Control Number: 2008940828

Denton Jubilee
The Church of Jesus Christ of
Latter-day Saints
Denton, Texas

CONTENTS

DEDICATION

This book is lovingly dedicated to

John W. and Margaret Porter

who truly magnified their callings
to establish the Lord's church in Denton
and nurture it to maturity.

PREFACE

In May of 2005, Elder Neil Anderson, one of the Presidents of the Seventy, and Elder Keith R. Edwards, of the Second Council of the Seventy, were General Authority visitors to a stake conference in the Denton Stake. The two visitors were Saturday night guests in President Andrus's home, and at breakfast on Sunday morning, Elder Anderson expressed curiosity about the origin and development of the Church in Denton. As part of the conversation, President Andrus told about the arrival of John and Margaret Porter and their roles in getting things started. He also made mention of the timely influx, through baptisms and move-ins, of leaders having just the right qualities and capabilities that were needed by the fledgling branch. Elder Anderson was fascinated.

"Has the history of the Church in this area been written?" he asked. "You must have it written," he added, "and when you do, I want to read it."

At one of the conference sessions that day, Elder Anderson further demonstrated his interest by publicly referring to some of the events of the early years, and he even referred to some of the principal participants by name.

A year and a half later, in the latter part of the year 2006, Elder Anderson and James Martino, former president of the Denton Stake, were in company with one another, and Elder Anderson still remembered about the Church's unique beginnings in Denton.

"Has that history been written yet?" he inquired of Brother Martino.

As a direct result of those conversations, the history of the Church in Denton now has been written, and I was given the special opportunity of writing it. The title, *When the Saints Came Marching In*, reflects those portions of the story that appealed especially to Elder Anderson. For Denton, the time and the season had arrived, and the saints truly did come marching in from many directions to quickly build up this part of Zion.

The story of the LDS Church in Denton is a remarkably unique story, and the hand of the Lord has been very evident in the things that transpired. In addition to building the Church from an almost zero beginning, those early LDS saints set an outstanding example of excellence for the dubious citizens of Denton.

The timing of this history is also significant. In November 2009, the Church in Denton will celebrate the fiftieth anniversary of its founding, dating back to the Sunday School organized by John and Margaret Porter. It is hoped that this history will be an integral part of the anticipated celebration.

Having been born and raised in Denton, and having done considerable exploring into Church history since my wife and I were baptized in 1951, I have a very special interest in the local history of The Church of Jesus Christ of Latter-day Saints in Denton. Compiling this history has been a spiritually uplifting experience for me, and I hope that those who read it will also find it spiritually rewarding and inspiring.

Finally, my greatest concern in compiling this history has been the realization that I would omit mention of people who really should be included. To these many dedicated and faithful members who fulfilled callings and blessed those about them, I offer my apologies in advance. I have tried to be all-inclusive in this, a daunting task.

— *George U. Hubbard*

The Church of Jesus Christ of Latter-day Saints
Milestones in Denton, Texas
1958 - 2008

The Formative Years

- Porter Family Baptized In Ft. Worth (12/6/58) — 1958
- Porter Family Moves to Denton (3/_/59) — 1959
- Denton Sunday School Organized (11/_/59) — 1959
- Denton Dependent Branch Organized (8/14/60) — 1960
- Denton Independent Branch Organized (1/22/61) — 1961
- Chapel Ground Breaking (3/2/63) — 1963
- Ragsdales Baptized (9/_/65) — 1965
- Chapel Dedicated (5/6/66) — 1966
- Denton Ward Organized (2/12/67) — 1967

The Development Years

- Elieson Family Arrives (8/_/67) — 1967
- Ft. Worth Stake Created (9/24/67) — 1967
- Martinos Baptized (12/7/67) — 1967
- Nobles Baptized (5/21/71) — 1971
- Building Addition Dedicated (11/10/74) — 1974
- Denton Ward Divided to form Denton 1st & Denton 2nd (7/20/75) — 1975

(continued next page)

Overall Timeline *(continued)*

The Growth Years

Timeline (1976 – 1992):

- Ft. Worth North Stake Created (11/14/76)
- Lewisville Stake Created (4/12/81)
- Denton 2nd Ward Divided to form Denton 3rd (11/14/82)
- Dallas Temple Dedicated (11/15/84)
- "Denton" Stake Center Dedicated (5/28/89)
- Denton Stake Created (5/3/92)

| 1976 | 1977 | 1978 | 1979 | 1980 | 1981 | 1982 | 1983 | 1984 | 1985 | 1986 | 1987 | 1988 | 1989 | 1990 | 1991 | 1992 |

The Expansion Years

Timeline (1993 – 2008):

- Denton 5th Branch Created (1/17/93)
- Regional Conference With Pres. Hinckley (3/17/96)
- Institute Building Dedicated 10/18/96
- Denton 4th Ward Divided to form Lake Cities Ward (2/18/97)
- Lake Cities Ward Divided to form Lake Cities 1st & 2nd Wards (10/13/02)
- Denton Sixth Branch Created (12/14/03)
- Justin Ward Created; Overall Realignment (1/1/07)
- Frisco Stake Organized (5/4/08)

| 1993 | 1994 | 1995 | 1996 | 1997 | 1998 | 1999 | 2000 | 2001 | 2002 | 2003 | 2004 | 2005 | 2006 | 2007 | 2008 |

Part One
IN THE BEGINNING

Introduction

*P*rior to 1958 when John W. and Margaret Porter moved to Denton, very little LDS church activity had taken place in Denton. The Dallas Stake was organized in October 1953, and Denton was geographically included within the Ft. Worth Ward, but there was no LDS organization in Denton.

From time to time, isolated LDS families lived for short periods in Denton, and a few LDS students attended the city's two universities. Although it is unlikely that the names of all the LDS families who sojourned here in those early years will ever be known; those that are known include the Fraims, the Hubbards, and the Thompsons . . . and representatives of those families are still here.

Before 1959, the only formal church organization in Denton was a Sunday School organized in October 1956, when the Merkleys of Logan, Utah, and the Ballards from California came to Denton. The Merkleys came for a year of graduate study at North Texas State College (now the University of North Texas). The Ballards, whose daughter was a student at Texas State College for Women (now Texas Woman's University), came on a temporary work assignment. Almost a year later, these two families left to return home, and shortly thereafter the Sunday School was disbanded for lack of priesthood leadership.

The Beginning Years of
The Church of Jesus Christ
of Latter-day Saints in Denton
Before 1958

Denton Events	Year	Area Events
	1952	
Fraims move to Denton Hubbards begin one year in Denton	1953	Dallas Stake Organized 10/19/53
Thompsons in Denton for a few weeks	1954	
	1955	
Merkleys & Ballards arrive First Sunday School Organized 10/21/56	1956	
Merkleys & Ballards leave 8/ /57 Trudie Swanson Baptized 9/19/57 First Sunday School Disbanded 9/ /57	1957	

CHAPTER 1
Creating the Dallas Stake

When the Fort Worth Branch was organized as part of the Texas Mission, Denton, along with Gainesville and Decatur, were among a large number of cities and towns included in the Branch's geographic jurisdiction.

As conversions increased and as church members moved into the area, it eventually became appropriate to organize the first Texas stakes outside of El Paso. In 1953, Apostles Mark E. Petersen and Delbert L. Stapley came to Texas and performed that task. Organizing the Dallas Stake on October 18, 1953, and the Houston Stake the preceding week, these two apostles set into motion an accelerated growth of the Church in Texas that has been magnificent to behold. The Houston and Dallas Stakes, the second and third stakes organized in Texas, followed the El Paso Stake which was organized in September of 1952.

Ervin W. Atkerson was called to be the first Stake President of the Dallas Stake. The Fort Worth Branch became the Fort Worth Ward, and Branch President Frank Hart became Bishop Frank Hart. The Fort Worth Ward's boundaries included Denton.

CHAPTER 2

Early LDS Presence in Denton

The Fraims

Jennis Fraim is the first known member of the Church to reside in Denton on more than a temporary basis. A life-long member of the Church, Jennis was born in McCornick, Utah,

where her father at one time was the bishop. Failing to survive drought and the economic effects of the Depression years, the community of McCormick ceased to exist, and Jennis' family soon found themselves in Salem, Utah, where Jennis spent most of her youth.

In her early twenties, Jennis moved to Salt Lake City to find employment, and it was while there during World War II that she met Roger Fraim, a native Texan,

Roger and Jennis Fraim
Jennis is believed to have been the first permanent LDS resident in Denton.

who was stationed as a soldier just outside of Salt Lake City. Following his discharge from the army at the end of the war, Roger brought Jennis to Texas where they were married on October 18, 1945. The newly-weds lived in several locations before finally settling in Denton in 1947. Their first child, Diana, was born in Corsicana before their move to Denton; whereas, their other three children, Dorcas, Janice, and Roger Jr. were born in Denton.

In 1949, four years after arriving in Texas, Jennis wrote to her father saying that in all that time she had never seen a Mormon church nor met a Mormon missionary. Her father quickly wrote to the mission office in Houston, and shortly thereafter, two LDS missionaries came from Dallas and knocked on the Fraim's door. Jennis happily accepted their gift of a *Book of Mormon,* as she had been without one since moving to Texas.

Wanting to canvass the Denton area for possible investigators, the missionaries asked if they could stay with the Fraims for a few days. They slept on the divan and Jennis included them in the morning and evening family meals. Having the missionaries in the home, however, was hard on Jennis. She had three young girls, and at that time she was pregnant with Roger, Jr. After a week, Jennis' husband, Roger, told the missionaries they would have to move on, and since they had not aroused interest from anyone in Denton, they went back to Dallas. Jennis was again without LDS contact until 1956 when the Merkleys and the Ballards arrived.

The Thompsons

Doyle Thompson Sr. and his wife, Nona, both grew up in Denton, and Doyle's parents owned the land where the Denton Stake Center on Old North Road now stands. Seeking opportunities in the north, Doyle, Sr. and Nona moved to South Dakota, and Doyle became a wheat farmer. None of the Thompsons were members of the Church at that time.

It was while they were living in South Dakota that an elderly Swede named Iver Sandberg introduced Doyle, Sr. and Nona to the Church. After reading all he could find about various Christian religions, Iver encountered a *Book of Mormon* which he read and believed. "Knowing" that the book was true, Iver traveled to Salt Lake City and requested baptism. Then back in

South Dakota, he took advantage of an opportunity to discuss Mormonism with Doyle Sr. and Nona.

"I know that the Church is true," Iver declared on several occasions.

"You may believe," Doyle Sr. remonstrated each time, "but you have no right to say that you know."

"I know it is true, and you can know it also," Iver always countered with a reference to Moroni 10:4.

Because of Iver's strong testimonies and his persistence, Doyle Sr. and Nona finally decided that they must put Moroni 10:4 to the test. Kneeling in fervent prayer one night, they promised to join the Church if the truthfulness of the gospel could be made known to them. Manifestations occurred that evening in their sleep, and before dawn, both were sitting up in bed saying "I am ready." Iver Sandberg performed the baptisms on Easter Sunday in 1948.

In short order, Iver and the Thompsons gathered, taught, and baptized about 15 families. A branch was organized at Gettysburg, South Dakota, where the Thompsons were living, and Doyle Thompson Sr. became its Branch President.

Pleasant memories of Denton remained with the Thompsons, however, so in the fall of 1954, they decided to return to Denton. Nona and four of their children came first. With no organization of the Church in Denton, the Thompsons attended church in the Fort Worth Ward, and they appealed to Bishop Hart to send missionaries to Denton. Prior missionary efforts in Denton had been quite unsuccessful, and missionaries were not sent at that time. Recognizing the need for a close church relationship in their lives, Doyle, Sr. came down to Denton, not to stay, but to gather Nona and the children who were here, and take them back to South Dakota.

where the Church was already established. The Thompsons remained in South Dakota for another eighteen years.

In 1972 when Doyle Sr. retired from farming, a Church unit now existed in Denton, and he and Nona returned to the Denton area and settled on family property in Argyle. Four of their six children also established homes in the Denton area.

As a postscript, five of the Thompsons's six children joined the Church shortly after their parents joined. Doyle Jr., however, saw no need for it in his life, and he held out for a number of years. In 1969, Doyle Jr., along with his wife, Joyce, also came into the church as a result of some very special spiritual experiences in their family.

Following his father's retirement, Doyle Jr. took over the farming operation in South Dakota, and he and his family lived in Denton during the winters and in South Dakota during the farming seasons. Doyle Jr. eventually became the first bishop of the Denton Fourth Ward when it was created in 1985.

The Hubbards

In August 1953, George and Billie Hubbard, along with their two infant children, returned to Denton. George had been born and raised in Denton, and he met Billie when she was a student at Texas State College for Women (now Texas Woman's University). Following his graduation from the University of Texas in June, 1950, George worked briefly in the east Texas oil fields, and then answered the call in December of that year to serve in the army during the Korean conflict. Two months later, as soon as Billie graduated from TSCW, she and George were married in Colorado Springs, Colorado, with parents and a few relatives attending.

The Spring of 1951 was very wet, and extensive floods wreaked havoc in parts of eastern Kansas and western Missouri.

George, who was assigned to a Corps of Engineers battalion, was sent to Fort Riley in Kansas to help clean up and make repairs. While he and Billie were living in an apartment in Junction City, Kansas, the missionaries came down the street knocking on doors. George and Billie both accepted the Gospel immediately. Billie was pregnant with their first child, and she was concerned that she had not yet felt life in the child, so she made a special request of the Lord. "If the Gospel is true," she prayed, "let me know by having the baby move." Shortly thereafter, when she lay down for a nap, she received a very definite kick from the baby. There were no more movements for a few weeks, and she again thought that the baby might be dead. It wasn't. But the continued lack of movement reinforced the "kick" that was the answer to her prayer.

George was transferred back to Colorado Springs where he and Billie were baptized on December 30, 1951. The interesting part of their baptism is that they had to request it; the missionaries never suggested it. A year later, George received the Melchizedek Priesthood, and he and Billie and their one child (at that time) were sealed in the Salt Lake Temple.

Following George's discharge from the army in December, 1952, the family spent eight months in Provo, Utah, where George, who was searching for what to do with his life, studied history at Brigham Young University. Although offered jobs at the Geneva Steel plant in Orem and with an electrical engineering construction firm in Ohio, George and Billie felt impressed to return to Texas and for him to prepare to become a school teacher. This they did, arriving back in Denton in August 1953.

While in Denton, the Hubbards attended church in the Fort Worth Branch which met in the LDS chapel on West Seventh Street in Fort Worth. After attending there for three or four months, George was called to teach the genealogy class in Sunday School. Then the following July, the Bishopric (Fort Worth was then a ward) approached George and asked if he would be willing to try to locate some Church members believed to be living in the Denton area.

With an assignment to locate three persons, George spent several days searching and visiting, and he succeeded in finding all three. One was a young man named Marion Hiskey, an Idaho golfer attending North Texas State College on a golf scholarship. Marion had a very promising future as a golfer, but unfortunately he was killed in a car accident the following year. The names of the other two members, however, are not remembered. One was a middle-aged lady living with her non-member husband in one of the tiny cottages that then existed on South Locust Street just south of Eagle Drive. The other was an elderly widow living in Krum. In all three cases, friendly conversations occurred, and a good spirit was felt.

What follow-up occurred after these visits is unknown. Shortly after reporting back to the Bishopric, George graduated from North Texas and left Denton to become a school teacher in Carlsbad, New Mexico. Billie had already left to spend a few weeks with her parents in Baytown, Texas, before giving birth to their third child.

CHAPTER 3

Organizing Denton's
First Sunday School

*O*n the fall of 1956, two LDS families — Charles and Margaret Merkley and John W. and Agnes Ballard — arrived in Denton for temporary sojourns. The Merkleys, who were faculty members at Utah State University in Logan, Utah, came to Denton to do graduate work in the School of Music at North Texas State College, as it was then known. John Ballard came for a temporary work assignment with a pharmaceutical firm in Dallas. Even though John was working in Dallas, the Ballards chose to make their home in Denton because they had a daughter who was enrolled in Texas State College for Women.

Having located a few other church members living in Denton, Brother Ballard made a request to Ervin Atkerson, Dallas Stake President, for missionaries to labor in Denton and for permission to organize a local Sunday School. Both requests were granted.

On October 21, 1956, seventeen people gathered in the home of Roger and Jennis Fraim at 1024 South Locust Street, and under President Atkerson's direction, they organized the first LDS Sunday School in Denton. After becoming organized, the group held weekly meetings at the Woman's Club building on Oakland Avenue.

The Sunday School organization continued in effect for the next eleven months. But when both the Merkley and Ballard families left Denton to return to their homes, the

Denton's First Sunday School
The home of Roger and Jennis Fraim, 1024 South Locust Street, where the first
LDS Sunday School in Denton was organized on October 21, 1956.

missionaries were removed from Denton, and the Sunday
School was discontinued for lack of Priesthood leadership.

With an organized Church unit no longer available in
Denton, the Fraims traveled to Fort Worth to attend Church
meetings of the Fort Worth Branch on West Seventh Street.
When the children were old enough, they were baptized, and
shortly thereafter, Roger also entered the waters of baptism.
Roger and Jennis and their children became stalwarts in
supporting the early development of the Church in Denton.

Just after the Sunday School was discontinued, the
missionaries baptized a Denton resident named Trudie
Swanson. It is believed that Trudie was the first person baptized
into The Church of Jesus Christ of Latter-day Saints in Denton.
She joined first, and eventually her husband, Riley, and four of
their six children also joined.

The Swansons' conversion story is similar in many aspects
to that of Joseph Smith's family. The Swansons were a religious

Trudie Swanson
with baby Ray

family. They were church attenders, and they were regular readers of the Bible. Frequently they read together, but sometimes Trudie would read to the younger children and Riley would read to the older children. The children became well acquainted with the Bible stories and with the characters in the Bible. Righteous living, along with honesty and integrity, were taught in the home, and Trudie taught her children that when faced with difficult decisions, to ask, "What would Jesus do?"

One Sunday afternoon the family was sitting around the dining table discussing what the preacher had said that morning, and family members became heated in disagreement with what they thought the preacher had meant by his message. Ellen, only five or six at the time, thought, "What's so hard about this? Just do what Jesus would do."

The Swanson Children
Ray (9), Margie (11), and Ellen (13) sitting at the table where
the missionaries taught them about five months later in 1960.

The Swansons' Home
at 1218 Avenue A, where the missionaries taught them.

Because Trudie was raised in a Baptist home, Riley had joined the Baptist church after marrying her. The Swansons, however, were not satisfied with any of the churches they knew. Just as Joseph Smith's family was searching for the right church, the Swanson family began a two year search. They sampled several churches searching for the "right" church. In her diary, Trudie wrote that she found good in all of the churches, but none of them seemed to be fully right.

Then one hot summer day Trudie looked out the window of her home at 1218 Avenue A, and she saw two young men dressed in suits trudging up the hill toward her house. They looked very hot and tired. Then came a knock on her door. Through the screen door one of the young men said, "We are from The Church of Jesus Christ of Latter-day Saints. May we come in and have a word of prayer with you?" Trudie sensed that there was something different about these two young men above and beyond their being dressed in "Sunday clothes," and she invited them into her home and immediately offered them ice water to drink.

The missionaries returned several times for discussions during those hot days, and Trudie thought to herself, "They must think a lot of my soul to go through all this suffering for me and for others." She was particularly impressed that they were doing this voluntarily and at their own expense.

Most of the missionary discussions were just with Trudie. Riley was not interested at that time. However, the three younger children, Ellen, Margie, and Ray, while staying out of sight, made sure they were close enough to hear everything, and they believed what they were hearing. Ellen, especially, recognized the truthfulness of the missionaries' messages, and she has written of her feelings and of an earlier event that gave rise to her feelings.

At the age of seven, Ellen attended church at one of Denton's Baptist churches, and on one Sunday she became quite disturbed by the pulpit pounding and the hellfire and damnation sermon delivered by the preacher that day. Then the preacher called Ellen's Sunday School class to stand up in front of the congregation, and he publicly asked each child, "You want to be saved, don't you?" The expected answer was a loud "Yes" which each child delivered until it became Ellen's turn. From her Bible stories and her training at home, she believed that little children are pure and innocent, that repentance is for people who have done something wrong, and that she had not done anything wrong. Ellen was also very shy, so finding herself unable to audibly respond to the preacher's question, she looked downward and simply shook her head, "No." The preacher was stunned, then recovering his composure, he went on to the other children. That afternoon, he visited Ellen's mother, Trudie, and informed her of the embarrassment in front of his congregation that Ellen had caused. After the preacher left, Trudie called Ellen in and asked why she had done what she did.

"Because I haven't done anything wrong," Ellen responded. Shaking her head, Trudie went into another room, and the incident was never again mentioned.

The incident, however, marked the beginning of a search by Ellen, a search for the kind of church that Jesus would organize. It had to have a prophet and apostles. It had to have temples. It had to baptize by immersion. It had to have other characteristics consistent with the way things were done when Jesus was on the earth. It was a search that Ellen pursued for five years until at the age of thirteen, she found herself listening, with Margie and Ray, to the LDS missionaries as they talked with Trudie.

When the missionaries talked about the appearance of the Father and the Son to a fourteen-year-old Joseph Smith, Ellen thought how true that was to patterns in the Bible. When she heard about baptism by immersion, she thought that is the way Jesus was baptized. To Ellen, the concept of apostles and prophets fit the pattern of the church Jesus organized. This church was "what Jesus would do." She prayed that her mother would join this church and not another that she was also investigating. In later life, Ellen commented that for the first time she was hearing about a church that was just like the one Jesus had organized, and that she was hearing answers to the various questions she had had about churches and religion.

Margie and James Swanson were equally religiously minded. Even before the missionaries contacted the Swansons, Margie, at the age of six or seven, had special feelings about attending church on Sundays.

"The whisperings of the Spirit led me to feel that God was pleased with me for going to church. I felt joy and peace as these feelings came to me," Margie has written.

Trudie accepted the gospel message as taught by the missionaries, and she was baptized on September 19, 1957. Even

Riley Swanson

though her husband, Riley, was not yet ready to join the Church, he surprised her by consenting to her baptism. He further surprised her by driving her to Dallas for the baptism in the LDS meeting house on Turtle Creek Drive. The family then began attending church in Fort Worth. (Baptisms for the other family members would come later.)

One evening, when the family was in their car at a grocery store, Margie asked if she could roll the window down because her father was smoking. Riley replied that she needed to get used to it because "your husband will smoke."

"No, Daddy, because I am going to marry a Mormon," she declared.

Little did Margie realize at the time how prophetic her declaration was. A few years later, when a student at BYU, Margie saw a young man who had a familiar look. Greeting him, she discovered that his name was Norman S. Lyman and that a few years earlier he had been a missionary in Denton and Gainesville. Margie recognized him from those earlier years. It didn't take long for that recognition to lead to romance and then to marriage in the Salt Lake Temple. Margie did, indeed, marry a Mormon.

The family continued attending church in Fort Worth until March 1959, when Denton's second Sunday School was organized. As will be seen, Trudie, and children Ellen, Margie, and Ray, were charter members of the Sunday School organized by John W. and Margaret Porter.

Part Two
THE FORMATIVE YEARS

Introduction

The period from December 6, 1958 to February 12, 1967 can be defined as the Formative Years of The Church of Jesus Christ of Latter-day Saints in Denton, Texas. The former date is the day John and Margaret Porter and their three children were baptized in the Ft. Worth Ward. The latter date marks the organization of the Denton Ward.

Three months after their baptism, the Porters moved to the Denton area, and under the auspices of the priesthood leadership of the Dallas Stake and the Ft. Worth Ward, the Porters immediately set about identifying and gathering Saints in Denton. From these efforts a Sunday School evolved in Denton, then a Dependent Branch, then an Independent Branch, and finally the Denton Ward.

Throughout these formative years, John and Margaret Porter were the prime movers, both in terms of missionary zeal and financial support. Margaret is quick to say, "We didn't do it. The Lord did it." While acknowledging the spiritual truth of her statement, it is nevertheless true that the Porters were the instruments the Lord used.

With stimulation from the Porters, a "can do" attitude prevailed among the small but enthusiastic local membership leading to the procurement of a temporary meeting facility and then to the construction of their own permanent meeting house. And the Porters' missionary zeal, which was high, extended not only throughout the Denton area, but also to Decatur, Gainesville, and Lewisville.

During these formative years there were many conversions and there were many move-ins. It was as though the Branch was a magnet attracting additional members. The following table, gleaned from the historical records in the Church's historical department in Salt Lake City, gives a good idea of the growth that took place in the Denton Branch.

Year	1961	1962	1963	1964	1965	1966
Total Membership	110	141	199	210	259	320
Convert Baptisms	25	20	16	20	40	38

Among these additions, special mention must be made of the conversion of Richard and Pat Ragsdale and their family, and of the arrival of Art and Carol Joy Cooper from southern Utah. Their stories will be given in separate chapters.

The following timeline will show the major events of this formative period and their time relationships to one another.

The Formative Years of
The Church of Jesus Christ of Latter-day Saints
in Denton
1958-1967

Denton Events	Year	Area Events
	1958	Porter Family Baptized 12/6/58
Porter Family Moves to Denton 3//59 **2nd Sunday School Organized 11/1/59**	1959	
Relief Society Organized 1/17/60 McKinney Street Building Obtained **Dependent Branch Created 8/14/60** Primary Organized 12/4/60	1960	
Independent Branch Created 1/22/61	1961	
Wilsons Baptized 3/28/62	1962	Meetings Began in Decatur, dependent on Denton Branch
Chapel Ground Breaking 3/2/63 First Meeting in Chapel 11/3/63	1963	
John R. Porter, First Missionary from Denton 6//64	1964	
Ragsdales Baptized 9/6/65	1965	Meetings Began in Gainesville, dependent on Denton Branch
Chapel Dedicated 5/6/66 Coopers Arrive 8//66 Institute Classes Began 9/28/66	1966	
Denton Ward Created 2/12/67	1967	Dallas Stake Divided and Fort Worth Stake Created 9/24/67

CHAPTER 4
Arrival of the Porters

John and Margaret Porter can appropriately be called the founders of the LDS Church in Denton. In November 1959, they were authorized to establish Denton's second Sunday School which, under the Porter's nurturing care, grew to a branch, then to several wards, and now to several stakes.

The story of the Porters begins with their meeting one another on a blind date in 1942. John, a captain in the U.S. Army Air Force stationed at Goodfellow Field in San Angelo, came to Dallas in the latter part of that year to visit friends at Southern Methodist University. Margaret Gorsuch was a student at SMU at the time. John's friends, who were acquainted with Margaret, suggested that he take Margaret out on a blind date, but when they approached Margaret with the idea, she balked.

"You don't have to marry him," the friends urged. "Just date him."

John and Margaret Porter

John and Margaret quickly found that they had several interests and characteristics in common, one of which was to act quickly if they felt something was right. On New Year's Eve, one month after their first date, John and Margaret were married. San Angelo became their first place of residence together.

During this same time period, an aunt and uncle of John's moved from Mackinaw, Illinois, to San Antonio for their health. In San Antonio, Aunt Kate and Uncle Lee became acquainted with some LDS families and began attending church with them. On occasional trips to San Antonio to visit his aunt and uncle, John would attend church with them. This was his first introduction to Mormonism. Although John knew nothing about the LDS doctrine, he was impressed with the friendliness of the people and with their strong family orientation.

Toward the end of his service in the Air Force in World War II, John had a very interesting, but very "hush-hush," assignment. Stationed at Wendover Field in the salt flats west of Salt Lake City, John found himself in an environment quite different from the other air bases where he had previously served. The strictest security measures were in force, even to the point of discharging a few servicemen of questionable integrity. In response to Margaret's questions, John could only respond that "you will hear about it in the news one day, and you will immediately know what it is."

On August 6, 1945, Margaret knew. While on a visit to some of John's relatives in Mackinac, Michigan, Margaret heard the radio news reports of the dropping of the atomic bomb on Hiroshima, Japan. Colonel Paul Tibbets flew the bomber which he had named the Enola Gay after his mother. John's role had been to engineer the bomb bay mechanisms so that the bomb would detonate exactly 1,000 feet above Hiroshima. A master at improvising and fixing things, John did his work to perfection. Following a second strike three days later at Nagasaki, the war ended, and our boys started coming home.

After being discharged from the Air Force, John and Margaret lived in several places in Texas, including a brief sojourn in Denton. Returning first to San Angelo, John leased and operated the parking garage at the Cactus Hotel. With a love for buying and selling, he next went into the used car and the surplus war material businesses. With his knack for successful buying and selling, John made several trips to Texarkana to buy surplus properties at the government disposal depot, and he usually had the items sold in San Angelo before his checks to the government cleared. During the war John and Margaret had amassed substantial savings in war bonds which greatly helped them during this period of transition. Margaret adds that this proclivity for saving served them well throughout all their later years. Soon, they had saved enough money for John to buy his first automobile dealership.

John started with a Lincoln-Mercury dealership in Graham, Texas. His preference, however, was to own a Chevrolet dealership which he eventually obtained in Munday, Texas. Munday, a small town, had a bumper crop of wheat that year, and money was plentiful. John sold everything he got his hands on. After several visits to the Dallas Chevrolet office and with a spectacular sales record, John acquired the Chevrolet dealership in Dallas on Mockingbird Lane across from the Dr. Pepper bottling plant. His star was rising high.

John was willing to sell almost anything for the right price. One day, the right price came along for his Dallas dealership, and he sold it. (The facility, now known as Friendly Chevrolet, still exists.) After selling the Dallas dealership, John and Margaret moved to Sherman where they met Dick and Pat Ragsdale. A life-long friendship blossomed between the two families which later was to have a significant bearing on the rise of the Church in Denton. While living in Sherman, John bought a Pontiac dealership in Fort Worth, and the family moved to Denton where they bought a house at 517 Roberts Street. Then two years later, John acquired a Buick dealership in El Paso. Commuting to El Paso, even on an occasional basis, was out of the question, so the Porter's next move was to El Paso.

In El Paso, John and Margaret were quite active in the Methodist church, and they each taught Sunday School classes. During this time, however, they both became quite inquisitive about religious doctrine, and they began searching for a faith that would satisfy their beliefs and their questions. When their own Methodist pastor was unable to respond satisfactorily to their questions, they became even more inquisitive. Gathering pamphlets and other literature from a variety of Christian faiths, they read and they studied, but satisfying answers to their questions were still not forthcoming. Then in April 1956, John's Aunt Kate reentered the scene.

Aunt Kate, now an LDS member herself, had been in the Los Angeles area serving a Church mission, her husband having previously died. On her way back to San Antonio following her release, she stopped in El Paso, thinking to spend two days with John and Margaret. Noticing the variety of church literature the Porters were studying, Aunt Kate knew they were searching, and her planned two day visit turned into two weeks of intensive questions, answers, and discussions. This time, however, things were different. John and Margaret were getting satisfying answers to all their questions. The Porters had never before heard of Joseph Smith and the story of his vision of the Father and the Son, nor of the appearances of the other heavenly messengers who appeared to him in western New York between 1820 and 1830.

"Aunt Kate, surely you don't believe those things," the Porters insisted.

But she did believe it, and she assured them that she knew them to be true. Margaret thought to herself, "I would give anything to be that sure of my beliefs!"

Kate gave the Porters a copy of *The Book of Mormon* when she left to return to San Antonio. Margaret and John both read the book, and the Spirit bore witness to them that the book was true. From that point on, the LDS Church would be the church for them.

Soon after Aunt Kate's visit, the Porters moved to Fort Worth where John had purchased a Pontiac dealership. But even though they lived within walking distance of a Methodist church, they discontinued their church attendance. Each Sunday morning their three children, Ann, Betty, and John R., put on their church clothes and walked to church without their parents. When asked if you are going with us, John and Margaret simply said, "No." The children were bewildered and concerned.

The Porter Children
Ann, John R., and Betty

Then on Christmas Eve of 1957, John and Margaret called their children together in a family council. They explained why they had not been going to the Methodist church with the children. They told the children about the new gospel – the gospel as taught by The Church of Jesus Christ of Latter-day Saints – which Aunt Kate had taught them. They rehearsed to the children the story of Joseph Smith and the First Vision. They explained about the *Book of Mormon*, its teachings, and its account of God's dealings with the peoples of the Western Hemisphere. For slightly over a year and a half, they (John and Margaret) had been prayerfully considering all these things, and now they were wholehearted believers. Then they made their grand announcement.

"From now on we are going to the Mormon church."

It was a family council that still provides poignant memories for John R., Ann, Betty. John R. still remembers lying in bed that night pondering on the things his parents had related.

"It was so strange, — so bizarre," he remembers, "and yet so compelling. One thing I knew for sure," John R. continued, "I knew that my parents fully believed it."

Although the Spirit began to bear witness to John R. that night, it never occurred to him (almost thirteen years old at the time) that he would later serve a full-time mission, become a branch president, and then be a bishop in this new church.

Now the children understood why their parents had stopped attending church, and they understood why there would be a change of direction. Even so, they were not very happy about leaving their friends at the nearby Methodist church, but after their first Sunday at the Mormon church, they became enthusiastic about the change. They said, "At this church we didn't just color. We really learned something."

The Porters found the LDS people to be friendly and welcoming. John and Margaret attended the Investigator's Class which was taught by a man also in the automobile business, so he and John spoke the same language. When asked about having the missionaries visit them, the Porters said it wasn't necessary because they were already converted.

After attending church meetings at the Fort Worth Ward for a year, the Porters were ready to make a lifetime commitment. Much of the credit for their decision goes to Dean Hatfield and Marcus Peterson and their families, who tirelessly friendshipped the Porters. The parents and all three children were baptized at the same time on December 6, 1958. It was two and a half years since Aunt Kate's visit in El Paso.

John and Margaret had become fully committed to the gospel, as evidenced by his feelings about working on Sunday. Acting against almost everyone's advice that he would "lose his shirt," John decided that his automobile agencies should be closed on the Sabbath day. He and Margaret both agreed in later years that instead of losing customers, his business volumes actually increased after taking that action.

In March 1959, three months after their baptism, John and Margaret Porter returned to their house at 517 Roberts Street in Denton. (This is the location where a second branch of the Church would be organized later that year.) Because there was no operating unit of the Church in Denton at that time, the Porters drove from Denton to Fort Worth twice on Sundays for Priesthood and Sunday School in the mornings and Sacrament Meeting in the late afternoons. They also made three other trips each week to Relief Society, MIA, and Primary.

"It was a lot of driving, but it was so worth it," Margaret later reported.

The Methodist minister in Denton remembered John and Margaret from the first time they had lived there, and when he learned that they were back in town and that they had joined the Mormon church, he called on them.

"How could you let two nineteen-year-old boys influence you to that extent?" he queried. "And you should have given me equal time to teach you."

"We weren't taught by nineteen-year-old boys," Margaret responded. "And as for equal time, I have been a Methodist for 38 years, and very little doctrine did I hear."

It would be appropriate to close this chapter on the Porters with Margaret's testimony written in 2007.

The Church of Jesus Christ of Latter-day Saints is true. Our family thanks Heavenly Father every day for our membership, and we have learned and experienced so much in the past 48 years.

The truth is restored to earth through the Prophet Joseph Smith with all of its powers, authorities, and keys. We revere him and all of those who have followed him as apostles and prophets of God bearing witness that Jesus is the Christ, and this is His church.

CHAPTER 5
Organizing Denton's Second Sunday School

After arriving in Denton in March 1959, the Porters continued attending church in the Fort Worth Ward because there was no Church organization in Denton at that time. Additional Latter-day Saint families, however, were now believed to be living in the Denton area, and President Atkerson of the Dallas Stake felt that the Porters were the right people for another "search and find" operation. He accordingly passed a list of names to Bishop N. Marcus Peterson, the Fort Worth Ward's second bishop, with the suggestion that the Porters try to make contact with the people listed.

The Porters went to work in earnest. After contacting most of the names on the list, they also went to Denton's two universities and located LDS students by checking student names and religious preference information in the registrar's offices. Delighted with the Porter's report, President Atkerson felt that enough people had been located for another Sunday School to be organized in Denton. He also felt that John and Margaret Porter were the right ones to lead the Sunday School.

On Sunday, November 1, 1959, twenty-three people met in the Porter home at 517 Roberts Street in Denton to organize Denton's second Sunday School. In addition to Bishop Peterson and the three members of the Dallas Stake Sunday School Superintendency, the attendees included John W., Margaret, John R., Ann, and Betty Porter; Bill, Myrtle, Pamela, and Karen Pate; Alvis Melchior; Trudie, Ellen, Margie, and Ray Swanson.

Planting the Permanent Roots
Home of John and Margaret Porter, 517 Roberts Street, where the
second LDS Sunday School in Denton was organized on November 1, 1959. It was this Sunday School that grew into the Church
organization that now exists in Denton.

From North Texas State University, Martin Guillot, Bill
McGinnis, and Carol Wilhite attended, along with Ann
Musgrove and Pat Thompson from Texas Womans' University.
The group was organized into a dependent Sunday School to
be attached to the Fort Worth Ward. John W. Porter was called
to be the local presiding authority. Although the Denton saints
would still have to travel to Fort Worth to attend other types of
meetings, they considered their new Sunday School a giant step
in the right direction, and they were delighted.

Instead of being satisfied with what they had already
accomplished, the Porters went out with added enthusiasm,
and within the week, they located additional LDS families,
including the Fraim family of Denton and the May family of
Keller. It quickly became apparent that the Porter's home did
not have sufficient space for the Sunday School meetings, and
a larger facility was needed.

Looking around Denton, Brother Porter located a vacant
two-story building (the former Jack Schmitz Mortuary) at 111

Planting the Permanent Roots
Early meeting location (as it looks in 2008) for the Denton Sunday
School and the Denton Branch, 111 West McKinney Street.
Formerly the Jack Schmitz Funeral Home.

West McKinney that he felt would be suitable for the meetings,
classes, and social functions of the Denton saints. John
succeeded in making arrangements with the Denton County
National Bank, owner of the building, to let the Sunday School
meet there free of charge. Having a meeting facility for their
exclusive use proved to be a significant strengthening factor
for the Sunday School. Before long, however, the bank found
a buyer for the building, and when the bank announced its
intention to sell, the Porters knew that losing this building
would be a severe blow to the functioning and growth of the
church in Denton. After searching in vain for another suitable
meeting facility, John bought the building himself so that the
Sunday School would not have to be displaced.

Now that it was their own building, the Saints were free to
do some remodeling, and considerable improvements were
needed. There had been a musty smell throughout. The roof
leaked, and when rain water got onto the upstairs red carpet,

the red leaked through and stained the downstairs ceiling. Kenneth Arrington, who was present at the time, tells of one meeting during which the rain was coming down heavily. As the speaker spoke about Christ's blood atonement, drops of red liquid began descending down the walls of the room. It made quite an impression on those in attendance.

Another unique oddity involved an old microphone system that the members used in their meetings. The police station was only a half block away, and occasionally the microphone system picked up police calls and broadcast them to the congregation at inappropriate times such as during the sacrament or during prayers.

There were other surprises from time to time. For example, while some of the youth were exploring the building, they found a child's casket that had been tucked away in a closet and left behind and forgotten. Ann Musgrove, a TWU student, taught a class of eight- and nine-year-olds in one of the upstairs rooms. Whenever the children would begin to lose interest, Ann could quickly regain their attention by discussing some of the embalmings that must have taken place in that very room.

Nevertheless, it was now their own building, and they set about making needed improvements. The chapel was downstairs, and the upstairs rooms were outfitted for Primary and Sunday School classes. It wasn't the best of facilities, but the Denton saints felt blessed to have a home of their own. It was a place for worship and also a place for sociality. The sociality even extended out of doors when they would erect a volley ball net and play in the parking lot on the west side of the building.

For the Porter family, Saturday activities always included going to the "mortuary" to clean it and prepare it for the Sunday services. Margaret insisted that the folding chairs in the chapel be lined up perfectly and that hymn books be laid out squarely on every other chair. She also used Saturdays to print the Sunday Bulletin on the primitive copying system available to her. Because the "mortuary" did not have a baptism font, special arrangements had to be made to accommodate converts who were ready to join the church. Frequently, those involved traveled to the Fort Worth Ward building on Seventh Street in Fort Worth. Brother Porter also made arrangements with the Christian Church on Fulton Street in Denton to use their font. Friendly relations existed between that church and the Mormons.

The three young Swanson children, Margie, Ellen, and Ray, were among the first baptisms. They had wanted to be baptized ever since their mother, Trudie, had joined the Church. Now that all three had reached the age of accountability, Margie expressed her desire to Brother Porter. He felt, however, that they should first have a deeper understanding of the gospel, so again, the missionaries began to visit and teach in the Swanson home. Margie, Ellen, and Ray were baptized in 1960, almost three years following their mother's baptism. Riley, their dad, was still not quite ready.

The Porters, as new converts, had no prior experience in administering the affairs of the Church, and the Lord provided help at the time when it was needed. Having Alvis Melchior as one of the charter members of the Sunday School was a Godsend. He was helpful to the Denton saints in many ways. Although no one remembers where he came from nor when he arrived in Denton, Alvis and the Porters found one another.

"Alvis Melchior was a rock," Margaret Porter declared in describing Alvis' contributions to the early Church in Denton. He was a high priest, and he and his wife were life-long church members. "He was the only one we had who had prior experience in the Church and who knew how the affairs of the gospel should be administered," Margaret added. "We relied on him greatly, and he was a wonderful help."

As one example, Brother Melchior understood the concepts and objectives of home teaching (then, ward teaching), and he taught by example as well as by counsel. At a later date, when the Ragsdales joined the Church, Alvis Melchior became their ward teacher.

"Alvis was one of the best ward teachers we ever had," reminisced Dick and Pat Ragsdale. The Ragsdales reported that Alvis always came with a message for the children, and he always came with a paper bag containing some kind of surprise for the children.

"We never had any trouble gathering the children when he came," Dick chimed in. "When he came, the children were excited to see him."

Besides being a stalwart in those early days of the Sunday School and the Branch, Brother Melchior had a reputation for being able to fix anything. A tin smith by trade, his skills were much in demand. It is said that Alvis always took his hammer, saw, and tool kit when visiting Branch members. For example he made several ninety mile round trips up to Sivells Bend on the Red River to fix home appliances for one of the Branch members. He also made a portable cabinet on wheels to contain the Church library at that time, and the cabinet was wheeled each week to the inner entrance of the meeting hall so its contents could be made easily available to all who came. He is also remembered for having used his tinsmith talents to make a replica of the golden plates according to his understanding of how they might have looked.

As the Sunday School organization increased in size and strength, the saints began to function in additional capacities.

For example, on January 17, 1960, sixteen sisters met together and, under the direction of the Priesthood, organized a Relief Society for Denton with Margaret Porter as President. For the first year they held meetings at night. Their work meetings were devoted mostly to making things to sell at bazaars which they held annually on the side walk in front of the old J. C. Penney store on the north side of the "Square."

Following the organization of the Sunday School, LDS missionaries were again assigned to Denton, and under their direction, local Sacrament Meetings were held for the first time. As a result of proselyting by the full-time missionaries and also by the Porters, Church membership in Denton grew, and by the end of the summer of 1960, it was time for the Denton Sunday School to become the Dependent Denton Branch. Only a year and a half had elapsed since the second Sunday School was organized.

The Branch continued meeting in the mortuary building until their new building on Malone Street was completed four years later.

CHAPTER 6
Organizing the Denton Branch

*B*y the end of the summer of 1960, the Denton Sunday School had grown sufficiently for the unit to carry out a full church program. Therefore, on August 14 of that year, Dallas Stake President Atkerson returned to Denton and organized the Denton Branch which would be a dependent unit attached to the Fort Worth Ward. John W. Porter was installed as Branch President of the dependent branch.

The Relief Society was already organized and functioning, and within a few weeks, the Primary (for 3-11 year olds) and the Mutual Improvement Association (MIA) (for teenagers) were also organized. The Branch followed the typical meeting schedule in use at that time: Priesthood and Sunday School were held on Sunday mornings, and Sacrament Meeting was held on Sunday afternoon. The other auxiliaries met on weekdays.

The Denton Branch remained a dependent branch for only five months. By January 1961, it had sufficient membership and priesthood strength to function independently. So

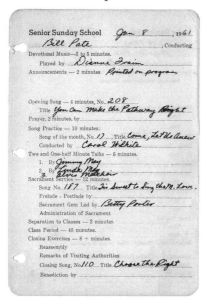

Sunday School Planning Agenda
for the Denton Branch,
January 8, 1961

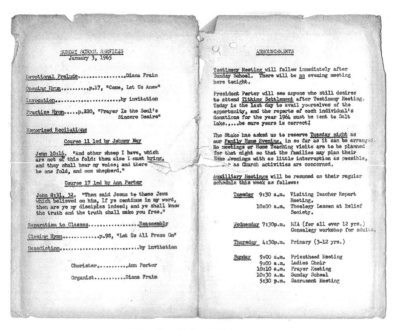

Sunday School Program
for the Denton Branch, January 3, 1965

President Atkerson came again, and on January 22, 1961, the Denton Branch became an independent branch to function and thrive under its own leadership. A full Branch Presidency was organized with John W. Porter as Branch President, Maurice Arrington as First Counselor, and Billy Joe May as Second Counselor. Bert Murphy became the Branch Clerk. (Alvis Melchoir later replaced Brother May in the branch presidency.)

Maurice Arrington, of whom more will be said in a later chapter, was a life-

Original Branch Presidency of the Denton Branch
John W. Porter, president; Bert Murphy, clerk; Maurice Arrington and Billy Joe May (counselors).

time member of the Church, having grown up in the Kelsey colony in east Texas. Maurice and Edleweis White, the girl he would eventually marry, lived only two miles apart during their youth. Raised in the Church of Christ, Edleweis joined the LDS church in 1949, five years after marrying Maurice. In 1962, they sealed their marriage in the Salt Lake Temple.

Although far removed from the center of Mormon activity in Utah, the Kelsey saints were a proud group of members descended from early converts in Georgia and Alabama. When migrating from Alabama to join the main body of Saints in the Great Basin, these converts found east Texas so much to their liking, that many of them decided to settle there. And their descendents are still there. Discounting Lyman Wight's ill-fated colony that settled in the Austin, Burnet, and Fredericksburg areas, the Kelsey saints claim to have been the first loyal LDS settlers in Texas and the oldest continually functioning LDS colony in Texas.

Billy Joe May and his family were baptized in Fort Worth in 1954. Although moving to Arlington and then to Keller where Bill still lives, the Mays continued attending the Fort Worth Ward until 1959 when Bishop Peterson suggested that Brother May and his wife, Virginia, could be a

The May Family
Another of the pioneer families in the
Denton Branch
Back Row: Jim, Billy Joe (dad), Linda
Middle Row: Mary, Virginia (mom), Ann
Front Row: John, Paul, Kathy

big help to the fledgling Denton saints by meeting and participating with them in Sunday School and in their other activities. The Mays accepted the call and began driving to

The Murphy Family
Bert and Joyce, with daughters
Terri Ann and Kelli.

Denton each Sunday for Church meetings. Sister May also drove their children from Keller to Denton each mid-week for Primary.

Bert and Joyce Murphy arrived in Denton in August of 1960, and stayed for four years. Bert came as an Air Force officer assigned to the Air Force ROTC at North Texas State University. One of their two children, Terri Ann, is the first child born into the Denton Independent Branch. Joyce, who is a niece of Alvis Melchoir, remembers attending lots of spaghetti dinners and bazaars in the branch.

"We loved Denton. We loved the people there," she recalls.

The Pate family also deserves special mention as stalwarts in the Branch. As charter members of the Sunday School when it was organized in 1959, the Pates were among the leaders in the newly organized independent branch. In the Branch Conference held on June 30, 1961, Myrtle Pate was sustained as Relief Society President, following Margaret Porter who became Young Women's President. Bill Pate was sustained as Sunday School

The Pate Family
Above, Bill with daughters Pam and Karen; below, Myrtle with Karen and Pam.

Superintendent, following John Porter. Virginia May was sustained as Primary President.

"It was a fun time," Myrtle remembers. "I especially enjoyed the testimony meetings."

The Porters, while still the main catalysts, were receiving needed help.

Membership in the Branch grew. Twenty-four convert baptisms were reported in 1961, including those of Jeanette Turner, wife of Doug Turner, on August 26, and Roger Fraim, husband of Jennis Fraim on December 31. Convert baptisms numbered twenty in 1962 and included Hoyt and Clara Wilson on March 28. Sixteen more converts were added in 1963.

Church attendance at the mortuary in Denton also included a few members who drove in from Decatur. Luke and Anna Parrish came from Decatur when there was no Church

Luke Parrish

organization for them there. Brother Parrish quickly became a favorite among the youth in the Denton Branch. Known as the "Candy Man," he always had a pocket full of candy, which he delighted giving to the kids.

With regard to music, the Denton Branch started with almost nothing. Carol Wilhite, a UNT music student, provided the only trained musical leadership. Ten year old Diana Fraim, whose feet could barely reach the pedals, provided the piano accompaniment. Carol organized a branch choir, and she taught the members how to sing. To teach the untrained choir members to make pleasant sounds while singing, Carol urged them to sing as though they had a "hot potato" in their mouths, thus keeping their mouths open and round. Initially a choir of sisters, they practiced each Sunday morning while the brothers met in Priesthood Meeting. Later when male voices were added, the choir became a source of intense pride within the Branch. They were especially thrilled when invited to provide the music for a Dallas Stake conference, and they became a special feature at branch and ward conferences.

The Milk Maids . . .
Ellen Swanson, Diana Fraim, Margie Swanson and Ann Porter provided memorable entertainment.

. . . and their Cow
as interpreted by
Janice and Dorcas Fraim.

On one occasion, the Branch responded to an invitation to provide entertainment during a break at one of the stake dances. Such entertainment was a common custom at that time. Four young Denton women, Diana Fraim, Ann Porter, Margie Swanson, and Ellen Swanson, performed a number called, "The Milk Maids," which Ann Musgrove, one of the Branch members who was a dance major at TWU, choreographed for the occasion. Any skit involving milk maids would, of necessity, need a cow also. Janice Fraim and her twin sister, Dorcas, with appropriate costuming, served as the front end and back end of the cow. The experience gave Branch members an elated and well deserved feeling that they could do anything the larger wards could do.

"Papa and the Playhouse"
Presented by the Dallas Stake, the production featured Denton participants.

Even in their infancy as a branch, the Denton saints participated in as many stake functions as possible. Individuals drove frequently to Dallas to participate in Dallas Stake productions such as "Promised Valley" and "Papa and the Playhouse." "Promised Valley," produced in the summer of 1963, evokes special memories among Denton participants because of Clayne Robison, who played the lead role of Jed. Brother Robison, a member of one of the Dallas wards, mesmerized the other cast members with his commanding presence and voice. He later became a Professor of Voice at BYU, and he is an author and lecturer in the science of creating beautiful music. Denton participants in "Papa and the Playhouse" included Margaret Porter and Don Clements in the cast along with Ellen Swanson and Dorcas Fraim assisting with scenery construction.

DeLynn Decker, another of Denton's early converts (1965), also made contributions for which she is well remembered. Having a flair for drama, DeLynn helped write scripts for roadshows and skits.

DeLynn combined with Keith Myrick, another Denton convert, to write the script for "Lil' Red and the Riding Hood," which told the traditional story in a modern-day setting. The set included a large lighted sign flashing "Granny's." Audiences roared with delight when Myrick, playing the part of the hood, roared onto the stage on a motor bike. Diana Fraim, clad in a red sequin body suit, was Lil' Red, and John R. Porter played the part of the wolf.

DeLynn remained in Denton until 1967 when she left to study English and drama at BYU. In 2009, she plans to retire as a high school English teacher in the Provo public school system.

Brother Myrick also wrote poems of a humorous nature which became regular features at branch social functions. His poem, "A Song to the Saints," is a typical example.

A Song to the Saints

Hey, Ma, look at them Mormons, ain't they fine?
A workin' an' a teachin' and a helpin' all the time.

You kin be a Mormon, Ma, they ain't much to it.
Jest knuckle down, buckle down, an' do it, do it, do it.

You kin be a Mormon, Ma, Yessiree bob.
But if you git to be one then yer gonna git a job.

Like them missionaries, ain't they swell?
Teachin' and a preachin an' really givin' folks …lessons.

Jest lookit them Elders, ain't they neat?
Knockin' them door panels up and down the street.

Up town, down town, workin' for the Lord.
Passin' out Mormon books, and settin' up flannel boards.

An' lookit them Deacons, ain't them little dickens cute?
Some's dressed up in they Boy Scout suits.

Mowin' that grass an' pullin' them weeds.
Sprucin' up the Church yard, an' a doin' good deeds.

Lookit that Seventy, Ma, ain't he a dude?
Workin' genealogy and storin' up food.

Lookit them Stake Boards travelin' them miles.
Shakin' folks hands and a givin' out smiles.

Tryin' to help the Wards out, tryin' to show the way.
So we kin do the Lord's work better ever day.

An' lookit that Gleaner gal, ain't she sweet?
Waitin' for an ex-missionary to sweep 'er off 'er feet.

Lookit them home teachers, ain't they a crew?
Visitin' them families like they supposed to do.

Cheerin' up the sick, and helpin' the poor,
Some does everything – others does more.

Say, lookit that Bishop, Ma, ain't he a stepper?
Livin' on peanut butter, prayers and Dr Pepper.

Solvin' folks' problems, writin' to their kin.
Preachin' to they children, and gettin' crops in.

Jest lookit them High Priests, ain't they a winner?
Settin' here and eatin' this free for nuthin' dinner.

How about them High Priests, ain't they fine?
Workin' them group sheets, a generation at a time.
Here ya go, High Priest, you kin do mine.

Jest lookit them Mormons, Ma, ain't they grand?
You kin be a Mormon, Ma, jest takes a little sand.

You kin be a Mormon, too, they ain't much to it.
Jest knuckle down, buckle down, an' do it, do it, do it.

Another of Brother Myrick's poems pays tribute to John Porter with typical Myrick humor.

Let John Do It

Way back yonder, when we was a Branch
We had an old widow woman who lived on a ranch.
And when she needed help, did the brethren hop to it?
No, they all sat back and said,
"Let John do it."

Well, time rolled on and we became a Ward
With lots more work to do for the Lord.
Didn't them Priests and Elders just wade right through it?
Nope, they all sat back and said,
"Let John do it."

Well, some years came and some years went —
And soon our new stake needed a President.
So the General Authorities came
And before anybody knew it, they'd all said,
"Let John do it."

Well, you know the day came
When all the brethren were waitin' in line
In front of them pearly gates so fine,
But the gates was locked and couldn't anybody undo it,
Then the voice of the Lord said,
"Let John through it."

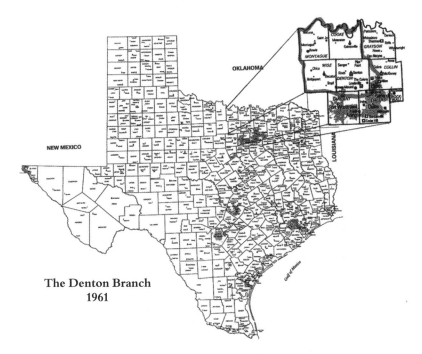

**The Denton Branch
1961**

The Denton Branch covered an extensive geographical area. It went to Grapevine and Colleyville on the south, and to Decatur and Bowie on the west. The Red River constituted the northern boundary, and McKinney marked the eastern boundary.

Bill May, who traveled with John Porter on Branch Teaching visits, reports that two trips and about 300 miles were required each month to visit their six families. Their route included families in Decatur, Alvord, Bowie, and Bolivar. Brother May also reports that they were 100% every month. Things were no easier for the sisters. Virginia May's Visiting Teaching route covered 287 miles each month.

Assisted by full-time missionaries, the Porters and other branch members actively proselyted throughout the Branch's area, and dependent Sunday Schools were soon established in Decatur in 1962 and in Gainesville in 1965. Although both of these locations had severe growing pains over the years, each city now has a flourishing ward and a lovely building in which to meet.

As was typical in most branches, a few individuals held several callings simultaneously in the Denton Branch. In addition to being Relief Society President, Margaret Porter was involved in everything else. Alvis Melchior served in several capacities and later became a counselor in the Branch Presidency. He even served as chorister when needed. He knew nothing about leading music, but he got the congregation to sing. Ann Musgrove taught in Sunday School, Primary, and Relief Society. Carol Wilhite served as Branch Chorister and Choir Director for four years until graduating from college. These charter members of the Sunday School and Branch organizations continued making their contributions as long as they were in Denton.

And they started young in some callings. Linda Barnett (née May) became a Primary teacher at the age of twelve. Diana Fraim was only ten years old when she became the Branch Organist. As she grew and became able to use the foot pedals, Diana's repertoire increased. She functioned as organist for several years, and when the saints eventually moved into the Malone Street building, she successfully made the transition from piano to organ.

A musical void was created when Carol Wilhite graduated from NTSU and left the area. Having no one else available with musical skills, John Porter, as Branch President, turned to Margaret and said, "I guess it's going to be you, honey."

"I don't know anything about this," she replied.

"It couldn't be that hard," John countered. "Look right here in the book. It just says 1, 2, 3, 4, … 1, 2, 3, 4. What you don't know about it you just make up with BODY TORQUE!"

With no formal musical training, Margaret Porter stepped forward and became the musical leader of the Branch and Ward in Denton. Margaret read books, she attended workshops, and she took classes. She studied intensely, and she became an outstanding and highly loved and respected musical leader. Margaret's daughter, Ann, remembers many nights at home when Margaret would be at the piano until the wee hours of the morning practicing and honing her musical skills. On other nights, Margaret could be seen sitting at the kitchen table reviewing and annotating musical scores. Even driving down the highway, Margaret's arm would frequently be directing an imaginary choir. Margaret not only became the Branch's musical leader, she remained the leader and she commanded the respect of the other accomplished musicians who subsequently arrived on the scene.

Margaret's daughters, Ann and Betty, became her students, and she taught them her same high standards. Ann and Betty served as chorister and pianist for Primary held weekdays after school. With ten year old Diana Fraim as Branch Organist, Ann, at age twelve, began leading the music in Sunday School and Sacrament Meetings.

"I received constructive criticism of my leading from Mom," Ann reminisced, "and she would be especially upset if I let my elbows 'flop around' while leading rather than keeping them appropriately tucked to my side."

Evidences of Brother Porter's generosity and concern for other people will be seen frequently throughout this book, and generally, his philanthropic deeds brought about positive results with regard to the Church in Denton. A case in point is Carol Wilhite. As a student at North Texas State College (NTSC), Carol needed a job to help pay her expenses. John went to Cletus Knight, who had just opened a title company, and said,

"Cletus, I'm sure you need some good part-time help." Cletus agreed, and Carol got the job. Knowing that Carol was LDS, Cletus asked her one day to tell him a little about the Church. Two hours later, he had received an ear full. Since he was paying Carol only a minimum wage, Cletus later commented that his introduction to the church cost him $3.45. The missionaries then became involved, and Cletus' wife, Clifford Ann, was baptized on October 30, 1966. Although Cletus attended fairly regularly with his wife, he waited sixteen years following his wife's baptism before he also took that step. Bishop Richard Ragsdale commented, "He has attended so many Gospel Essential classes, he ought to be teaching them."

Cletus Knight's baptism in 1982 had a unique aspect. Cletus had believed the gospel for a number of years, but he was afraid to go through the baptismal procedure. A paraplegic, Cletus was not at all ambulatory. He was also a very large man — three hundred pounds would be a conservative estimate of his weight. So how would it be possible for him to get into the baptism font, be immersed, and then get back out? For this reason he avoided the issue for several years until the brethren finally convinced him that it could and should be done.

On the appointed day, the brethren assigned to assist placed Cletus in a prone position onto a wooden gurney and strapped him to it for safety. With six brethren assisting, they lowered Cletus into the font, immersed him, and brought him out again. The plan was then to carry Cletus, still on the gurney, to Clara Wilson's house across the street from the Malone church building. (Clara was Hoyt Wilson's widow.) There he would have his wet clothing removed and his regular clothing placed on him. For the trip across the street, the brethren protected Cletus from getting too cold by placing a white sheet over him. Vaughn Andrus was one of eight brothers carrying Cletus, just as pallbearers would carry a casket. With the white sheet over Cletus, Vaughn was sure that any neighbors who might be watching would be convinced that the Mormons were really baptizing their dead.

In June, 1964, the Branch sent out its first full-time missionary, John R. Porter, son of Margaret and John W. Porter.

Elder John R. Porter
Denton's first full-time
missionary, 1964-1966

Elder Porter's call was to the Western Canadian Mission. Going to Salt Lake City to begin his mission, Elder Porter met and was set apart by John Longdon, an Assistant to the Council of the Twelve. After visiting for several minutes, Brother Longdon performed the setting apart and gave Elder Porter a blessing. During the blessing, Brother Longdon paused and then urged Elder Porter to work hard on his mission with the promise that the Branch in Denton would grow and prosper according to the effort Elder Porter put into his missionary work.

"I had the privilege of seeing that prophecy literally fulfilled," John R. later reported. "When I came home from my mission, the Branch had grown so much, I didn't know half of the people there."

Roger Fraim, son of Roger and Jennis Fraim was Denton's second missionary. From his mission in Uruguay, Elder Fraim wrote a letter to his close friend, Jim Martino, telling Jim all the reasons why Jim should go on a mission. The letter is now one of Jim's treasured mementos of those earlier years. (Jim, along with the full Martino family, will be introduced in a later chapter.)

Following Elder Porter and Elder Fraim, several additional young Elders entered the mission field from Denton. Among these were (alphabetically) Joe Arrington, Kenneth Arrington, David Baria, Rick Baria, Glenn Davis, Jimmie Jones, David Martino, Jim Martino, John May, Paul May, Mark Ragsdale, and Rick Ragsdale.

Hoyt and Clara Wilson were converts in the Denton Branch who deserve special recognition. Hoyt has to be compared to J. Golden Kimball. Both were characters. But in different ways. J. Golden Kimball was a character for his colorful language and his forthrightness in "telling it like it is." Hoyt Wilson was a character

for his missionary zeal and boldness in proclaiming the Gospel to others. Just as Church members love to hear J. Golden Kimball stories, no history of the Church in Denton can be complete without a few Hoyt Wilson stories.

Hoyt Wilson

Hoyt's introduction to the Gospel had a unique aspect. Coming home from work late one Sunday afternoon in March 1961, Hoyt was tired and hungry, and he wanted only to eat and go to bed. But the LDS missionaries were there visiting with his wife, Clara.

"I decided to listen for a few minutes, only to be polite, and then I would excuse myself and let them talk to my wife."

Although Hoyt had been searching for a religion which he could fully embrace, he had never knowingly met a Mormon, and he knew nothing about Mormon beliefs.

"Everything the missionaries said from the very first moment, I knew was true beyond any shadow of a doubt," Hoyt later recalled.

At that time, the missionaries had six lessons which they hoped to give in six visits. But not so with Hoyt.

As the missionaries prepared to depart after giving the first lesson, Hoyt was so taken by the message of the restoration and the need for a Savior, that he insisted that they stay and give the next lesson immediately. Although the missionaries were supposed to be back in their apartment by a certain time, they yielded to Hoyt's insistence and gave the second lesson. Hoyt then wanted the third immediately, then the fourth. Finally, at midnight, Hoyt and Clara had received all six lessons, and he and Clara were ready to be baptized as soon as a place could be found.

"I want to do it tomorrow," Hoyt announced.

Feeling that the baptism should wait until everyone was sure of the depth of Hoyt's conversion, the missionaries consulted their mission president, Ralph J. Hill. President Hill agreed that more time should elapse, but then he said, "Have President John Porter interview Mr. Wilson. If he can convince John that he is converted, then you have my permission to go ahead."

President Porter was equally amazed at the quickness of Hoyt's conversion, but he also sensed that it was real. The Wilsons were baptized in the Turtle Creek Chapel in Dallas on March 28, 1962, three days after receiving the six lessons.

Hoyt was a very missionary minded new convert, and as a member of the Denton Kiwanis Club, he was not at all shy about letting it be known that he was a Mormon. At the Club's weekly luncheon meetings, Hoyt made it a practice to sit with someone new whenever possible. He would turn his coffee cup upside down and then ask the person next to him, "Do you know why I turned my coffee cup upside down?"

"I suppose it's because you don't want to drink coffee," was the usual response.

"It's because I am a Mormon, and Mormons don't drink coffee. What do you know about the Mormon Church?"

Sometimes Hoyt would get a gospel conversation going and sometimes he wouldn't. But he was always trying. He is credited with helping bring over one hundred people into the Church.

On one occasion while watching a television news broadcast, Hoyt was quite taken by a news segment featuring the plight of a mother in a Lewisville hospital who had tragically lost a child. Responding to a feeling that came over him that this woman needed the gospel in her life, Hoyt picked up a *Book of Mormon* and some other Church literature and went to the hospital. After introducing himself to this woman who was a perfect stranger, he talked to her about the plan of salvation and left the reading material with her. Hoyt then had the missionaries follow up. It is reported that the woman took the missionary lessons and became a faithful member of the Church.

Hoyt loved people and would do almost anything to be helpful. In later years when Pearl Yates lived near the Wilsons, Pearl remembers that Hoyt would make it a point to be out in his driveway on frequent mornings to give a cheerful greeting to Pearl's daughter as she walked to school. As a home teacher, Hoyt was "always there."

Hoyt was also a "do-er." He bought a large tract of land in Oklahoma, built a lake on it, and made it available for church outings. He even dreamed of making it into a Mormon community with its own ward and everything, but that dream died with Hoyt's untimely death early in 1980.

Jan and Judy Martin, already members of the Church, came to the Denton area in 1964. When Jan, a Delta Airlines pilot, learned that he was being transferred from New Orleans to the Dallas/Fort Worth airport, he made a phone call inquiring about where to live. Talking to the wife of one of the Dallas bishops

(Jan doesn't remember her name), Jan asked, "If you were moving to Dallas at this time, where would you choose to live?"

"I believe I would choose to live in Denton," she responded.

As a result, the Martins bought a house from John and Margaret Porter on Crawford Road in Argyle, and they brought additional Church experience to the Denton Branch.

CHAPTER 7

The Arringtons Bring
Needed Gospel Maturity

*I*t would be hard to overemphasize the contributions Maurice and Edleweis Arrington made to the Church in Denton during its early years. It would also be hard to overemphasize the love and respect with which they were regarded by the Denton saints. In addition to the Arrington's spirituality and commitment to the gospel, they brought experience in how a Church unit should function.

Edleweis and Maurice Arrington

It would appear that the Arringtons were foreordained to work with the Denton saints. When Maurice took a job with General Dynamics in Fort Worth in 1950, the Arringtons moved from east Texas to Colleyville, where they lived for several years. They attended church with the Fort Worth Ward on Seventh Street in Fort Worth.

The Porters and the Arringtons first became acquainted when both families attended Church meetings in the Fort Worth Ward in the mid 1950s. Because of Maurice's lifetime in the gospel, President Porter of the Denton Branch and Bishop Peterson of the Fort Worth Ward both saw the strength the Arringtons could provide to the fledgling Denton Branch.

Upon being asked, Maurice and Edleweis agreed to start attending in Denton. Therefore, in late 1959 or early 1960, the boundary between the Denton Branch and the Fort Worth Ward was changed to run down the street which the Arringtons' home faced. The Arringtons' side of the street became part of the Denton Branch while the other side of the street remained in the Fort Worth Ward. Denton, at that time, was still a dependent branch attached to the Fort Worth Ward

Although this new alignment constituted a sacrifice for the Arringtons, they were willing to do it. They now had to drive thirty-two miles to church, and trips were made on Sundays for regular meetings, on Tuesdays for Primary, on Wednesdays for Mutual, on Thursdays for Relief Society, and occasionally on Saturdays for special activities. Frequently they would drive first to Keller and pick up members of the May family. Somehow they managed to cram several extra bodies into their red Volkswagen for the trip into Denton and back. Their commitment to the gospel, which formerly had been somewhat lukewarm, now became a "driving" force in their lives.

Another indication of the Arringtons' new commitment to the gospel came when President Porter visited the Arringtons one Sunday and interviewed them about paying tithing. The Arringtons' budget was so tight, they knew they could not afford tithing, but President Porter persisted.

"I have a testimony that you can pay it," President Porter declared, "and the Lord will bless you and make you eligible to serve in the branch presidency if you do."

The Arringtons made the commitment, and the next week at work, Maurice received a pay raise that more than compensated for the tithing he was now paying. The commitment came first, and the way was then opened. As already mentioned in an earlier chapter, when Denton became an independent branch in 1961, Maurice Arrington was called to be a counselor in the branch presidency.

During this tithing interview, President Porter noticed that Brother Arrington had been bitten by a black widow spider. Maurice had a big welt on his foot, and he could not walk.

"Why don't I give you a blessing for that foot you've got?" President Porter suggested. The next morning the foot was better, and Maurice could put a shoe on. This was President Porter's first experience in giving blessings—a faith-promoting experience for him.

Finally, in 1967, the Arringtons decided that they needed to live closer to Denton in order to ease the transportation to Church meetings and activities. Leaving Colleyville, they came north and settled on Crawford Road in Argyle on land they bought from John Porter. They lived temporarily in a small house just west of Art Cooper (where the Turners now live) while building a new home just east of Art Cooper.

Along with other Denton members who were committed to the Church's home teaching program (as it is now called), Maurice traveled hundreds of miles each month making his visits just as he had done earlier in the Fort Worth Ward. His son, Kenneth, says, "Dad never missed a month."

The Arringtons, along with the Melchoirs, were the only Church members in Denton at that time with any experience in operating a Church unit. Although it was the Porters who were called to be the leaders, it was the Arringtons and the Melchiors who provided the experience and gospel maturity that were sorely needed. The Lord truly provided!

With regard to the Arringtons, Maurice served as a counselor to three bishops in Denton, and he served on the first High Council of the newly created Fort Worth Stake in 1967. Maurice and Edleweis both served on the Fort Worth

Stake Sunday School Board. Edleweis also served a stint as Primary president in Denton, and she was at the forefront in all the branch and ward activities. They were a pillar of strength.

More will be said in a later chapter regarding a special aspect of Maurice's callings and contributions.

CHAPTER 8

Building a Meeting House

By the end of 1960, it was apparent that the Denton Branch would need a permanent building of their own if they were to continue growing and functioning with the full programs of the Church. Although it had been only a year and a half since the Sunday School had been organized and only a half year since the Denton Dependent Branch was created, the local Saints were determined to move forward with a building program.

When Dallas Stake President Atkerson organized the Denton saints into an independent branch on January 22, 1961, he initiated the movement for a chapel by challenging the Branch to start a building fund. He then added incentive to the challenge by pledging himself to match the first $1,000 collected into the building fund. The branch members immediately pledged what they felt they could afford, and John Porter, in his typical style, pledged the rest. Margaret Porter reports, "We got his (President Atkerson's) money before he left that very day."

A building site was needed, and it was generally felt that a site near the Denton High School would be advantageous to the early morning seminary students. John Porter's search for a suitable site was fruitless until the Rayzor family, knowing of John's search, offered to sell him a three-acre plot at the northwest intersection of University and Malone.

"How much?" John asked.

"Fifteen thousand dollars."

"We'll take it," John responded.

After the Church Building Department gave their approval, John Porter once again rose to the occasion. He personally purchased the land, and shortly thereafter he sold one of the acres to Whataburger for $25,000. He then donated the remaining two acres to the Church. The Branch now had two acres of land free and clear plus over twelve thousand dollars for their building fund. The address became 1801 Malone Street.

Having Whataburger next door to the new LDS building proved advantageous in at least one respect. When the priesthood failed to bring bread for the sacrament, President Porter would send someone over to Whataburger to buy bread. On a few occasions, it was hot buttered rolls that were used for the sacrament.

At this time, the Church Building Department was studying a variety of possible plans for new types of building architecture. The brethren in Salt Lake initially saw the construction process for the Denton building as a three-phase operation. Phase 1 would be the chapel. Phase 2 would be the north corridor leading to and including the Primary Room. Phase 3 would be the cultural hall, kitchen, and additional offices and class rooms. The Denton saints, however, wanted Phases 1 and 2 done at the same time in the initial construction step. There was also a difference of opinion, however, between the Denton leaders and the Church's Building Department regarding the design of the roof. For this reason, approval to begin construction kept being deferred. The local membership had already raised fifty percent of the cost of the building in pledges and labor commitments (as was required in those days), and they were ready to start construction. They only needed an O.K. from Salt Lake.

The Malone Street Chapel
Artist's Conception

Two related and helpful things happened at this time. One was that John and Margaret Porter went to Salt Lake City to receive their endowments in the Salt Lake Temple. The other was that Karen Peterson, a daughter of N. Marcus Peterson, Bishop of the Fort Worth Ward, married Richard Moyle, a son of President Henry D. Moyle of the First Presidency. Since the Porters and the Petersons were already well acquainted, John and Margaret were invited to the Moyle home in Salt Lake City for a post-wedding brunch. John and President Moyle became acquainted, and John managed to let President Moyle know about the slowness in getting approval to start construction of the church building.

About ten days later, John got a very cooperative phone call from the Building Department. He then made another trip to Salt Lake City, and everything he wanted was quickly approved. Ground breaking took place on March 2, 1963. Local membership stood at 140 members.

As the Denton saints wanted, Phases I and II were constructed simultaneously. Thus the initial building housed the chapel, some offices, baptistry, two rest rooms, a small

Ground Breaking for the Malone Street Chapel
Clockwise from bottom left: Alvis Melchior, John Porter (Branch President),
Si Ragsdale (Denton Chamber of Commerce), Lars A. Warner (Construction
Supervisor), Ervin W. Atkerson (Dallas Stake President), Ernest D. Wright
and Gilman J. Housley (Counselors to President Atkerson).
Photo courtesy of the *Denton Record-Chronicle.*

kitchen, and classrooms. Also included were the foyer on the
north side of the chapel and the overflow area at the rear of the
chapel.

Lars A. Warner and his wife came from Mesa, Arizona, to
supervise the building process and to guide the local volunteer
labor which was used as much as possible. Joyce Murphy was
Denton's Relief Society President at the time, and Sister Warner
became one of Joyce's counselors.

"Sister Warner, with all her experience in the Church, was
a tremendous help to me. I loved her dearly." Joyce has
acknowledged.

Malone Street Chapel Groundbreaking
Outside of program

"The World Has Need of Willing Men"

The world has need of willing men,
Who wear the worker's seal;
Come help the good work move along,
Put your shoulder to the wheel.

Chorus

Put your shoulder to the wheel, push along;
Do your duty with a heart full of song.
We all have work; let no one shirk;
Put your shoulder to the wheel.

The Church has need of helping hands
And hearts that know and feel;
The work to do is here for you;
Put your shoulder to the wheel.

Repeat Chorus

PROGRAM

MARCH 2, 1963   4:00 P.M.

Welcoming Remarks .... President John W. Porter

Opening Song .... *The World Has Need of Willing Men*

Invocation .... Bert T. Murphy

Remarks .... Members of the Stake Presidency

Dedicatory Prayer .... Ervin W. Atkerson
President of the Dallas Stake

Malone Street Chapel Groundbreaking
Inside of program

The only unusual incident during the construction process occurred one night when the beams on which the roof was to be placed collapsed and had to be replaced. Anti-Mormon feelings were quite prevalent among Dentonites at that time, and when the townspeople learned of the collapse of the roof supports, there was considerable laughter among the "I told you so" groups.

Construction proceeded at a rapid pace, with Church members providing much of the labor. Riley Swanson, a carpenter and a cabinet maker by trade, did the detail woodwork at the front of the chapel.

Riley was the husband of Trudie Swanson, believed to have been Denton's first convert. Having been a heavy smoker, Riley resisted the gospel for about five years after his wife's conversion. Then in 1962, James, the Swansons' third oldest son, returned home from military service in England. After listening again to the missionaries, James and Riley decided it was time for them to join the church, so together they quit smoking "cold turkey," and they too entered the waters of baptism.

Riley's commitment to the gospel was total. When construction began on the Malone Street building, Riley quit his regular day-time job and spent full-time assisting Brother Warner in constructing the building. Riley then worked evenings for his own customers, making just enough money to pay the household bills.

Riley did all the beautiful woodwork in the front of the chapel, and he experienced joy in so doing. People today can appreciate the simplistic beauty and the excellent workmanship that is still evident in the pulpit and the surrounding paneling. The completed job was a source of real pride to Riley.

However, it was a difficult routine for Riley, who was a diabetic, and his strenuous and irregular schedule had its detrimental effects. Sadly, Riley suffered a debilitating stroke after finishing the chapel woodwork, and he died shortly thereafter.

Alvis Melchior did most of the work on the air conditioning ducts. By November 3, 1963, construction was far enough along for the Branch to start holding meetings in the new building. Moving in on the first Sunday in November, exactly four years from the establishment of the Sunday School, the congregation were cold on the outside, but very warm on the inside. Although it was a cold wintry day and the heating system was not yet functioning, the Saints were ecstatic about being in their own building. Seventy-seven members of a total of 196 members were present that day.

The building construction (Phases 1 & 2) was completed in January, 1964. The total estimated cost of the building at that point was $230,000. Although the actual cost may have varied somewhat from the estimated cost, the branch made its final payment of one half the final cost in January 1966. Now that the building was completed and paid for, it could be dedicated.

The chapel had a sacred aura, and it featured a fine organ which President Atkerson and his wife donated from their home. Elder Bernard P. Brockbank, an Assistant to the Quorum of the Twelve, came and dedicated the building on May 6, 1966. President Atkerson of the Dallas Stake and President Sanfred Elieson of the Texas Mission also attended and spoke. Local membership was now up to 325 members. As part of his remarks, Brother Brockbank predicted that the time would soon come when Denton would be a stake in Zion. It was a difficult expectation for the small group of Saints in Denton at that time.

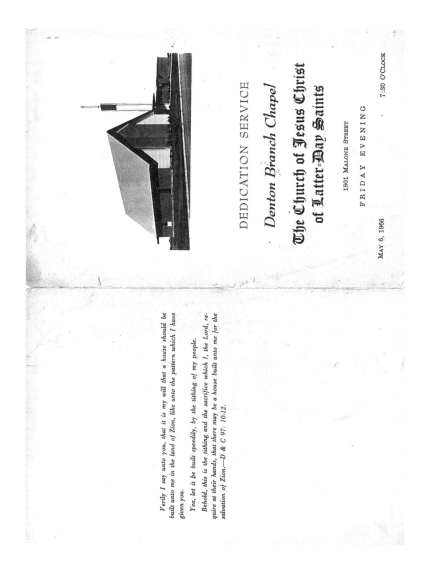

Dedication of the Malone Street Chapel
Outside of program

History of the Denton Branch

On October 21, 1956 seventeen people gathered in the home of Jennis and Roger Fraim, Jr. at 1024 S. Locust, and formed a Sunday School which was to meet weekly thereafter at the Woman's Club Building on Oakland Street. In August of 1957 the group disbanded when most of its members moved away at the termination of the school year, the majority having been here in connection with the universities.

By the fall of 1959 there were enough Latter Day Saints in the area to warrant another Sunday School, and, at the direction of the Stake President, Ervin W. Atkerson, 23 members assembled at 517 Roberts, the home of John W. Porter, on the first Sunday of November, 1959. The Denton Dependent Sunday School was organized by Bishop N. Marcus Peterson of the Fort Worth Ward and Ronald Whiting, Stake Sunday School Superintendent.

The following week a vacant two-story building at 111 W. McKinney was procured through the generosity of the Denton County National Bank, and all meetings were held at that location until the completion of the Chapel. During the time of occupancy, the building was sold and it was then rented from the purchaser who remodeled it to suit our needs.

As the membership grew, the various Church programs and auxiliaries were added, and on January 22, 1961 the group was made an independent Branch in the Dallas Stake by President Ervin W. Atkerson and his Counselors, Ernest D. Wright and Gilman J. Housley.

Immediately a Building Fund was set up, and preparations made for a meeting house to be erected in Denton which would be adequate for the growing membership. The site at 1801 Malone Street was selected and approved, and correspondence began with the Church Building Department, and plans selected for this Chapel. With the details finalized and funds raised to meet the requirements, the Construction Supervisor, Lars A. (AL) Warner and his wife, Veva, were assigned to the project, and on March 2, 1963, ground breaking services were held. Construction proceeded, with much of the labor donated by the local membership which numbered approximately 140.

The first meeting was held in the new Chapel on the first Sunday of November, 1963, although the building was not fully completed until January 1964. The final payment was made in January of 1966, and application submitted for dedication. The current membership of 325 is anticipating the addition of a cultural hall to be used in the fields of drama, dance, music, and sports in keeping with the recreational programs of the Church.

With the knowledge that the Church exists for two purposes — the development and perfection of the individual members, and the spreading of the Gospel throughout the world —— we, in the Denton Branch, pray that this building may be used to these ends. May this Chapel, and the lives of those who worship herein, stand as strong witnesses of the restoration of the Gospel of Jesus Christ.

PROGRAM

Devotional Prelude - - - - Diana Fraim
Branch Organist

Opening Hymn - - "Jehovah, Lord of Heaven and Earth"

Invocation - - - - - Alvis H. Melchior
Counselor in the Branch Presidency

Welcoming Remarks - - - - John W. Porter
Branch President

"Prayer of Thanksgiving" - - - Denton Branch Choir
Dr. Richard W. Ragsdale, Conductor

Remarks - - - - Ervin W. Atkerson
Dallas Stake President

Remarks - - - - Sanfred W. Eliason
Texas Mission President

Vocal Solo: "If With All Your Hearts" - - Carol Willhite
Joan Northcutt, Accompanist

Dedicatory Address and Prayer - - Bernard P. Brockbank
Assistant to the Council of the Twelve

Closing Hymn - "The Spirit of God Like A Fire Is Burning"

Benediction - - - - H. Maurice Arrington
Counselor in the Branch Presidency

Dedication of the Malone Street Chapel
Inside of program

CHAPTER 9

Enter the Ragsdales

$\mathcal{A}$s the Denton Branch continued to grow, additional strong and able leadership was needed, and it came. With the Porters leading the way in proselyting and fellowshipping, they soon were able to begin sharing the load with others. Over a ten year period in those early years, convert baptisms averaged twenty-seven per year. Among those early converts were Richard and Pat Ragsdale.

Dick and Pat Ragsdale met and became friends with the Porters when both families were living in Sherman. In 1956, the Ragsdales moved to Denton where Dick became an optometrist associated with Texas State Optical. He later owned

Pat and Richard Ragsdale

his own optometry facility. Pat was well-known in Denton for her participation in civic affairs. As examples, Pat was a charter member of the Denton Benefit League, a ladies' organization that provides annual grants totaling several hundred thousand dollars to a large number of local charitable and cultural organizations. She served a year as president of that organization, and she also served a year as chairman of

Denton's United Way. In addition, Dick and Pat both held responsible leadership roles in the Methodist Church.

About a year and a half after the Ragsdales' arrival, the Porters moved to the Denton area (for the second time) and bought property on Crawford Road in Argyle. The two families rediscovered each other and became very close friends. This time, however, the Porters had already joined the Church, and they were zealous in their efforts to share the gospel with their friends.

For three and a half years, the Porters invited the Ragsdales to cottage meetings, social functions, and Church meetings. Dick and Pat had been Methodists all their lives, and they weren't interested in making a change. Dick and Frank Martino were co-superintendents of the local Methodist Sunday School, and Pat was a Sunday School teacher. But on the other hand, the Ragsdales were disturbed by some of the teachings and practices of the Methodist ministry in Denton, and in a way, they were looking for something more closely related to what they really believed to be right.

Although the Ragsdales attended some of the Branch's spaghetti dinners and frog leg dinners, they had no interest in the cottage meetings or the church meetings, and they used every possible excuse for saying "no" when invited to attend. But the Porters persisted, and finally, after three and a half years of saying "no," the Ragsdales decided they would have to go to a cottage meeting or sever their friendship with John and Margaret. So one Sunday night in 1965 they acquiesced and attended a cottage meeting at the Porters' home in Argyle. The Church missionaries were there, and Sanfred Eliesen, president of the Texas Mission, was there with his wife, Virginia. John and Margaret both bore strong testimonies, and then they turned the meeting over to Sanfred who reviewed the Joseph

Smith story. The Ragsdales were favorably impressed. The missionaries, who had fasted all day, gave a *Book of Mormon* to the Ragsdales and asked them to read it, which Dick and Pat did. Again, they were impressed. Pat knew immediately that it was true.

"No boy with a third grade education could have written a book like that," she later proclaimed.

Shortly thereafter, the missionaries challenged the Ragsdales to live the Word of Wisdom for two weeks, and Dick and Pat agreed to do it.

"I got headaches and all kinds of pangs," Dick reports, "but I did it."

Then at the end of the two weeks, the missionaries asked the Ragsdales to go another two weeks living the Word of Wisdom, and Dick said, "No way. I'm going on a hunting trip to south Texas. There is going to be beer and coffee there, and that's what I am going to be doing." It was an annual affair that he had thoroughly enjoyed in previous years.

Leaving home on a Saturday, Dick joined his friends in the Valley, but the anticipated enjoyment wasn't there. The next day he phoned home and told Pat, "I'm coming home."

"Why? What's the matter?" she asked.

"The coffee and beer taste terrible. I'm miserable, and I'm coming home." Then he added, "We need to do some talking."

Together again, Dick and Pat both expressed their feelings that the Church was true, that the *Book of Mormon* was true, and that they needed to join. Scheduling their baptism on Labor Day, September 6, 1965, they went into the water, and at their request, John Porter performed the ordinance. Their two sons, Richard and Mark, who had been taught by the missionaries separately from their parents, were also baptized at that time. Their daughter, Stacy, at three years of age was too young.

Following their baptism, Dick and Pat reported to their Methodist minister to tell him of their action. His reaction was almost exactly the same as he had expressed seven years earlier when the Porters joined the LDS church.

"I have only one regret," the minister said. "You didn't give me equal time to tell you all about the Methodist Church."

"I've been a Methodist for over forty years," Dick retorted. "You have had plenty of time."

Even though they were new converts, the spiritual strength and maturity displayed by Richard (Dick) and Pat Ragsdale was outstanding, and it was just what the little Branch needed. Consider, for example, that Dick Ragsdale became a Bishop of the Denton Ward in 1967, only two years after his baptism. Six years after that (1973), he was called to the stake High Council, and in another three years (1976), he became the Stake President of the newly created Fort Worth North Stake. In 1984 Brother Ragsdale was called to be a temple sealer and to serve as First Counselor to Ivan Hobson, first president of the Dallas Temple. Dick and Pat have served additional missions as presiding missionaries at the Liberty Jail visitors' center and as temple workers in the London Temple. That quality of spiritual leadership ability is rare, and the Denton Saints were the principal beneficiaries.

CHAPTER 10

Art Cooper Moves to Denton

*A*bout a year after the Ragsdales' baptism, another special family appeared on the scene. Although the zeal of new converts is great in any organization, the depth of leadership and spiritual maturity that can be provided by dedicated lifetime Mormons was also needed. And it was provided.

Jed Arthur (Art) Cooper

Art Cooper, a lifetime Mormon from Panguitch, Utah, arrived in Denton in the late summer of 1966 along with his wife, Carol Joy. The Porters, along with the entire branch, had been praying earnestly that Denton's two universities would be a source for attracting strong and capable additions to Denton's tiny Branch. Art, a college professor at the University of Arizona in Tucson, was the first to arrive in Denton in response to those prayers. (Many others also came, as listed in Appendix 5.) Art came to North Texas State University to teach in the College of Education, having applied there and also at Weber State College in Ogden, Utah. Both schools wanted him, but the North Texas offer came first.

Before making his final decision to come to Denton, Art looked in the Church Directory and learned that Denton had a branch of the Church and that John Porter was Branch President. On a Sunday afternoon, Art picked up a phone and called the Porter home. Because John was in Decatur at the time, Art got to talk with Margaret. After explaining his LDS background to Margaret and telling her that he was considering moving to Denton, Art asked about the strength of the Church in Denton. With her usual degree of enthusiasm, Margaret shouted back, "We have the best unit in the whole Church!" Art reached his final decision then and there.

Art brought with him a lifetime of Church and leadership experience. And he was not new to Texas, having served a mission in the Spanish-American Mission headquartered in San Antonio. As a missionary, Art served as bookkeeper, as mission secretary, and for six months as a counselor in the mission presidency. As a resident of Tucson before coming to Denton, Art had been a Branch President, and in earlier years in Utah, he had also served a term in the Thirty-third Session of the Utah State Legislature.

The Coopers arrived in Denton on a Friday and moved into a new rental home on Crescent Street. Arriving a few days before their furniture, they spent Friday and Saturday nights sleeping on the floor. On Sunday morning, Art walked a few short blocks to Priesthood Meeting at the Malone Street building where he enjoyed the liveliness of the assembled priesthood brethren. He especially enjoyed a rousing rendition of "Onward Christian Soldiers" with Dick Ragsdale playing the melody on a "rinky dink" piano. Branch President John Porter and his First Counselor, Maurice Arrington, were there along with Bill Biggs, Hoyt Wilson, Doug Turner, Jan Martin, Thomas Wright, Roger Fraim, Riley Swanson, Robert Vann, Gene Giles, and Roy Odom. It was a lively and congenial group.

Returning home, Art announced to Carol Joy, "I attended the swingingest priesthood meeting of my life."

John and Margaret Porter called on the Coopers that afternoon, and upon seeing that there was no furniture in the house, John insisted that the Coopers move, at no charge, into a motel the Porters owned on Dallas Drive, and stay there until their furniture arrived. Such was the generosity of the Porters.

Almost immediately after the Cooper's arrival, Art was called to be High Priest Group Leader in the Denton Branch. It was not a difficult calling because Alvis Melchoir was the only other high priest in the Branch. He was also called to teach an Institute class for NTSU and TWU students, and to teach early-morning seminary for the high school students in the Branch. Additional leadership callings were to come later.

As far as Art is concerned, the Denton Branch really was "the best unit in the whole Church." He and Carol Joy quickly learned to love the Branch members. In reminiscing over those early years in the Branch, Art has spoken especially about the strength and steadiness of Roy Odom and his wife and their gentle, sweet spirit.

Carol Joy became a teacher in Relief Society and in Primary. She also made significant contributions as the Sunday School chorister. Carol Joy was very much appreciated in that calling because she supplemented the song practice sessions with historical and spiritual backgrounds of the songs being learned. When the General Sunday School later urged such an approach to song practice, Carol Joy was already doing it in Denton. Thus, we have another example of leadership ability and gospel maturity arriving when needed for building up the "kingdom" in Denton.

In 1967, about a year after their arrival in Denton, the Coopers expressed their desire to live in a more rural setting, and John Porter offered to sell them some of the land he owned on Crawford Road in Argyle. Except for a parcel he had already sold to the Arrington family, Brother Porter owned all the land on the north side of Crawford Road from U.S. Highway 377 on the east almost to Interstate 35W on the west. The Coopers bought a parcel immediately to the west of the Arringtons. Shortly thereafter, Doug Turner and his wife, Jeanette, bought property immediately to the west of the Coopers. Additional sales were made to LDS families, and soon Jan Martin and Sue Manning were also living on Crawford Road. John and Margaret Porter were also living there at the time on the eastern-most parcel.

Thus, for a while, six LDS families were living on Crawford Road at the same time, along with a non-Mormon family living on the western-most parcel, and Crawford Road became known unofficially as "Mormon Row." A standing joke soon emerged that seven families were living on Crawford Road, and all of them were Mormons. Actually, it was the six LDS families just named plus one non-LDS family whose last name happened to be "Moorman." A little poetic license was taken in their case.

During his thirty-five year stay in Denton, Art filled significant leadership roles. He responded to four different calls to serve as a stake high counselor. He served as a counselor in the Denton Ward bishopric, then two different times as a counselor in the Denton Second Ward bishopric, and later as a counselor in the Denton Fourth Ward bishopric. He was Denton's first Institute of Religion teacher. Art also served for ten years on the school board of the Argyle Independent School District. Art's Church-oriented background was indispensable in those early years of the Church in Denton.

In 1998, Art retired from the University of North Texas, and three years later he returned to Panguitch, Utah, the home of his boyhood. Although Art returned home with every intention of living a typically retired life, his second grade school teacher welcomed him by saying, "Art, we need you. You must run for City Council." Complying with her request, Art ran and was elected to the Panguitch City Council in 2003. Two years later he was elected mayor of Panguitch. In his retirement years, Art Cooper is probably the busiest, and happiest, person in Panguitch, Utah.

Part Three
THE DEVELOPMENT YEARS

Introduction

On February 12, 1967, the Denton Ward was created as a result of the growth that had taken place in the Denton Branch. From that date until July 20, 1975 when the continuously growing Denton Ward was divided, we have what can be considered as the Development Years of The Church of Jesus Christ of Latter-day Saints in Denton, Texas. This period begins with the creation of the Denton Ward and closes with the division of the Denton Ward into the Denton First and Second Wards on July 20, 1975.

The entire Dallas Stake was also growing. On September 24, 1967, Elder Harold B. Lee of the Council of the Twelve, presided over the creation of the Ft. Worth Stake from a division of the Dallas Stake. Denton was included as a unit in the new stake.

During its first four years as a ward, the Denton unit showed the following growth pattern as gleaned from the historical records in Salt Lake City. Total membership growth slowed, although there were still significant numbers of convert baptisms.

Year	1967	1968	1969	1970
Total Membership	392	331	390	381
Convert Baptisms	24	26	16	27

One of the keys with regard to the development of the Church in Denton lay in the spirituality and leadership abilities of many of the new converts and move-ins. Among the move-ins, the Sanfred Elieson family has to receive special mention. They brought needed strength to this area, and they stayed, making the Denton area their permanent home. Later move-ins include the families of Newell Kay Brown, and Al White, both of whom became bishops after coming to Denton. Jim and Maureen Richards came from Utah and added invaluable strength. Jim and one of his sons, David, also became bishops in Denton.

Converts in large numbers brought additional strength and vitality during these development years. Among these converts were the Martino and Nobles families whose conversion stories and contributions will receive special attention in this history. Converts Ralph and Sarah Davis, and Bill Williamson also deserve special mention.

Because of the rapid influx of new members, it soon became apparent that the time had come to add the planned Phase III expansion to the Malone Street building. In only seven years, the saints had outgrown the original two-phase building.

Throughout this development period, the Denton saints worked together, worshipped together, and socialized together in what was truly a harmonious environment. Bazaars, picnics, and special celebrations all worked together to promote a happy unity among the Denton saints. And when there wasn't anything special to celebrate, the saints got together anyway for pot luck dinners. These activities, along with the spiritual uplift gained from the Church meetings, cottage meetings, missionary activities, home teaching, and visiting teaching helped the Denton saints develop into a ward mature enough and large enough for division in 1975.

The following timeline will show the major events of this development period and their time relationships to one another.

The Development Years of
The Church of Jesus Christ of Latter-day Saints
in Denton
1967-1975

Denton Events	Year	Area Events
Denton Ward Created 2/12/67 Eliesons Arrive 8/ /67 Martinos Baptized 12/7/67	1967	Fort Worth Stake Created 9/24/67
Davis' Baptized 8/16/68 Richards' Arrive 8/ /68	1968	
	1969	
	1970	
Nobles Baptized 5/21/71 Browns Arrive 8/ /71 Nielsens Arrive 8/ /71	1971	
Steiners Arrive Sorensons Arrive 8/ /72	1972	
Meeting House Addition Began	1973	
Meeting House Addition Dedicated 11/10/74	1974	
Denton 1st & 2nd Wards Created 7/20/75	1975	

CHAPTER 11

Development of the Denton Ward

A New Ward and an Expanded Building

On February 12, 1967, the Denton Branch became the Denton Ward. Branch President John W. Porter became Bishop John W. Porter, and Maurice Arrington and Alvis Melchior, both of whom had served as counselors in the branch presidency, became first and second counselors in the new ward bishopric. This bishopric functioned together for only seven months, however, for on September 24, 1967, Elder Harold B. Lee created the Fort Worth Stake from a division of the Dallas Stake, and Bishop Porter was called as First Counselor to President John Kelly of the new Fort Worth Stake. On that same date (and only two years after his baptism), Richard Ragsdale became the new bishop of the Denton Ward, with Maurice Arrington and Art Cooper as his First and Second Counselors.

Harold B. Lee issued the calls to Brothers Ragsdale, Arrington, and Cooper. Some insight into the contributions, many of them behind the scenes, that Brother Arrington made to the Church in Denton, is gained from his interview with Elder Lee. The substance of the interview came to light many years later when Kenneth Arrington, one of Maurice's sons, quizzed his dad about why he had always played a supporting role and had never been called to be a bishop himself.

Three Denton Bishops
John Porter   Robert Nobles
Richard Ragsdale

Maurice responded, "When Harold B. Lee called me to be a counselor to Bishop Ragsdale, he told me, 'Your calling is not to be the bishop. Your calling is to *train* the bishop.'"

In his supporting role, Brother Arrington fulfilled his special calling and contributed invaluably to the early growth and development of the Church in Denton. He served as a trainer and counselor to three bishops in Denton – John Porter, Richard Ragsdale, and Bob Nobles.

Brother Cooper's tenure as a counselor to Bishop Ragsdale lasted only three months, for he was then called to the Fort Worth Stake High Council where he served for the next three years.

As the Church continued to grow in Denton, it was not long before the need for the Phase III portion of the building was felt. Phase III would consist of a cultural hall and stage along with additional classrooms, rest rooms, a full kitchen, and offices. So in 1973, only nine years after completing the first two phases of construction, the local authorities requested approval to proceed with the final construction phase. Denton was now a ward in the Fort Worth Stake, and Richard Ragsdale was still Bishop of the Denton Ward.

The need for a cultural hall became apparent as members traveled back and forth to Fort Worth to participate in such dramatic productions as *Promised Valley* and *Papa and the Playhouse*. The space was also needed for socials and athletic events. On the other hand, however, a building addition also meant loss of space behind the building for softball games. The need outweighed the loss.

With the approval process already in motion in 1973, Bishop Ragsdale made a trip to Salt Lake City to attend General Conference. While there he visited the Church Building Department to ascertain the current status of plans and to make sure that everything was all right.

Bishop Ragsdale was told that even though the first phase was built with interior walls made of brick, the Church was going to use drywall construction on the next phase.

"We don't want drywall," Bishop Ragsdale insisted. "We want brick just like we have in the first phase."

"You don't understand the Church's position," they told Bishop Ragsdale. "The Church has to be economical in the use of its funds, and dry wall construction is cheaper than brick."

After thinking it over for a moment, Bishop Ragsdale made the following reply.

"We will accept the drywall construction and get the next phase built. Then after it is built and dedicated, we will tear down the dry wall and replace it with brick. And we will use our tithing money to do it."

The building department representatives went off into a huddle, and when they came back they said, "You will get your brick."

With the addition to the previously existing building, the Denton saints decided to replant the lawn. Out went the old grass, and in came new grass. John Porter provided an ample supply of manure to help the new grass grow. It is reported that the air in the neighborhood reeked for three or four weeks, but the new lawn proved to be beautiful.

Fourth of July Flag Raising Ceremony
in front of the Malone Street Building

A problem of a minor nature still exists in the front lawn with regard to the flagpole that R. B. Pennington designed and welded. The job of setting the flag pole in place in its previously dug hole and of applying concrete at the base fell to Kay Brown and Bill Williamson, and the task was not going well. With concrete on the surface of the ground as well as in the hole, Bill Williamson was on his knees scooping up concrete with his bare hands and pushing it into the hole. Over and over again, Bill was saying softly, "I'd never be doing this if I'd remained a Catholic. I'd never be doing this … ." Amused, Kay Brown started laughing, then Bill started laughing, and before they knew it, the concrete in the hole began to harden. A close look at the flagpole shows that it is not exactly straight up and down; it has a slight tilt.

The dedication of Phase III occurred on November 10, 1974, with Horace L. Leithead, President of the Fort Worth Stake, presiding. This last addition to the building was begun

The Malone Street Chapel
All three phases completed and rededicated November 10, 1974.

in Bishop Ragsdale's term and was completed under Bishop Ell Sorensen.

Ell Sorensen succeeded Richard Ragsdale on September 9, 1973, as bishop of the Denton Ward. Brother Sorensen came to Denton in 1972 as Dean of Students at North Texas State University. Thus, he was one of the fulfillments of the prayers of the Denton saints that the two Denton universities serve as a magnet for attracting capable LDS members and leaders.

Brother Sorensen came to North Texas State from Illinois State University. In Illinois, he was quite happy with his position at the school, yet he had a desire to return to his home state of Utah. Then one day early in 1972 his wife, Patricia, had a premonition.

"We are going to Texas," she announced. Texas was the last place Ell thought about going.

In the spring of 1972, Ell went to Denver, Colorado, to an educators' conference, and there two administrators from North Texas State interviewed him and offered him a position as Foreign Student Advisor. Toward the end of the summer, the administrators called Brother Sorensen and told him that things had changed and that they now wanted him to come as Dean of Men. That would be a significant step upward, both in prestige and salary. So the Sorensens came to Denton in the fall of 1972.

The Sorensens loved the ward in Denton. They had moved around quite a bit in the past, and Ell relates that the saints in Denton were friendlier and more congenial than in any other place where they had been. In addition, he was completely relaxed and absolutely certain that he would never be called as bishop because of the plethora of talented and capable members in Denton at that time. Then on one Sunday in the chapel, Ell had a spiritual experience (which shall remain personal and private) that let him know that things were about to change for him.

When Richard Ragsdale was released as bishop in September 1973, no one was named to replace him. But Ell Sorensen was asked to go to Dallas to meet with Apostle LeGrande Richards. It turned out to be a very unusual and memorable meeting.

Instead of being his usual jovial self, Elder Richards was all business. "Let me see your recommend," he said. Brother Sorensen pulled out his temple recommend.

"No, your recommend to be bishop," Elder Richards said.

Brother Sorensen not only didn't have that kind of recommend, he had never heard of such a document.

"I don't have anything like that," he replied. Elder Richards was not amused.

"Who is your stake president?"

"John Kelley."

"Where is he?"

"In Iran."

Elder Richards was even more not amused.

"Who is his First Counselor?"

"Philip Besseliever."

"Where is he?"

"In Fort Worth."

Then to someone else, Elder Richards ordered, "Get him on the phone."

To President Besseliever, Elder Richards said, "What's the idea of sending this man down here without a recommend to be bishop? How do I know that he doesn't drink or smoke or chase bad women?"

After being assured that Brother Sorensen was indeed the right man, Elder Richards concluded by saying, "When I go home and report to the brethren, if I get excommunicated for not following proper protocol, it's your fault." And with that, he hung up the phone, and then he proceeded to ordain Brother Sorensen a bishop and set him apart to be bishop of the Denton Ward.

Brother Sorensen served as bishop of the Denton Ward until its division on July 20, 1975. At one time Ell considered building a home on land he and Roger Fraim had jointly bought east of Denton, but largely because of the impending death of his father, Ell resigned his position at North Texas and moved back to his home state of Utah.

On many occasions Brother Sorensen has expressed his love for Denton and for the Church members in Denton.

"We loved the people of Denton so much," he has said in retrospect. "We have never forgotten the beautiful people. The kindnesses that the people exhibited were so impressive. My time in Denton was the highlight of my life!"

Love and Devotion to the Gospel
Unity and *Esprit d'Corps* in the Ward

The Denton saints enjoyed the high degree of closeness and togetherness that is typical, in varying degrees, of small wards and branches. These qualities existed in exceptionally high degree among the Denton saints. Without exception, those who are still available speak with sincere nostalgia of the love and enjoyment they experienced during those development years in the Denton Ward. They were years of love, activity, spirituality, and enjoyment.

Bill May reports that it was one of the closest groups he could imagine. He detected no animosity among any of the members. They loved one another, they enjoyed one another, and they did many things together. Bill Biggs has characterized the oneness everyone felt by saying, "It was a tight group." Janice Fraim has "really good memories" of the Denton Ward and of the Branch that preceded it. "It was a close group. It was a good time." Kaye Calabrese, who joined the Church in 1969, remembers the feeling that the Denton saints were "one big, happy family." Kaye also remembers the enjoyment of pot luck dinners almost every week.

A large measure of credit for this feeling of closeness and enjoyment goes to Margaret Porter. Everyone was caught up by Margaret's warmth and enthusiasm for whatever they were doing. "She was so warm and lively and enthusiastic," reports Dayonne Work, who, with her husband, Pete, moved to Denton in 1970. "Margaret treated us all as equals. There was no one beneath her. We had fun and we were happy together." Praising Margaret on another occasion, Dayonne said, "She taught us to love one another."

One characteristic that Margaret taught by example as well as by precept was that anyone who attended church – visitor or new member – should be welcomed warmly.

"Get out of your comfort zone and introduce yourself," she frequently admonished.

Credit for the closeness of the early Denton saints also goes to Margaret's husband, John, who as Branch President and then as Bishop, shepherded the flock with love and devotion. In addition to his many philanthropic deeds, some of which have already been cited, John also loved the people and he gave of his time. According to Sister Calabrese, "John always had time for everyone."

Devotion and Commitment

With the Porters as role models, the early saints in Denton developed and exhibited outstanding practices of devotion and commitment to the gospel. With the Fort Worth Stake extending from the Oklahoma Border on the north to Temple and Killeen on the south, a large geographic area had to be covered. Maurine Richards relates one such example when Denton was part of the Fort Worth Stake.

"Margaret Porter was Stake Relief Society president. I was a counselor in the Stake Primary presidency. We decided to visit the Relief Society and Primary in Killeen and Temple together. Margaret picked me up very early in the morning in her station wagon. It was still dark! We had a bed in the back for my two pre-school kids, Dana and Louise. We carried them out of my house and just put them to bed in the back. We had to be in Temple in time for their 10:00 am Relief Society meeting. After that meeting, we had lunch and then drove to Killeen for Primary at 4:00 pm and then back to Temple for a night Relief Society meeting for women who worked. Then the long ride back home. We put the kids back into their station wagon bed and got home very late. Those kids of mine always referred to that experience as their two day trip with Margaret Porter."

Margaret Porter was the "designated driver" to almost all Stake activities. Betty Cochran, one of Margaret's daughters, remembers many trips with her mother and others to stake meetings on Saturdays at the Dallas Stake Center on Kiest Boulevard. As was Margaret's usual custom, she picked up the Denton attendees at their homes, drove them to Dallas for meetings that occupied most of the day, and then brought them home, sometimes after the Saturday night dances. It was also Margaret's custom, after an already long day and evening, to stop at Goff's for hamburgers so the teenagers could get in another hour of socializing with Stake friends prior to the drive back to Denton.

Special Activities
County Fairs and Bazaars

The saints in Denton never missed an opportunity to make themselves visible in a positive light to the Denton community. One of the ways of doing this was the annual bazaar held on the sidewalk in front of the old Penney's store on the north side of the Square. Baked goods and crafts of all kinds were sold, and in addition to the good will established, profits were made for the building fund. The Relief Society, with help (when needed) from the priesthood, spent countless hours each year preparing for these bazaars. Besides benefiting community relations and the ward's building fund, these activities contributed immeasurably to binding the sisters ever closer in gospel unity.

Another community involvement occurred each autumn at the Denton County Fair. The Denton Ward was there each year with a food concession booth in which they sold frog legs, among other things. Doug Turner and his scouts provided the frogs and did the cooking while Hoyt Wilson did the "barking." "Yummy, yummy, yummy. Tickle your tummy," Hoyt would call out as he successfully enticed people to patronize the booth. It proved to be a popular concession, and they sold out every night. They also made a significant amount of money for their building fund.

A Special Pioneer Day Celebration

These were years of fun and enjoyment, and the Denton saints tended to do things on a grandiose scale leading to interesting results. A case in point is their Pioneer Day celebration on the weekend of July 24, 1973

The Ward planned a three day affair that would be representative of the pioneer days. Beginning with an overnight family campout at the Nobles' farm on Friday, the twenty-first, the celebration featured a Saturday trail ride into the fairgrounds in Denton and then an all-out celebration on Monday evening, the twenty-fourth, also at the fairgrounds. This celebration would consist of food, craft exhibits, demonstrations of pioneer skills, a rodeo, musical presentations, and a variety of games.

On Saturday, the trail riders left from the Nobles' ranch and traveled on US 380 into Denton. They walked, they rode in wagons, and some pulled homemade handcarts. As a result of prior arrangements, a lane of US 380 was blocked off from traffic for their exclusive use.

Don Clements was the designated trail boss for the ride into Denton. When the starting time arrived, Don mounted his horse and gave the starting signal, At that same instant, his foot slipped from the stirrup, he fell from his horse, and he broke his ankle. That was accident No. 1. Accident No. 2 occurred when Jackie Carpenter, driving a two-wheel cart pulled by one of Earl Cochran's donkeys, was easing the cart out onto the road. At that moment, a tire blew out on a passing car, and the loud explosive noise sent the donkey into a panic.

"Bail out!!" Jackie yelled to her son, Brent, who was sitting in the back of the cart.

Brent jumped, and the donkey ran with the cart down a ditch with Jackie unable to gain control until the donkey crashed into a fence. It might have been considered a dangerous situation had the onlookers been able to control their laughter. Despite that auspicious beginning, the trail ride continued, and the group made their way to the fair grounds.

At the fair grounds on Monday, the saints in their pioneer costumes had an exciting time. The area looked like a mini county fair with booths displaying crafts and home production of varying types. They also had food booths with lots of fried chicken and frog legs. Contests included apple dunking, three-legged races, wheel barrow races, wet sponge throwing, and a variety of other fun activities.

Toward evening they had a rodeo featuring greased pigs and a wild cow milking contest. Following the rodeo, they had a musicale in which a chorus sang songs featuring music arranged by Kay Brown. Finally they capped off the day with a pageant in which they told the story of the Mormon migration to the Salt Lake Valley through the medium of songs and dances. Rock Oakason, of the Denton Second Ward, composed the songs for the pageant.

The celebration was advertised throughout Denton, and an estimated 100 to 150 non-LDS citizens accepted the invitation to attend. It is also reported that they appeared to be very interested and impressed by the festivities.

The activity that Bob Nobles remembers best was the "wild cow milking contest." With the cows, furnished by the Nobles and the Porters, roaming freely inside the rodeo arena, teams of two men each had to catch and milk a cow. More precisely, one of the team members had to catch and hold a cow while his partner milked it by squirting the milk into an empty Coke bottle. The first team to fill a bottle with fresh milk would be the winner.

Joe McWilliams and Frank Martino constituted one of the teams, and they were assigned to the wildest cow in the bunch. Those who knew Joe McWilliams will more fully appreciate what happened. Joe went into the arena and grabbed his cow by the horns. Not liking what Joe was doing, the cow started running and shaking while Joe held on for dear life. He was dragged all around, but he refused to let go. No cow was going to get the better of Joe McWilliams. Finally, the cow accepted the inevitable, and Joe held her while Frank did the milking.

Who won the "wild cow milking contest?" No one remembers. But the old-timers who were there still talk about what a great experience it was and about the unifying effect of the various activities of the day and how they strengthened the bonds that Church members already had for one another.

Athletics

While basketball, followed closely by volleyball, is the sport of choice for most latter-day saint participants, the young men of the Denton Ward excelled in several sports. In basketball, the Denton Ward teams, with former college players such as Wally Cochran and Tony Wright, were frequent stake champions, and in the late 1960s they won several stake and district championships.

Social Activities

Members of the Denton Ward enjoyed one another, and they enjoyed socializing with one another. One could always count on good food and good entertainment when they got together. Fish fries, frog leg dinners, pot luck meals, and box suppers were always popular. Fried chicken dinners after ward conferences became a tradition. Yolanda Fernandez was famous for her chicken enchiladas.

The occasions for socializing were frequent. They had monthly ward dinners. Get-togethers could also be expected on such occasions as Valentine's Day, the Fourth of July, Pioneer Day, Harvest Hoedown, Halloween, Thanksgiving, the Christmas season, New Year's Eve. They also got together for work parties and for dances such as the Gold and Green Ball.

In addition to the good food and the enjoyment of one another's company, musical and dramatic entertainment was often featured. Group singing along with skits and floorshows could usually be counted on to provide mirth and enjoyment.

Scouting

Although Doug Turner never occupied one of the more visible leadership positions in the Denton Ward, he played one of the more important parts by being what many old-timers refer to as "the best scoutmaster Denton ever had."

Born to an LDS family in Tennessee, Doug met his future wife, Jeanette Miller, while stationed in Fort Worth in the military. As a fairly young couple, the Turners came to the Denton area in the early 1960s. Buying property from John Porter on Crawford Road in Argyle (immediately to the west of Art Cooper), they moved a house onto the property and later added on to the house. It is still their home. The Turners met with the Denton Branch in the old funeral home on McKinney Street. Doug, who loved camping, hunting, and fishing, became the Church's first scoutmaster in Denton, and he continued in that calling for several years.

Under Doug's leadership the boys went on hikes, survival trips, and high adventure outings. Returning home from one high adventure outing to Tennessee, rain forced the group to spend one night in the shelter of a cave, and as a result, several returned home with severe cases of poison oak. Their survival trips were designed to teach the boys to live off the land. In addition to water and sleeping bags, the boys could take anything else they wanted as long as it would fit into a band-aid can. The boys also became adept catchers of frogs, which they provided in abundant numbers for the many frog-leg dinners the branch/ward sponsored.

Doug Turner's scouts also excelled in scoutcraft competitions and camporees and summer camps. Under Doug's leadership, they learned their scouting skills, and they became quite adept in putting them into practice.

The accomplishment for which Doug is most noted occurred in February, 1968, when six of his scouts attained the rank of Eagle all at the same time. Their names are Joe Arrington; Kenneth Arrington; David Baria; Richard Baria, Jr.; Roger Fraim, III; and Richard Ragsdale. Their names can be seen on a plaque mounted inside the Denton Stake Center.

Doug's boy scouts had an *esprit de corps* which can be envied by most other troops. As an indication of the love and esteem they had for their scoutmaster, the boys worked together on one occasion earning enough money to buy Doug a new suit of clothes as a token of their feelings for him. The Denton LDS scout troops have been blessed with a number of excellent scoutmasters over the years, but none are remembered with any higher degree of esteem and love as Doug's scouts felt for him.

Dividing the Denton Ward

At the beginning of 1975, Denton Ward membership was nearing 600 members, and it was apparent that a ward division was imminent. On July 20, 1975, Fort Worth Stake President Horace Leithead came to Denton and presided over the division. The Denton First and Second Wards were created with Newell Kay Brown and Robert H. Nobles, respectively, called to serve as bishops.

Dividing the Denton Ward was a traumatic occurrence in the minds of many of the Denton members. It was as though a very happy family was now being split asunder. But the accelerated growth that normally follows a ward division also occurred in this case. Although a separation was taking place, the Denton saints rose to the challenge, and both new wards prospered.

CHAPTER 12
Music and Drama Abound

*A*ppropriate music has always been an important aspect of worship in the Church. Music and dancing have also been a fundamental aspect of LDS recreation and culture. Dramatic activities, ranging from small skits to roadshows to full sized productions, were also integral parts of the cultural side of Mormonism The early Denton Ward (and the earlier Denton Branch) built inner strength by participating fully in such activities.

Music

Except for Carol Wilhite (a UNT student discussed in an earlier chapter), skilled musical talent was simply not available among the saints in those early years in Denton. So the Porters, along with others, prayed for it to come. And it came.

The Branch in general, and the Porters in particular, prayed for membership additions that would have expert musical talents. The results were impressive. When Sarah Davis was baptized, the Branch had an outstanding pianist. Susan Myatt, a superb singer, pianist, and organist moved in. Kay Brown came as a music professor at NTSU, and his wife Myrna was a professional with the flute. Kevin Dartt, with her excellent singing voice, was baptized. Patricia Diers and her harp were featured in most of the musical performances. Dallin Pack, a noted jazz pianist, was another welcome addition to the Church's collection of musical talent in Denton. His arrangement of "I Am a Child of God," became a popular choir selection in Denton. There was no longer a shortage of musical talent in those early years.

Even with the arrival of these musical artists, Margaret Porter remained the musical leader of the Denton Stake for many years. Because of her enthusiasm for music and the self-training she had accomplished, the incoming musicians were happy to work with her.

As a choir leader, Margaret knew what she wanted, and in her own enthusiastic way, she demanded and got excellence. During choir practices, whenever Margaret stopped waving her baton and started beating it on the music stand, choir members knew that improvements were going to be demanded. In addition, she insisted they pronounce the lyrics correctly.

"You can't sing as though you were drinking from a Dixie cup," she would admonish.

Under Margaret's direction, the ward choirs (and later the stake choirs) sang for sacrament meetings, ward conferences, stake conferences, and other functions. One group, known as The Singing Mothers, performed annually with a huge variety show which Margaret directed. They also made public appearances whenever possible. For example, the Singing Mothers visited and sang in senior citizens homes and for a Habitat for Humanity benefit.

Margaret also directed full choir performances singing in the community at every opportunity including performing for eleven years as a major part of Denton's annual Festival of Christmas Carols, a gala event heralding in the Christmas season. Beginning on a small scale in the mid-1970s, the Festival was held first in the Texas Woman's University's Redbud Auditorium. Then as it grew in scope and attendance, it was moved to TWU's Margo Jones Auditorium, and then to the

North Texas State University's main auditorium.

The Festival featured choirs from the various Denton churches and schools, with each choir taking its turn on stage to perform two or three numbers. Under Margaret Porter's direction, the Denton Stake provided the largest of the choirs, and the quality of their renditions was such that Carol Lynn Mizell, Denton's music director for the event, would put the LDS choir last on the program to give the ending of the program the greatest impact.

With Margaret Porter leading a cast of ward members possessing a host of musical as well as other creative talents, the Denton Ward established a standard for the other wards in the metroplex area with regard to music and drama. In addition to possessing superb talents, the ward members participated enthusiastically because Margaret made it fun. She never had a problem recruiting singers for choir performances. People wanted to sing for her.

In addition to setting a standard of excellence in sound, Margaret's choirs also set a standard in appearance. Margaret insisted that each female choir member be attired in a black skirt and white blouse. The men were to be dressed in matching attire. And to make sure that this standard was maintained among the women, Margaret kept a rack of black skirts of various sizes to be loaned to whoever needed one.

Mention of a special experience regarding one of Margaret Porter's choirs is appropriate at this point. When the new Fort Worth Stake Center on Loop 820 was dedicated on February 18, 1973, a youth choir sang under Margaret's direction. Sitting toward the rear of the congregation, one of the attendees, Joan Bently, looked carefully at the choir because she was hearing many more voices than could be accounted for by the choir she saw. Sarah Davis, at the piano, also noticed the difference.

Following the dedication program, Sarah told Margaret, "I looked up from the piano, and I saw another choir of youth standing behind your choir."

Drama

Drama in the Denton Ward and Branch took on many forms. They produced skits and floor shows for ward socials and for entertainment at stake dances. Even though they were a small and relatively new unit of the Church, the Denton Ward produced roadshows that regularly won first place in stake competitions.

"We were bold enough to think we could do anything the big wards could do," Ann Andrus reminisced. And they did! They participated with quality.

The Denton Ward also produced full plays and musical dramas as a contribution to the citizens of Denton as well as for themselves. It cannot be said frequently enough that they had fun in all these efforts.

Skits and Floor Shows

Humor was the key focus of Denton's skits and floor shows. Initially these productions were the creation of Margaret and her son, John R. Later, people such as Leah Beedle, Sherrie Dutson, and others to be mentioned, added their talents to the mix.

When Margaret and her son, John R. Porter, conjured up a skit, hilarity was a foregone conclusion. If the phrase "When comedy was king" can be applied to the Porter combination, Margaret has to be the queen and John R. the crown prince. They put out some masterpieces.

One of the best remembered skits, performed at a ward

social, was titled, "Ahab, the Arab" (pronounced A-hab, the A-rab). A parody of Ray Stevens' famous song of the same name, the skit pantomimed the words of the song. Patricia Diers remembers it for its hilarity. "Whenever Margaret and John R. put their heads together," Patricia recalled, "you knew the result would be funny."

The skit was a pantomime accompaniment to a recording of the actual words and music of the song. Sarah Davis, playing the part of Fatima, and John R., as Ahab, kept the audience laughing throughout the performance. In the song, the "sheik of the burning sands," named Ahab, rides up on his camel, named Clyde, to have a clandestine visit with Fatima. Fatima, the Sultan's favorite dancer, is in her tent "eating on a raisin, and a grape, and an apricot, and a pomegranate, a bowl of chitterlings, two bananas, three Hershey bars, sipping an RC Cola, listening to her transistor, watching the Grand Ole Opry, and reading *Mad Magazine* while singing 'Does Your Chewing Gum Lose Its Flavor'." When Ahab (John R.) brought his camel to a screeching halt (with sound effects), alighted, and opened the flap of Fatima's (Sarah Davis') tent, the audience howled at the scene Sarah presented.

The "Milk Maids," with varying personnel, continued to provide entertaining song and dance for many floor shows at stake and ward functions. James Swanson playing the guitar with some of the girls backing him up in such numbers as "Why Do Little Birds Fall in Love," were also frequent entertainers. Other favorites at the early ward socials and variety shows included Arden and Lorraine Hopkins, Gary and Cheri Case, and Ferrell and Craig Nelson,

A parody on Elvis Presley proved to be another popular skit. Several old-timers still remember and laugh about Vic Nielsen's portrayal of Elvis, complete with body gyrations and lips moving in sync with the recorded music.

Skit themes were varied and ranged from country western ("Pistol Packin' Mama") to food storage. Leah Beadle and Clara Wilson also wrote many of the scripts.

One further skit should be mentioned. When Wally Cochran, John R. Porter, and Jimmy Ray Jones did a lip sync parody of the Singing Mothers, again there were laughs galore.

The ward members knew how to have fun.

Roadshows

Virtually the entire branch/ward participated in producing roadshows. They wrote scripts; they made costumes; they constructed scenery; they arranged transportation; and they did the acting and singing. Keith Myrick was one of the early prime movers in these productions. He wrote scripts, he acted in many of them, and he helped significantly with transportation to performances in Dallas and Fort Worth. Clara Wilson made many of the costumes using fabrics provided by the Martinos. Sherrie Dutson made much of the scenery. Margaret Porter, of course, was everywhere, and she infused everyone with enthusiasm for what they were doing. DeLynn Decker, who left Denton in 1967 to study English and drama at BYU, says that "Margaret Porter was the cohesive force behind almost all of the things we did in MIA."

Costumes, scenery, and music left little to be desired. These were quality performances, and Denton was a perennial winner in the eyes of the judges.

Comedy and fun were very much a part of the dramatic productions. In one roadshow (no one seems to remember its title), Hoyt Wilson, dressed as a bumblebee with a flashing light in his tail, stole the show as he danced and flitted about on the stage to the supposed dismay of the other performers. Because of the audience's enthusiastic reaction to Hoyt's performance, his bumblebee act was purposely written into subsequent roadshows for the next three or four years.

"I have seen roadshows from California to Washington, D.C.," Bishop Ell Sorensen once commented, "but in Denton they are done right. Denton is the Broadway of the Mutual roadshow."

Plays

The Denton saints continued to be quite active in dramatic productions. Several youth from Denton participated in "Saturday Night Warrior," produced in 1975 by the Fort Worth Stake. From Denton, Allen Stewart, Lynne Williamson, Beth Cole, Carol McCutcheon, Vicki Martin, Debbie Ragsdale, and Adrian Work participated in the production which was staged for the public in the Landreth Auditorium on the campus of Texas Christian University.

The Denton wards produced performances of "My Turn on Earth" staged in the NTSU main auditorium for the general public. Later, Dallin Pack and Sarah Davis combined to create a play called, "Where's Dad?" which traveled to senior citizens' centers and to service clubs. Participation in drama of various types not only helped strengthen the Denton saints, it also served as a means of contributing to the community and of gaining respect and interest from the community.

CHAPTER 13
The Eliesons

*O*n August of 1967, just before John Porter was released as Bishop of the Denton Ward, Sanfred and Virginia Elieson and their family moved to the Denton area. It would be difficult to imagine a more welcome or valuable addition to the Church in Denton.

Sanfred had just been released from serving three years as President of the Texas Mission, a mission that included the entire state of Texas except the El Paso area. No strangers to Denton, they had visited the Denton Branch several times during their tenure as presiding authorities of the Texas Mission, and they liked the Denton area so well that as soon as Sanfred was released as mission president, he and Virginia returned to Salt Lake City, sold their home there, and returned to make Texas their permanent home. And as life-long members of the Church, they brought with them a wealth of Church experience and Gospel knowledge.

Sanfred and Virginia Elieson

As a young boy in Salt Lake City, Sanfred grew up with Bruce R. McConkie. They developed a lifelong friendship as they played together, went to school together, and studied the scriptures together. Sanfred served a mission in the Southern States where he had close associations with LeGrande

Richards, the mission president. A young lady, Virginia Shurtliff, waited for his return, and in 1937 they were sealed in the Salt Lake Temple by Melvin J. Ballard, Virginia's uncle.

In the early 1940s Sanfred and Virginia moved from Salt Lake City to Los Angeles where Sanfred's parents were then living. Sanfred quickly found employment as an accountant with Vega Aircraft Company, a subsidiary of Lockheed. During their fifteen year stay in Los Angeles, Sanfred served on two high councils, and he played a leading role in getting a Bishops Storehouse established in that area. As the first bishop of the newly created Morningside Park Ward, Sanfred felt the need of greater coordination among the priesthood and auxiliary leaders of the ward, and he brought them together in council meetings on Sunday mornings. Out of this innovation grew the Ward Council meetings that are now a staple of ward administration throughout the church. During this time, Sanfred became a close friend of Robert L. Simpson, who later became a counselor in the Presiding Bishopric.

During their Los Angeles years, Virginia, who had a flair for interior decorating, developed a clientele among movie stars and other notable persons. Virginia's Los Angeles clients included Judy Garland, Doris Day, and Ronald and Nancy Reagan. She was good at what she did.

The Eliesons returned to Salt Lake City in 1958 and remained there until Sanfred's call in 1964 to serve as president of the Texas Mission. During this time Sanfred became affiliated with Beneficial Life Insurance Company, and he worked with M. Russell Ballard in land development projects. Virginia did interior decorating projects for several of the General Authorities including David O. McKay and Gordon B. Hinckley. They fulfilled various Church callings, and they engaged in serious study of the scriptures. One has only to view Virginia's Bible and *Book of Mormon* and observe the thoroughness of her notes, colorings, and markings to know that she was no casual student of the scriptures.

During this period, the Eliesons maintained close friendships with many of the General Authorities. For their missionary farewell prior to leaving to preside over the Texas Mission, M. Russell Ballard gave the invocation. Then in addition to Bill Elieson, son of Sanfred and Virginia, the speakers were Robert L. Simpson, LeGrande Richards, Spencer W. Kimball, and Gordon B. Hinckley.

Such was the measure of the family who decided to make the Denton area their home. It was as though a portion of Heaven had come down to become a nurturing father and mother to the Denton Saints.

In their several trips to Denton as missionaries, Sanfred and Virginia had been popular speakers at cottage meetings and in regular church meetings, and they were always happy to share their insightful understanding of the scriptures and of Church history. As mission president, Sanfred emphasized the use of the *Book of Mormon* as a missionary tool, and the missionaries throughout the mission used this approach with significant success.

Toward the end of Sanfred's term as Mission President, John Porter offered him a job if he and Virginia would come back to Texas after being released. The Eliesons had fallen in love with Texas anyway, so after settling their affairs in Salt Lake City, back to Texas they came.

True to his word, John Porter put Sanfred to work in a car agency in Bowie. The Eliesons stayed in Bowie for about a year and then moved to Jacksboro, where Sanfred owned his own car agency. But the automobile business was not for Sanfred, so after a year and a half in Bowie they came to Denton

County where they purchased land and built a home just northwest of Sanger. Sanfred resumed his former relationship with Beneficial Life Insurance Company, and he also sold financial plans and investments.

In Church service, Sanfred served on the High Council of the Fort Worth Stake until it was divided on November 14, 1976. He was then called as Patriarch of the new Fort Worth North Stake, a calling he held for twenty-three years (1976 – 1999) until becoming unable to function because of ill health in his declining years. When the Dallas Temple was dedicated in October 1984, President Hinckley set Sanfred apart as a sealer. Three years later, the Dallas Temple's second president, Robert L. McCook, requested Sanfred as his First Counselor and Virginia as a Matron. Sanfred and Virginia served in those capacities for the next three years in addition to Sanfred's calling as a stake patriarch.

Virginia taught in all the auxiliaries in the Denton Wards. Art Cooper remembers that he could hardly wait for each Sunday so he could enjoy the instruction and the spirit of her Gospel Doctrine classes.

One of the special contributions Sanfred and Virginia made in Denton was in organizing a study group that met twice a month on Sunday evenings. They had done this in Salt Lake City among the General Authorities, and it had worked well there. It worked well here also, so much so that even though the Eliesons have now passed on, the study group still continues to meet on the second and fourth Sunday evenings. For years it met at the home of Frank and Betty Martino. Now, Richard and Pat Ragsdale host the study group in their home.

Sanfred and Virginia were scriptorians without peer, and perhaps their greatest contribution in Denton was the way they expounded and clarified the scriptures in study groups, in cottage meetings, and in classes. In this manner they played a significant role in many of the conversions that occurred in Denton during the 1960s and 1970s.

Virginia Elieson died on February 6, 1999. In a consoling letter written by President Hinckley to Brother Elieson, President Hinckley said, "Virginia was a remarkable woman. My wife thought the world of her. She was extremely able in decorating and in many other things."

On August 29, 2000, Sanfred joined Virginia in the next life. Denton will ever be grateful for their many contributions.

CHAPTER 14
The Martinos

*I*t might be said that fate brought Frank Martino and Betty Newman together. It might also be said that this was a match made in heaven before coming to earth, and it was foreordained to happen.

Frank first met Betty on a blind date in Dallas, a date arranged by a very insistent friend of Frank's. It did not go at all well. But as students at the University of Texas at Austin in the late 1940s, their paths kept crossing, and soon Frank and Betty were dating again. It might be fair to say that at first, Betty tolerated Frank. But she also recognized the outstanding qualities he possessed, and soon that toleration turned into a deep and abiding love which he reciprocated.

Frank was always a doer and a leader. In college, for example, he joined the Sigma Phi Epsilon fraternity. As the fraternity's social chairman, he was in charge of the various dances held at the Student Union Building. He later served as president of the fraternity. Frank also served as an associate editor of the campus yearbook, *The Cactus*, and he was elected a member of the prestigious Goodfellows organization. Betty was also quite active on campus, and in her senior year, she served as house manager of her Chi Omega sorority.

Betty Newman's parents, with assistance from Holford Russell, owner of Russell's Department Store in Denton, had established a business of manufacturing and selling women's underclothes. After finishing college in January 1949, Frank served a brief stint selling clothing for a firm in Mississippi

The Martino family at the time of their baptism
Sons Rick, Trey, David and Jim standing behind Frank and Betty.

before being offered a sales position with Russell-Newman. Frank moved to Denton, Betty was graduated from college in June, and the two were married in Denton on July 23, 1949.

Over the intervening years in Denton, both Frank and Betty have been prominently involved in civic and political affairs. Betty, for example, has been president of the Petal Pusher Garden Club and of the Garden Club Council. She has also served as president of the Republican Women of Denton and as Vice Chairman of the Denton County Republican Party. Betty was a member of the prestigious Denton Benefit League, and she served one term as its president.

Frank, having risen to be Chairman of Russell-Newman, Inc., has been chairman, president, or director of numerous organizations including First State Bank of Texas, American Apparel Manufacturers Association, Southwest Apparel Manufacturers Association, Denton Chamber of Commerce,

Denton County Republican Party, TWU President's Council, and a host of other organizations and activities. Frank has been listed in several "Who's Who" categories, and he has received numerous awards from prestigious organizations.

You don't push the Martinos. They make sure of what they are doing, and when they are ready, there's no stopping them. Their conversion to The Church of Jesus Christ of Latter-day Saints serves as a classic example of this trait. The Martinos' introduction to the Church occurred in 1957 when two sister missionaries knocked on their door at 1222 Emerson Street in Denton. Their baptism, however, did not occur until ten years later, on December 7, 1967. A lot of things happened in between.

Having a deep religious commitment and being open and broad minded, Frank and Betty invited the sister missionaries into their home and visited with them. With great respect for the enthusiasm and dedication of the two sisters, Frank and Betty enjoyed the visit. But they already had their religion, the Methodist church, and the idea of making a change never penetrated their hearts on that occasion. Nor on other occasions.

The Lord, however, worked on the Martinos from more than one direction. There were additional visits on a yearly basis from missionaries, but it was the persuasive efforts of Dick and Pat Ragsdale, who had been converted to the Gospel some years earlier that effectively opened the door. After repeated invitations to attend church services, Sunday evening cottage meetings, and dinners, the Martinos finally decided that they should say yes to something as a token of their friendship with the Ragsdales. So they accepted an invitation to attend a (non-religious) book review at the LDS church building on Malone

Street. Touched by the spirit there, Frank attempted to give Pat a twenty-dollar bill to be used in any way the Church needed. Refusing to take the money, Pat, nevertheless took advantage of the opportunity.

"We have not invited you to come for funds, but we love you both so much, and we would like to share what has become the most important thing in our lives. If you would just read the *Book of Mormon,* we would be grateful. It is such a beautiful book, and we know you will enjoy it."

Frank and Betty accepted the challenge, but they both acknowledge that she was more serious about following through than he was. She read dutifully; he would start reading and then fall asleep.

About this same time, Frank's parents returned from a trip to South America and the Easter Islands. Commenting on Thor Heyerdahl's book, *Aku-Aku,* Frank's dad said it was the best book he had ever read. He told Frank about the book describing a light-skinned race and a dark-skinned race, and the dark-skinned race destroyed the light-skinned race about 400 A.D. That aroused Frank's interest, and he got serious about reading more of the *Book of Mormon.*

The LDS missionaries were now meeting regularly with the Martinos, two or three times a week, and as a result of their gentle urgings, both Frank and Betty completed reading the *Book of Mormon.* They both believed the book to be true.

"What are we going to do about it?" Betty asked.

"Nothing," Frank responded.

A short while later, coming home from Christmas shopping in Fort Worth on the Friday following Thanksgiving, Frank voiced a change in attitude.

"Betty," he said, "if the *Book of Mormon* is true and we don't do anything about it, the sin will be on our heads."

Betty agreed wholeheartedly. They were almost ready for baptism.

Although Frank and Betty had made their decision, breaking away from the Methodist church was not an easy move for people as involved as they had been. Frank had headed a committee to build the Wesley Center at North Texas State University in Denton, and he had just completed his obligations to that task. Betty had been Sunday School Superintendent for the church, and she began the process of turning that responsibility over to another person in an orderly manner. But there was resistance on the part of friends and Methodist church members. Scores of anti-Mormon reading materials began to circulate about Denton. George Hopkins, a Denton attorney and a close friend of the Martinos, said that their conversion to Mormonism caused more books on Mormonism to be sold in Denton than ever before.

On the other hand, the Martinos leaned more toward the Gospel because their Methodist ministers were suggesting new perspectives on several theological topics that seemed totally false. The LDS teachings seemed logical and right, and Frank and Betty had little trouble accepting them, although Frank had trouble for a short while with the concept that Joseph Smith was a real prophet of God. And unbeknown to the Martinos at the time, the mission president of the Dallas Mission kept Elder Ted Montayne in Denton for several months just so he could continue working with the Martinos, which he did successfully.

The die was cast, and when the Martinos announced their decision to be baptized to the Ragsdales, joy abounded. The date would be December 7, 1967. Dick Ragsdale baptized both Frank and Betty, and Sanfred Elieson confirmed them.

When the Martinos decided to be baptized, Dick Ragsdale, who at that time was bishop of the Denton Ward, wanted to be sure that Frank understood what he was getting into from a financial standpoint. Calling Frank into the bishop's office, Bishop Ragsdale conducted the following interview.

"Frank, as a member of the Church you understand you will be expected to pay one-tenth of your increase as tithing."

"Yes, I understand that."

"You will also be expected to contribute the cost of two meals each month to the Fast Offering."

"I understand that also."

"We have a ward budget you will be asked to contribute to."

"That's all right."

"And we also have a building fund for enlarging our meeting facility."

"That's all right also."

"We also have a missionary fund for helping to support missionaries in the field."

"That's all right also."

It was a rather unique way to welcome someone into the Church, but Bishop Ragsdale knew Brother Martino, and he had confidence in what the end result would be.

When Frank and Betty decided to be baptized, they called a family meeting to make the announcement to their sons. These meetings, commonly called "Councils of War," were a tradition in the Martino family. The parents told their sons that they knew that their decision was right and that they hoped that their sons would follow them, but it was a personal decision that each of the four boys would have to make for himself.

Responding to their parents' request, the Martino sons began taking the missionary lessons two days after their parents' baptism. David and Trey accepted the Gospel readily and were baptized two weeks later. Rick was only seven years old at the time, so his baptism had to wait for a few months. Rick enjoyed attending Primary, and upon reaching the age of eight, he was ready.

Jim, the eldest son, took a little bit longer. While not objecting to his parents and brothers joining the Church, he resisted making the move himself, as did his high school sweetheart, Jennie. Some readings in an advanced placement English class had left Jim with some unresolved theological questions, and he also had some misconceptions about LDS practices. He was under the impression, for example, that the Church members did not participate in athletics, and he loved athletics.

Jim continued attending the Methodist church, and he withdrew from meeting with the missionaries. He also began studying the Bible with the intent of proving that Mormonism was wrong. But the more Jim saw of the Mormons, the more impressed he became of their way of life, and after six weeks of resistance, he started attending the LDS meetings. Jim was especially impressed with his Sunday School teacher, Virginia Elieson. In addition, even before his baptism, he became a home teaching companion to Sanfred Elieson. These were associations not to be denied.

One last hurdle had to be overcome, and that was resolved by Elder Buterus, a missionary who also had an extended stay in Denton. When together for a family dinner in the Martino home, Elder Buterus asked, "Jim, why haven't you joined the Church?" Jim thoughtfully replied, "There are still two things that bother me. One is the denial of the priesthood to the blacks, and the other is polygamy."

"Those are fair questions," Elder Buterus responded, "and I'll answer them to your satisfaction. But first I want to ask you two questions, and when you respond to me, I'll then answer your questions."

Question number one from Elder Buterus was, "Was Joseph Smith a true prophet of the Lord?" Question number two was, "Is the *Book of Mormon* true?" Jim's prayerful inquiry was brief, as the Spirit bore witness to him. And when he responded "Yes" to both questions, his own questions became moot. Jim's conversion was complete, and he was baptized by his father on October 20, 1968.

Shortly after Frank and Betty were baptized, Frank became Executive Secretary to Bishop Ragsdale in the Denton Ward, and the Martinos have been major LDS leaders in the Denton area from that point on. Four years after his baptism in 1967, Frank Martino was serving on the Fort Worth Stake High Council (1971). Four years after that (1975), he became a counselor in the Fort Worth Stake Presidency, and in three more years (1979), he became Bishop of the Denton First Ward. In 1994 Frank Martino was called to be a sealer in the Dallas Temple. Then in 1998 he became First Counselor to Dallas Temple President Owen Jacobsen. When President Jacobsen had to be released early because of his wife's illness, Brother Martino became the president of the Dallas Temple. Frank and his wife, Betty, have also served a temple mission in the Nauvoo Temple.

Betty has served in many capacities such as ward and stake Relief Society presidents, and as Matron in the Dallas Temple. She was also one of the best of Denton's many seminary teachers. In her early years in the Church she graciously accepted a visiting teaching route that required over 150 miles of driving. The route included the Parrish family in Decatur, Sanfred and Virginia Elieson in Jacksboro, and Nina Salter in Bowie.

If Frank and Betty Martino are to be considered outstanding Church leaders in the Denton area, equal recognition has to go to their four sons, James (Jim), David, Trey, and Rick. Theirs is an example of an exceptionally outstanding family that has provided needed leadership and strength to the Church in Denton and elsewhere. All four sons, Jim, David, Trey, and Rick, have served full-time missions and have served on stake High Councils. In addition, David has twice served as a bishop and is now a counselor in the stake presidency. Trey has served in two bishoprics and as a counselor to two mission presidents in the Fort Worth Mission. He is currently (2008) serving as bishop. Rick, the youngest, currently serves on the Denton Stake High Council. Jim has served as a bishop, then as the first stake president of the Denton Stake, then as a mission president for three years in Venezuela. In the Church's General Conference of April 2008, Jim was sustained as an Area Authority Seventy. Not bad for a person who initially set out to identify the fallacies of the gospel his parents had just embraced.

Of all the many accomplishments of the Martinos in Denton, Frank's and Betty's greatest accomplishments can be said to have been within their family. All four sons are stalwart members and leaders within the Church. When Frank retired from Russell-Newman, the sons carried on unitedly. Jim serves as chairman of the board, David as president and chief executive officer, Trey as chief operations officer, and Rick as executive vice president. The parents and each of the sons and their families live in their own homes located together on property just west of Aubrey. Known as the "5M & R Ranch," the colony also includes the home of Richard and Pat Ragsdale as well as that of Merle and Dawn Egget, parents of Rick's wife, Connie. The Martinos have generously made the "5M & R

Ranch," with its many features, available for many stake and ward activities.

The Martinos are a very close-knit and united family. One time when a New York publication sent a reporter to interview the Martinos as one of America's outstanding families, she lost interest in the project when she could not find anything negative to include to balance her story.

Frank and Betty both died in the summer of 2007, he from a fall from a hotel balcony in Africa, and she, a few months later, from an illness. They essentially went together to accept a greater call to help build the kingdom on the other side of the veil.

The Martino Family
Summer 2007, following Frank's death

CHAPTER 15

The Nobles

Dr. Robert (Bob) Nobles, D.O. was a successful physician and surgeon in Denton. He even owned his own hospital on West University Avenue. Bob's avocation, and probably his first love, was raising cattle at his home west of Denton and on other lands he owned to the northwest of Denton. In many instances, he was a doctor in overalls.

Early in their marriage, Bob and his wife, Jimmie Lou, were church goers, but Bob felt uncomfortable on such occasions because he couldn't agree with many of the things being taught.

Jimmie Lou and Bob Nobles

"I felt like a hypocrite when I attended," he reports. So he and Jimmie Lou stopped going to church even though he knew that she really wanted to go.

Bob Nobles was also a Rotarian, and he attended Rotary Club meetings regularly. That is where he first encountered Mormonism.

In the Rotary Club at that time, the members took turns presenting the program, and periodically, the speaker's assignment would be to give a "classification" talk in which he described the ins and outs of his business or occupation to the assembled group. In 1969 the time came for Dick Ragsdale to give a classification talk. Ragsdale,who was Rotary Club president at the time, was an optometrist. He was also bishop of the Denton Ward. Standing before the group, Dick introduced his topic.

"I have two classifications. I am an optometrist. I am also bishop of the Denton Ward of The Church of Jesus Christ of Latter-day Saints, and that's the classification I want to share with you today."

At that point, according to Ragsdale, four ministers from other churches got up and walked out.

Dick did not make the presentation himself, but he had invited Sanfred Elieson to attend and talk to the group. Sanfred went to the microphone and gave the Joseph Smith story "from A to Z."

Following Sanfred's presentation, Bob Nobles was perplexed. In fact, he was troubled. Two thoughts went through his mind. First, he would give anything to know as surely as Sanfred seemed to know that the things he had heard were true. And second, "How can anyone in his right mind believe such things as I heard today?"

"At that point, the Spirit bore witness to me that what I had heard was true," Bob acknowledges.

But Bob Nobles wasn't yet ready for such a change in his life, and for the next two years he gave no further thought to the matter. And then his time came.

On the day before Easter in 1971, Bob was at one of his properties building a fence. The plan was for Jimmie Lou and the kids to come and join him for the weekend. Quite suddenly the thought of Sanfred Elieson's talk came to him along with the thought that he could make Jimmie Lou happy by taking her to church on Easter Sunday.

"And if I still feel the same way about it after going," he said to himself, "then I am going to investigate the Mormon church."

Bob immediately called Jimmie Lou and told her not to come to the ranch because he was coming home.

Easter Sunday came, and they went to church, but Bob didn't feel any better about being there.

"I was miserable," he reported. "I felt like I was sitting on a bed of hot coals."

The plan after church was for the family to have lunch in the cafeteria at Bob's hospital. They went there, then Bob excused himself and drove the few short blocks to the LDS chapel on Malone Street, hoping to see Dick Ragsdale come out when the Sunday meeting ended. Parking his car on the street, Bob waited, but Dick did not come out with the others. So the next day, Bob called Dick on the phone and said, "I need to talk with you."

The two met for lunch at a hamburger stand, and Bob said, "I need to know more about all this." Dick gave Bob a quick summary of LDS beliefs with emphasis on three things: (1) the preexistence, (2) this life as a probationary state, and (3) the three degrees of glory. These were things that Bob had believed all his life anyway, and he knew that this was the Church for him.

"What do I do now?" he asked.

"You need to take the missionary lessons," Dick responded.

Following lunch, Bob left to return to his hospital. Dick then called Hoyt Wilson, who dashed to the hospital and was waiting for Bob to arrive. Hoyt gave Bob a *Book of Mormon* and a copy of LeGrande Richards' *A Marvelous Work and a Wonder*.

Bob left the next day on a trip to Missouri, taking the books with him. After starting *A Marvelous Work and a Wonder*, he couldn't put the book down, and he read the entire book without stopping. Returning from his trip, he was ready for the missionary lessons.

At this point, it is appropriate to switch to Jimmie Lou and review the events that led her to becoming ready to have the missionary lessons. Her story, to this point, is quite different from Bob's.

Jimmie Lou was aware of the Mormon presence in Denton because of noticing the missionaries riding their bicycles on the streets, but she paid no real attention to them. Then one day, two missionaries knocked on the door of her home, and asked if they could leave a *Book of Mormon* with her to read. "We'll be back in a week to see what you think about it," they said. She accepted the book, but didn't read it. She was away from home when the missionaries returned, and she left the book on the front porch for them.

Some time later, while attending Hemisfair in San Antonio with some family members, Jimmie Lou stopped at the LDS booth there to look at their displays. She liked what she saw, but she declined to give her name and address. She was interested, and yet, she was not interested.

Then Jimmie Lou met Jo Ann Baria. Jo Ann had a house full of crafts the Relief Society had made for a bazaar, and Jimmie Lou was interested by it all. She and Jo Ann became close friends. Then when the time came for her and Bob to take the missionary lessons as serious investigators, they attended the LDS Church on a Sunday which happened to be Fast and Testimony Sunday. Jo Ann Baria bore a powerful testimony in that meeting, and the Spirit bore witness to Jimmie Lou that it was all true. She, too, was ready for the missionary lessons.

Bob and Jimmie Lou took the missionary lessons together, and then they were baptized on May 21, 1971, along with two of their daughters, Nancy and Beth.

In 1975, four years after his baptism, Bob Nobles became bishop of the newly created Denton Second Ward, and he had served on the Fort Worth Stake High Council before that. Following his tenure as bishop, Bob was called as first counselor to President Gordon Watts in the Lewisville Stake Presidency (1980). He is currently (2008) a sealer in the Dallas Temple, and he is also the Patriarch of the Denton Stake.

CHAPTER 16
God Will Provide

*C*arl "Red" Blake, coach of the Army (West Point) football teams during their glory years in the 1940s, once said, "Good football players are a dime a dozen, but a good leader is priceless."

When one considers the outstanding assemblage of leadership talent and gospel maturity that came together in Denton during the 1960s and early 1970s, one must acknowledge that more than just coincidence was involved. Mature and capable leadership was needed for the Branch to survive and grow, and God provided it.

"It was a miracle!!" declared Virginia Elieson in retrospect.

"We prayed them in," Margaret Porter rightfully claims.

And pray they did, with faith and conviction. In their leadership meetings as well as in their personal prayers, the Porters prayed for specific help. If they felt a need for people with skills in music or drama or anything else, they prayed for those specific types of persons to be made available through move-ins or conversions. They prayed that Denton's two universities might be a means of attracting members having exceptional skills of various types, and those prayers bore remarkable fruit. People who remember those years report that the prayers offered by the Porters and by others in the branch and ward brought undeniable results.

Accounts of families that formed the core of leadership in the Church's early years in Denton have already been presented in prior chapters. These families, the Porters, the Ragsdales, the Coopers, the Martinos, and the Nobles, were outstanding community leaders as well as outstanding church leaders. In fact, the conversion of the Ragsdale and Martino families sent ripples of incredulity through the elite of Denton.

As gospel and scriptural scholars, Sanfred and Virginia Elieson, both life-long members of the Church, made invaluable contributions in strengthening the local members and in attracting new converts by teaching from the scriptures with incredible knowledge and insight. Virginia's Sunday School classes were a highlight to everyone who attended.

The many services of John and Margaret Porter in getting things started in Denton have also been reviewed in earlier chapters. However, it would be well at this point to acknowledge their later calling to spend three years as President and Matron of the Sacramento California Mission (1981 - 1984).

Although it was the Porters who got things started in Denton, it has been noted in prior chapters that the Ragsdales played a major role in the conversions of the Martino and the Nobles families. These and other converts, plus the several families that moved in to Denton, not only built up the Church in Denton, they also played many prominent roles in the stake organizations.

And as has been indicated, bishops, stake presidents, patriarchs, mission presidents, and temple presidents have emerged from this beginning nucleus.

Not only did the Lord provide outstanding additions to the Church membership in Denton, he also sent outstanding missionaries to labor in Denton. Elder Rolfe Kerr, who labored in Denton during the early years of the Branch, is currently (2008) the Church Commissioner of Higher Education. Elder A. Roger Merrill was instrumental in the conversion and baptism of the

Ragsdales. His tenure in Denton was extended beyond its normal duration just so he could continue working with the Ragsdales until their expected baptism. Elder Merrill is now (2008) the General Sunday School President of the Church.

On one of their recent trips to Salt Lake City, the Ragsdales visited with Elder Merrill, and Pat Ragsdale exclaimed, "Brother Merrill, do you know what you accomplished when you were in Denton? You are responsible for conversions that have led to a large number of bishops and stake presidents and other leaders in our area." Smiling, Brother Merrill humbly thanked Pat for telling him that. "It is a fulfillment of a part of my patriarchal blessing," he responded. "My patriarchal blessing said my mission would make a difference in a lot of lives, and they, in turn, would bless my life." It was a prophecy magnificently fulfilled by Elder Merrill's missionary service in Denton.

Denton Leaders in the Fort Worth Stake

Fort Worth Stake Presidency, February 1974
Standing: Quinn McKay, 1st Counselor; **Frank Martino**, 2nd Counselor
Seated: Horace Leithead, President
(Denton member in bold type)

Denton Leaders in the Fort Worth Stake

Fort Worth Stake High Council prior to February 1974
Sanfred Elieson, Walter Carmony, Eugene Giles, Lloyd Redd,
Horace Leithead, **Victor Neilsen,** Otto Puempel, **Frank Martino**,
Hugh Martin, **Richard Ragsdale**
(Denton members in bold type)

Stake AP/YWMIA Board
Standing: **Richard Ragsdale**, Hugh Martin, Carolyn Bell, **Victor Nielsen**,
Dallin Pack, **Virginia Elieson**, Otto Puempel
Seated: Charlene Taylor, Jerri Weeks, **Betty Martino**
(Denton members in bold type)

Denton Leaders in the Fort Worth Stake

Stake Sunday School Board Members
Art Cooper, Glen Gryble, David Steiner,
Edleweis Arrington, Maurice Arrington
(Denton members in bold type)

Denton Leaders in Houston to attend the
Regional Conference with President Kimball
Dick Yates, Al White, James Martino, Wally Cochran

CHAPTER 17

The Porter Family Expands

$\mathcal{D}$uring the Church's development years in Denton (1967 to 1975) the three children of John and Margaret Porter reached maturity and married their sweethearts. All three — John R., Betty, and Ann — have produced families active and prominent in the affairs of the Church in Denton. With regard to the beginnings of these three families, their stories offer some unique aspects and some interesting conversions.

The Extended Porter Family
Photograph taken in 1986, shortly after John and Margaret
returned from their mission in Sacramento, California.

John R. and Susan Porter

John R. Porter and Susan Rowlett were high school sweethearts who looked forward to marriage in the not too distant future. Susan was not LDS at that time, and religion did not mean as much to her then as it did to John. When John was called as the first full-time missionary from Denton, he gave Susan a *Book of Mormon* and some additional Church literature and asked her to study them while he was away.

Upon John's return two years later, he was very disappointed that Susan had done very little reading and studying, and no noticeable progress had been made toward the conversion that he had hoped she would experience. After a few weeks, it was time for John to return to BYU, and he and Susan discussed the possibility of marriage.

Then taking Susan by surprise, John declared, "Susan, it won't work."

Startled, Susan responded indignantly, "You mean your church is more important to you than I am?"

"I don't want to say it that way," John replied, "but it simply won't work" And he departed for BYU.

While John was away, Susan dated another person who soon proposed marriage to her. Faced now with a momentous decision, she felt the magnitude of it all. Should it be John R. or should it be the new person? And was the Church true or not? She had to have more light and understanding than she then had.

Susan began reading the materials John had earlier left with her, and she was soon impressed to kneel and pray about it. "I need to know!" she pled. As Susan relates it, the instant she got up off her knees, her bosom was filled with a burning fire, and she knew! She immediately phoned Margaret Porter, and she began taking the missionary lessons. She then requested baptism.

John R.'s father, John W. Porter, was the Denton Branch President at the time, and he gave Susan a searching interview to be sure she was being baptized on her own testimony and not because of her love for John R. Susan passed the test, and she was baptized on October 15, 1966.

In Provo, John R. received a phone call from Susan that night. "I have something to tell you," she announced. "I was baptized today." One can only imagine the happiness they both felt. They became engaged when John was home for the Christmas holiday, and they were married the next year in August of 1967 in the Salt Lake Temple.

Over the ensuing years, John R. and Susan have served in numerous church callings. John's service has included being Branch President in Decatur and Bishop of the Denton Second Ward.

John and Susan have become the parents of six children and twenty grandchildren, with two more on the way.

Wally and Betty (Porter) Cochran

Wally Cochran, son of Earl and Doreece Cochran, grew up in the Argyle area and played basketball while a student in Denton High School and at Dallas Baptist College. He and Betty Porter dated one another in high school, and in June 1968, they became man and wife. Following their marriage, they moved into a house on Bonnie Brae Street next door to John R. and Susan Porter.

In 1970, a friend named Jimmie Jones was living with the Cochrans, and it was Jimmie's consuming curiosity about the gospel that served as the catalyst in completing Wally's conversion. Although Wally and Jimmie were non-members at that time, they and John R. (a returned missionary) were the best of friends. They loved playing basketball and other sports together, and they were virtually inseparable at other times.

One evening when visiting in the Cochran home, John R. told of a humorous experience he had had on his mission, an experience that involved giving a priesthood blessing to a woman.

Jimmie startled everyone by pouncing on the idea of the blessing. "Wait a minute," he exclaimed, "what gives you the authority to give a blessing?"

Jimmie's question was all John R. needed to launch into an explanation of the priesthood and divine authority from Jesus Christ. But John R.'s explanation elicited further questions. Jimmie was sincerely interested, and his questions kept coming. Sometimes the three would be together at Wally's house, and sometimes at John R.'s house. But wherever they were, the conversation would include religion. John R. would respond to the questions, and Wally would listen intently. Occasionally Wally, who had had many of the missionary lessons, would also respond to Jimmie's questions. These sessions became spiritual feasts for all three men, with the end result being that Jimmie Jones and Wally Cochran were both baptized on March 26, 1971. On April 5, 1972, Wally and Betty were sealed in the Salt Lake Temple, and their posterity now numbers three children and eight grandchildren.

Church service for Wally and Betty includes serving in two bishoprics for Wally, and serving twice as Stake Young Women's President for Betty. In addition, Betty deserves special recognition for longevity in a calling. Her twelve years as a seminary teacher is believed to be a local record in a single calling.

As a point of interest, it should be added that Jimmie Jones served a mission in the states of Washington and Oregon, and he later married and moved to Utah where he became a bishop.

Vaughn and Ann (Porter) Andrus

Vaughn and Ann Andrus moved to Denton in March of 1974. Actually, it was a "return" to Denton for Ann, one of the daughters of John and Margaret Porter.

Vaughn and Ann were both graduates of BYU where they became acquainted. They met again in 1969 while they both were living in the San Francisco Bay Area in California. Ann was living in California as an airline flight attendant, and she attended the Singles Ward in Berkeley. Vaughn, who was born and raised in the Church, visited the Berkeley Singles Ward one Sunday, and, recognizing Ann, became reacquainted with her. Romance quickly blossomed, and they were married in December 1971 in the Oakland Temple.

Vaughn, at that time, was employed by the Berkeley police force, and in his five years in that role, he experienced the anti-Viet Nam riots in Berkeley as well as the beginning of the hippie culture. Following his marriage to Ann, Vaughn spent two years as an undercover agent buying drugs and mingling with the drug culture. In this role he had to look the part which included a beard and shoulder-length hair. It was during this undercover period that Ann and Vaughn came to Denton to visit her family. Vaughn still chuckles about John Porter's embarrassment when introducing Vaughn as his new son-in-law.

"This is my son-in-law," John would say, and then after an awkward pause, "he has to look this way because of his job."

The Berkeley, California Undercover Vice Squad, 1972-1973
Vaughn Andrus (second from right, in hat)

Vaughn was always actively involved in the affairs of the Church. After moving to the Denton area, some of his callings included being a stake clerk, a high counselor, a bishop, and a counselor in the stake presidency. Brother Andrus was released on May 4, 2008, as president of the Denton Stake after serving eight and a half years in that position. He has since been called to serve as a counselor in the Fort Worth Mission.

In addition to his Church service, Vaughn has been very active in community affairs, both in the city of Krum and in Denton County. As president of the Farmer's and Merchant's Bank for twenty-nine years, he headed a financial institution known throughout the area for its integrity and solidarity. Personally, and through the bank, Vaughn did much for the community in terms of financial support for various projects, and he was a perennial fund raiser for youth livestock shows and fairs, supporting many youths from Krum and Denton County.

Vaughn and Ann are currently the parents of six sons and eight grandchildren. They are expecting a ninth grandchild in December 2008.

Aunt Gladys

Before leaving the Porter family, mention should be made of Gladys Bryan, Margaret Porter's sister. Known as "Aunt Gladys" to all the Porter generations and to the ward members, Gladys moved from California to Denton in 1965 following the death of her husband. Gladys, however, wanted nothing to do with that "strange religion" that John and Margaret had espoused.

"I'll never join that church," she is reported to have said. But gospel conversations with John and Margaret were inevitable, and Gladys also attended some church meetings and cottage meetings. Still she held out. Then one day while visiting the Porters in their Argyle home, John challenged her.

Aunt Gladys was not feeling well that day, and she was in a somewhat bad mood.

"Gladys," John said, "your problem is that you know the Church is true, and you aren't doing anything about it. You know you need to be baptized, and you aren't going to be fully happy until you do."

A few days later, Gladys went out and purchased baptism clothes, and on April 23, 1971, Gladys entered the waters of baptism. She was the only member of Margaret's family to do so. Aunt Gladys remained in Denton as an active member of the Church until her death in 1983.

CHAPTER 18

Further Additions to Church Membership in Denton

The late 1960s and early 1970s saw significant growth in the Denton Ward as the result of additional conversions and move-ins. They brought strength, maturity, leadership, and spirituality. It is impossible, however, to mention more than just a few in this history, but the people included in this chapter are people who cannot be overlooked in any history of the Church in Denton.

Ralph and Sarah Davis

Ralph and Sarah Davis became investigators of the Church in the late 1960s. Ralph had established a successful dental practice in town, and he and Sarah were staunch members of the First Baptist Church.

After acquiring a testimony of the Gospel, there was still a reason for Ralph and Sarah to delay their entry into the waters of baptism. Ralph had signed a pledge to donate a large amount of money toward the construction of a new Baptist meeting facility on Malone Street, and honoring that pledge plus paying 10% of his increase in tithing would put a severe strain on their family finances. A pledge was a pledge, and he would honor it.

Dick Ragsdale and Frank Martino saw things somewhat differently: Join the Church, pay your tithing, and trust the Lord to fulfill His promises. So Dick and Frank showed up at the Davis' home one night, and Frank was carrying a bucket of water. When Sarah opened the door, Frank showed her the water and he wasted no words, "Sarah, we are going to baptize you one way or the other."

Finally deciding that they had to say "Yes" to the Ragsdales' repeated invitations, Ralph and Sarah began going to early services at the Baptist church and then to LDS services at "the little church up the street." It was hard for Sarah to give up the soft seats at the Baptist church for the hard seats at the LDS chapel.

When Ralph and Sarah began reading the *Book of Mormon*, they both received a testimony of its truthfulness. Sarah had an especially moving experience.

"When I stopped to ask the Lord if it was true, my whole skeletal framework filled with intense light. I could actually see where the bones of my face were as though I was looking into them and into this bright light. At the same time I knew that some heavenly presences were there. I could not see them, but I could feel them."

The Davises had a testimony, and they joined the church even though they expected to experience financial difficulty for doing so at that time. Dick Ragsdale baptized both Ralph and Sarah on August 16, 1968, and their anticipated financial difficulties did, indeed, occur.

While beginning to pay their tithing, the Davises continued paying Ralph's pledge to the Baptist Church until his commitment was completed. In addition, Ralph's dental business dropped off sharply following his affiliation with the Mormon church. From a financial standpoint, the Davises were tested severely, and they passed the test. Ralph and Sarah gave liberally of their time and talents, and they provided needed leadership in many areas. Before long, additional dental patients began coming to Ralph, and their faith with works was rewarded.

Jim and Maureen Richards

The Richardses brought lifetimes of Church experience when they moved to Denton in 1968 for Jim to take a position on the NTSU faculty as an art professor. Upon the Richardses' arrival, they accepted an invitation to meet with some of the LDS members at the Arringtons' home in Argyle, and John and Margaret Porter took advantage of the opportunity to interview them and to become better acquainted. When John asked Maureen about her background in the Church, he and Margaret were especially impressed with Maureen's response.

"I've done a lot," she said, "and I can do anything."

Time proved her, for during their stay here, Maureen did almost everything, including serving twice as Ward Relief Society president – once in the original Denton Ward, and again in the Denton Second Ward when it was formed. At one other time she was a counselor in both the Stake Relief Society and Primary organizations at the same time. On one occasion, Bishop Ragsdale gave Maureen a bottle of perfume as a "thank you" for helping keep the ward records up to date. "I learned how to do that from Margaret," she explained, "who could find anyone, anywhere."

Jim was equally active and helpful. He served as a bishop and as a counselor in several bishoprics, and his experience and "know-how" were available at just the right times.

Maureen tells of a spiritual experience when teaching a lesson in a Gospel Essentials class in Sunday School. The lesson was on the restoration of keys in the Kirtland Temple, and she was using LeGrand Richards' book, *A Marvelous Work and a Wonder*. As she sat waiting to begin her lesson, she received a strong impression to see what Bruce R. McConkie's book,

Mormon Doctrine said about Elias. Finding that McConkie's explanation did not conform with LeGrande Richards' explanation, she felt moved upon to go with McConkie's version. Later, when a new edition of *A Marvelous Work and a Wonder* was published, LeGrande Richards' explanation of Elias had been changed to agree with Brother McConkie's explanation.

"I was just a Sunday School teacher in the Denton Ward, but the Spirit wanted to keep the doctrine pure. It was a great testimony to me that the Lord will help us do that."

Jim and Maureen stayed in Denton for nine years, until 1976 when they moved back to Utah. But Texas called again, and back they came in 1986 and stayed here ten more years until 1996.

The entire Richards family were stalwarts. Jim Richards was called to be bishop of Denton Second Ward from September, 1988 until September 1993, and Jim's oldest son, David was bishop of Denton Third Ward from May 1992 until April 1995. Both wards met in the Malone Street building. Thus, we have a father and son who were bishops at the same time and in the same building, a rather unique occurrence. They got along well together.

Newell Kay and Myrna Brown

Newell Kay Brown, along with his wife Myrna, came to Denton in 1971 as a music professor at the University of North Texas.

"We needed musical talent, and we prayed you in," Maureen Richards later told Brother Brown. Trey Martino remembers the specific prayer, given in a gathering of ward leaders in the Martino home. They prayed for a person having specific musical talents and also having a family with specific attributes. Shortly thereafter, Kay Brown and his family arrived with almost the exact qualities requested in the prayers. Margaret Porter became so excited about the Brown's arrival that she called her daughter, Ann, who was living in California at the time, to exclaim about the "celebrity" who had just moved to Denton in answer to their prayers.

Another lifetime Church member, Kay was also a composer of music, and his "I Hope They Call Me on a Mission" has

Chinese Version
One of eighteen languages into which it has been translated

"I Hope They Call Me On A Mission"
The song inspired loving lampoonery

inspired many a child and adult when sung in Primary meetings throughout the Church. This song, which Kay composed in the summer of 1970 in response to a request from the Church Music Committee, has been translated into at least eighteen languages, and it has been used in a historical musical production, "Zion..." as well as in the movies, "The Singles Ward" and "The RM."

Also an excellent pianist, Kay would occasionally mix a little humor with the classics. For example, he enjoyed entertaining friends by playing "Twinkle, Twinkle, Little Star" as it might have sounded if written by Brahms or by Beethoven or by Mendelssohn or by other classical composers.

In March 1984, the Church Music Committee sent Kay the text of the hymn "With Songs of Praise," and asked if he would compose the music for the hymn. And they gave him nine days in which to do it. The result is Hymn #71 in the 1985 edition of the Church's Hymn book. The Tabernacle Choir sang the hymn in their broadcast on September 23, 1984, and again at the following General Conference.

Because the music of each hymn is also titled, the Church Music Committee called Kay and asked him the name of his composition.

"It doesn't have a name," Kay responded.

"It must have a name," they told him.

"O.K., Call it 'Denton'. I composed it here in Denton."

On page 402 in the section on Tune Names in the Hymn book, one can see "Denton" as the tune name for Hymn #71.

Brother Brown became the first bishop of the Denton First Ward following the division of the Denton Ward in July 1975.

One of Kay Brown's more cherished memories, when he lived in Denton, pertains to attending the Solemn Assembly conducted by President Kimball in San Antonio. Brother

Brown recalls the experience as follows:

"Those of us who attended the Solemn Assembly in San Antonio on August 26, 1978, will never forget that nearly overwhelming feeling of singing "We Thank Thee O God for a Prophet" while the prophet himself, President Kimball, walked up the aisle to the pulpit. His counselors, Marion G. Romney and N. Eldon Tanner, were also present, plus Marvin J. Ashton of the Council of the Twelve and Vaughn J. Featherstone and George P. Lee of the First Quorum of Seventy.

"I was privileged to direct a priesthood chorus that evening which more than filled the choir seats. True to form and never wanting to waste a minute, President Kimball suggested that we join him in reciting the thirteen articles of faith while waiting for all the chorus members to arrive. We all did pretty well on the first two or three, but as our memories failed he proceeded to reprove us in a kindly manner. 'Come on, brethren,' he said. 'I memorized those as a youth while milking cows!' "

Vic and Marlene Nielsen

As another family "prayed in" to join the faculty of one of Denton's two universities, Vic and Marlene Nielsen arrived in Denton in the summer of 1971. Vic came as a professor of political science at NTSU. They both quickly became stalwarts in the Denton Ward, and in the Fort Worth Stake. Vic became bishop of the Denton Second Ward in 1984 after having served earlier as a counselor in two other bishoprics. In his stints as a counselor, he was released each time to become scoutmaster, a calling he thoroughly enjoyed.

Marlene was a leader also. While in Denton, she served three times as a Ward Relief Society president and once as a

Stake Relief Society president. She also had similar roles in Primary and in Young Women. Marlene had a reputation of being the one to ask if you wanted to know anything about what was going on in the stake. At the Denton Ward reunion held in 1979, Margaret Porter gave praise to Marlene by asking out loud, "If you need information, what number do you call?" In a loud response, the attendees shouted out Marlene's phone number.

Brother Nielsen was especially interested in genealogy, and he played the leading role in getting the Denton Family History Center established with Dayonne Work as its first director. Then when plans were made in the mid 1980s for building a stake center in Denton, Brother Nielsen took the lead in assuring that adequate space would be devoted to housing the family history center.

David and Mary Steiner

Even though they did not arrive in Denton until 1972, David and Mary Steiner quickly became stalwarts among the Denton saints. An orthopedic surgeon, David brought medical skills along with lifelong leadership experience in Church doctrine and procedures.

Mary was no less accomplished and experienced. Raised in Salt Lake City, Mary lived next door to Vaughn Andrus. It is likely that they played together as children.

David's very first calling after arriving in Denton was that of Stake Sunday School President. A sampling of his counselors will include Art Cooper, Maurice Arrington, and Ell Sorensen from Denton. David felt that he had wonderful counselors, but he couldn't keep them very long because they were continually being called to become bishops or high counselors or to other positions of authority.

In Denton, David later served as a counselor to two bishops, Bishop Sorensen and Bishop Nobles. He also served on the Fort Worth North Stake High Council. One of David's favorite callings, however, was that of scoutmaster.

When Ell Sorensen became bishop of the Denton Ward, he selected David Steiner and Bob Nobles as his counselors. Both counselors were medical doctors, and thus, both kept odd and uncertain hours in their professions. Their bishopric meetings had to be scheduled accordingly.

David Steiner, especially, liked to call Bishop Sorensen whenever he had an idea to be presented or discussed, and he frequently made those phone calls late at night or very early in the morning—when most people would be in bed asleep. Ell was very tolerant of these phone calls that usually awakened him from his slumber.

One night after getting home quite late from the hospital, Brother Steiner felt the need to talk to Bishop Sorensen, so he picked up the phone and called. When Ell answered, David started talking about whatever it was that he called about.

Interrupting, Ell asked, "David, do you know what time it is?"

"Yeah, it's three o'clock in the morning," David responded, and he went right on with what he called to talk about.

It goes without saying, however, that Bishop Sorensen loved his counselors, and they worked together in full harmony. David reports that "we all had some good times together, and we did some good things."

David had a rather unique relationship with his daughter, Allison. Allison seemed to feel that she was more of a boy than a girl. For example, she was more interested in playing with toy trucks than with dolls.

When only three or four years old, Allison and Justin Beedle were running all over the lawn after church one Sunday and creating a hazard for more elderly people trying to get to their cars. Seeing the situation, Pat Ragsdale called out to Allison to "come over here" so Pat could calm her down.

"I can't," Allison called back. "Justin and I are chasing girls."

David partially contributed to Allison's boyish tendencies by frequently taking her with him whenever he went on fathers and sons outings and priesthood activities. Wherever David went, Allison usually went.

It all came to an end, however, on Allison's eighth birthday when Dick and Pat Ragsdale visited the Steiners. Dick brought a birthday cake to Allison and Pat brought an orchid. Then Dick, as Stake President, explained to Allison, "You are eight years old, and from now on you are a girl. You cannot go to any more fathers and sons outings."

From that point on, Allison was a girl.

Pete and Dayonne Work

The Work family brought steadiness and dependability when they came to Denton in 1970. Pete was in the business of selling, installing, and repairing heating and air conditioning systems. He had a reputation for being able to fix anything, and he received frequent calls to demonstrate that ability.

With priesthood guidance from Vic Nielsen, Dayonne established the Denton Family History Center in the Malone Street building in 1978, and she nurtured it as it grew into an outstanding family history research facility. When the Denton Stake Center was in the planning stage, Dayonne worked closely with Brother Nielsen to assure that a Family History Center of the highest quality would be included. Dayonne served as director of the Denton Family History Center from its inception in 1978 until her departure with Pete in 2000 on a Church mission to Africa.

Lucile Guess

Lucile and her husband, Carl, came to Denton in 1973. When Carl, a West Point graduate and a career army officer, retired as a Lt. Colonel, he and Lucile chose to settle in Denton, partially because of the beauty of the area and partially because of their friendship with Pete and Dayonne Work, whom they had known when living for a short time in Tyler, Texas.

Lucile, a dynamo of energy and enthusiasm, quickly became known as the person you call upon when you want a difficult job done with excellence. With confidence and ability, she

Lucile Guess

frequently led the way, and Carl, though not a member of the Church, supported her fully.

Lucile taught in all the Church organizations, and she was called to teach early morning seminary on several occasions. She also served as a Ward Primary President and in other leadership capacities.

Two special projects Lucile led were Granny's Pantry and the feeding of workers during the construction of Eureka Park in the southern portion of Denton. Granny's Pantry, which will be discussed in a later chapter, was a huge fair demonstrating personal and family preparedness and security.

With regard to Eureka Park, the Denton saints responded to an invitation to support a community effort to build an ambitious playground in a time period of one week. The Denton wards took on the task of providing lunch for 1,300 workers on one of the work days. Who would be the right person to lead the effort of gathering food in advance, storing it, preparing it, and serving it at the right time? The answer, which came rather easily, said "Call on Lucile Guess." She organized; she got food donations; she got monetary donations; she got many people involved; and she led a very successful project to show the Mormons as capable and responsible members of the community.

One of Lucile's most treasured experiences occurred in 2007 just before she succumbed to the ravages of cancer. One of her grandsons, Tavita, along with his priesthood leaders, came into her bedroom where Tavita was ordained a priest in her presence. He then performed his very first priesthood ordinance by helping to administer the sacrament and passing it to his ailing grandmother.

Bill Williamson

Bill Williamson was one of the most loved of the Church members in Denton. When asked, "How are you?" he always responded in his cheerful voice, "Never better." His response became his trademark and his nickname. Everyone loved "Never better."

Another of Bill's traits was his forthrightness in expressing his opinions. He loved to talk, especially from the pulpit. As a High Counselor he always began his talks with expressions of love for the gospel and for the members, and then he would proceed to "lay it on the line," telling the congregation what they were doing wrong and how they needed to shape up. But he had a charm about him that prevented people from being offended. Bill was one of the most popular High Council speakers in Denton. People loved to hear him, and it is likely that many members did shape up after being thoroughly chastised by Bill Williamson.

Even though Bill's wife never joined the Church, Bill served several stints as a bishop's counselor and on stake high councils. He was also a Dallas Temple ordinance worker and he served for a while as a shift supervisor in the Dallas Temple. In addition, whenever there was a church event of large size such as a stake conference or a regional conference, Bill was always there as the lead usher.

For many years, Bill served as the stake physical facilities representative. Following the completion of the stake center, the Malone Street building underwent an extensive interior renovation which included, among other things, the replacement of the old pews with new pews in the chapel. Bill donated the old pews to the First Christian Church, the same church that had made its baptismal font available to the Mormons in the early days of the Denton Sunday School and Branch.

One of the things Brother Williamson did that was especially meaningful to him occurred also in connection with the renovation of the Malone Street building. In the cultural hall were six large and heavy folding room dividers. They had been very useful for partitioning the cultural hall into cubicles for Sunday School classes, but because of ward divisions and the existence of the new stake center, the partitions were no longer needed. Bill was instructed to get rid of them.

Normally a man of immediate action, Bill had a stupor of thought regarding the partitions, and he took no action for

FURTHER ADDITIONS TO CHURCH MEMBERSHIP IN DENTON   149

almost a year. Then one day in December 1999, while driving on Bonnie Brae Road toward Windsor Road, "a strong, silent voice said to me that the dividers should be given to the little church on the left just ahead."

Driving up to the "Church on the Go," Bill went in and introduced himself to the pastor, Mr. Garcia, and to Mrs. Garcia. Offering them the room dividers, Bill was overcome by the looks of incredulous joy that appeared on the Garcias' faces.

"Mr. Williamson, you don't realize what you have done. God has sent you to us."

Mrs. Garcia explained that just the week before, she and her husband had priced room dividers and had found them much too expensive for their little church. They had been praying throughout the week that in some way the Lord would help them and provide for their needs.

"Surely the Lord has sent you with this gift," she added.

A few days later, the men from the little church came to the Malone Street building and loaded the dividers into their vehicles.

In Bill Williamson's words: "One of the men, on the steps of our church, offered a prayer of thanks to God. It was BEAUTIFUL."

Shortly thereafter, Bill received a "thank you" card signed by all the members of the "Church on the Go." This card, along with Bill's written account of the occasion, are now in the Church Historian's Office in Salt Lake City.

Dick and Pearl Yates

Dick and Pearl Yates were Church stalwarts in many respects. Dick served at one time as a counselor to Bishop Kay Brown in the Denton First Ward. Pearl worked several years in the Young Women's program, and she also served as a Ward Relief Society president. But the callings they held for the longest time and which they remember with the greatest fondness were as leaders, both on ward and stake levels, of the Special Interest groups (now known as the Single Adults).

Pearl came to Denton in 1966 from Nashville, Tennessee, and she joined the Church in Denton in 1971. In Nashville she had been a close friend of Art and Carol Joy Cooper while Art was studying for his doctor's degree. Dick lived in Arlington. Both Pearl and Dick became products of broken marriages. As a result, they both became participants in Special Interest functions, and they met one another at one such function. Pearl was the answer to Dick's prayers, and they married in 1974 with Denton becoming their home.

Dick and Pearl Yates give special credit to Art and Carol Joy Cooper, who were also living in Denton at that time, for fellowshipping them and helping them over the rough spots. The two families, including the children, became very close

Being sponsors of the Single Adult program was a natural calling for Dick and Pearl. Having experienced divorce themselves, they had a special understanding and empathy for others in the same situation. They also knew and had experienced loneliness. Dick and Pearl stood as role models showing that happiness is still available after such experiences. This, plus the love and warmth they naturally felt for all people, made them the right people for the job.

Dick and Pearl opened their hearts and their home to the single adults. They were always available to them. On many Monday nights the single adults met in the Yateses' home for Family Home Evening. On Fast Sundays they gathered for a pot luck dinner. They had frequent weekend activities. On a stake level the Yates played leading roles in helping the Special

Interest groups stage a dinner theater at the Fort Worth Stake Center in Hurst.

Except for a three-year interruption when they went to the state of Washington, Dick and Pearl fellowshipped the Single Adults for over ten years until 2003 when they moved from Denton to Dallas to serve a mission in the Dallas Temple. Their contributions to the Single Adults in Denton were beyond measure.

Lee and Georgia Head

It took a fire to get Lee Head and his family into the Church. But the story begins before the fire occurred.

Following the end of World War II, Lee returned to Rice University in Houston to complete his bachelor's and master's degrees. In the process, he also married Georgia Spacil, who was also a student at Rice, and who had waited for him while he was overseas. With his college education behind him, Lee accepted a job with Ling-Temco-Vought (LTV) in Grand Prairie, and he and Georgia moved to the Dallas area. They lived there for a few years, and Georgia gave birth to four sons: Lee Jr., Paul, Greg, and Jeff.

Although theirs was a happy family, the Heads really wanted a rural environment. After searching the area in and around Denton, they found a desirable plot of land adjacent to Clear Creek west of Bolivar which, in turn, is west of Sanger. They bought the land, and in 1968 they built their dream home.

Two years after moving into their new home, two of the Heads' sons, Jeff and Greg, were doing some welding in the barn on their property, and some sparks flew in the wrong direction, setting the grass on fire. As the fire spread and seemed about to get out of control, it attracted the attention of John

Porter and his hired hands who were working on the Porter's property immediately north of, and adjacent to, the Head's property. Very quickly, a pickup truck came roaring onto the Head's property, and John and his workers jumped out and helped extinguish the blaze. After the excitement subsided, John and Lee introduced themselves to one another.

Now, to go back in time, Lee's secretary at LTV was an LDS church member named Josephine Troxell. Sister Troxell happened to be acquainted with John and Margaret Porter, and some time after the Heads had moved to their new home, Sister Troxell told the Porters about them. So it came as a complete surprise to John when he realized, after the fire was extinguished, that he has just met the family Sister Troxell had told him about. John asked permission to visit with the Heads and talk about some matters of religion, and Lee readily granted it.

Things progressed fairly normally from that point. Gospel discussions with the Porters ensued, and the Heads attended several cottage meetings. Lee became very interested in learning about the Gospel, but Georgia was not interested at that point. Having been raised a Catholic and then having attended the Baptist church with Lee, she announced that she was not about to change churches again.

The cottage meetings and discussions continued, however, and one cottage meeting in which Carlos Asay spoke especially impressed the Heads. Elder Asay, who was president of the Dallas Mission at the time, spoke about the restoration and the fact that the true gospel was again on the earth. Jeff Head was especially touched because he was a fourteen-year-old boy hearing about another fourteen-year-old boy who saw the Father and the Son.

Lee and Jeff were baptized on September 19, 1970. Georgia waited another month. With some questions she wanted to explore, Georgia visited a Mrs. White, who was a staunch Baptist friend, and the conversations resulted in Georgia's deciding that baptism into the LDS church was for her also. Georgia and Lee, Jr. were baptized on October 16. Paul followed on October 11, and Greg completed the family transition on October 23, 1970.

One further item should be mentioned with regard to Lee and Georgia. In 1995 they were called on a mission as a senior missionary couple. The unique aspect of this mission is that they were sent to the same locality in Alabama where Lee had grown up. Some of his relatives and some of his former friends were still there. Lee and Georgia were busily involved in correcting some erroneous practices that had crept into the branch and in increasing the branch membership and attendance.

The branch met in a rented store space at one end of a strip mall. On one occasion, a fire started at the other end of the mall, and as it spread rapidly toward the store unit in which the branch met, one of the firemen cautioned Georgia to be prepared to lose the unit to the fire.

"You just keep squirting your water," Georgia retorted. "This is the Lord's church, and He is not going to let it be destroyed." And as Georgia predicted, the fire stopped and was extinguished just before reaching the store unit that was the local branch's home.

Ray and Leah Beedle

Ray Beedle's conversion to the Gospel was bound to happen. Numerous contacts with the Church prepared him for eventual teachings from the missionaries. Ray's earliest awareness of the Church came when watching a "Route 66" television program. References to Mormons in some sequences set in Salt Lake City made a favorable impression on him. Later Ray made visits to Kirtland, Ohio, when living a portion of his life in Cleveland. In later years he made business trips to Salt Lake City where he noted the high moral standards that prevailed. Visits to Temple Square impressed him. In his business meetings and socials, he observed the differences between those who drank cocktails and those who didn't, and that also impressed him. He enjoyed listening to the Tabernacle Choir. To top things off, Ray's LDS secretary gave him a copy of the *Book of Mormon*. So when the opportunity came to meet with the missionaries, Ray was prepared.

Not so with Ray's wife, Leah. Joining the Church would mean giving up the wine she so enjoyed at dinner time, and she was not at all interested in that kind of commitment. Then one night, Leah had a dream of a special nature. It was dark, and she was being pursued by men in dark clothing. There was an evil aspect to it, and she was desperately trying to get away from them. Even though she was running in terror, they were gaining on her. Suddenly she saw the opening of a cave and she dashed into it. Inside the cave, Leah encountered another group of people, but the environment was totally different. There was light, and the people were dressed in white. They were loving as they offered her friendship and protection. She felt the peace and security that prevailed, as opposed to the terror from which she had just escaped.

That dream was all Leah needed. She had no more desire for wine, and she was ready to join the church. The first time they attended church they sat next to Sanfred Elieson, and they felt his loving spirit. Everyone treated them in a warm and loving manner.

"We were loved into the Church," Ray and Leah said.

The Beedles attended cottage meetings in Denton, they met with the missionaries, and they were baptized in 1974.

For several years the Beedles' home, on a large piece of property in the southern outskirts of Argyle, served as the site of many Church socials. Bonfires, barbeques, ball games, sing-alongs provided enjoyable activities for all age groups. Earl Cochran would bring his wagons and horses for hay rides. For several years, church members gathered at the Beedle's for Pioneer days, Halloweens, Thanksgivings, and other occasions. They were very unifying and enjoyable times.

R. B., Lena, and Mabel Pennington

In 1957 Mabel and Smith Pennington, who lived in Athens, Texas, bought a farm in Aubrey. Mabel and her children were members of the Church. On weekends and during much of the summers, the Pennington family would travel from Athens to spend time on their Audrey farm.

As relative newlyweds, R. B. Pennington and his wife, Lena, moved from Athens to his parent's Aubrey farm in 1970, and they have been living there ever since. R. B. grew up in east Texas and was baptized in 1957 in the Longview Ward. Lena, a life-long member of the Church, grew up in Lehi, Utah.

Lena remembers the first sacrament meeting she attended in Denton; it was a missionary farewell for Jim Martino, who was leaving for a mission in Guatemala.

"I was there with a three-day-old baby (Raquel)," Lena recalls fondly, "and everyone wanted to hold her. They literally took her away from me."

Lena knew she was with friends, and she likes to recall the camaraderie and unity she found in the Denton Ward in those early years. A special closeness grew between the Penningtons and the Arringtons (Maurice and Edleweis) and the Fraims (Roger and Jennis) who were especially outgoing in welcoming the Penningtons into the ward.

Lena also had a special feeling for Bob Nobles, who became the Pennington 's family doctor. When Lena was ready to give birth to her second child, she and R. B. picked up Hoyt Wilson and took him to the hospital so Hoyt could care for little Raquel while R. B. stayed with Lena as long as he could. It was a spiritual experience for her when Dr. Nobles came into her hospital room before the delivery and had prayer with the family.

Over the years, both R. B. and Lena have been actively involved in church service. R.B. had the honor of being ordained an Elder by Richard L. Evans, and to the office of a Seventy by Spencer W. Kimball. He has served as a counselor to Bishop Martino in Denton First Ward. He has also been a High Priest Group Leader three times, a stake missionary, and a Gospel Doctrine class teacher. Lena has been a Primary president, Relief Society president, and she has served in the Young Women's programs for many years. In later chapters, additional contributions of the Penningtons will be noted.

Behind only the Ragsdales and Martinos, the Penningtons are believed to be the most tenured members of Denton First Ward.

George and Billie Hubbard

A brief account of the conversion of George and Billie Hubbard, along with their temporary sojourn in Denton prior to the Porters' arrival, has been given in an earlier chapter. Returning to Denton as permanent residents in February 1980 as a result of George's transfer by IBM to Las Colinas (in Irving,

Texas) from the Bay Area of California, they moved into the geographic area of the Denton Second Ward.

Expecting some kind of calling after arriving, Brother Hubbard waited, — and waited. Finally, his bishop, Bishop Nobles, asked him, "Has the stake contacted you yet?"

"No. No one has contacted me."

This question and answer exchange occurred two or three more times over the next few weeks, and then on a Saturday in late May, Bill Biggs, the Stake Executive Secretary, called Brother Hubbard and asked him to come down to the stake center in Hurst. George had just gotten out of the hospital from a gall bladder surgery (old style with a long incision), and driving himself was out of the question, so his wife, Billie, drove him. He was called to become the Ward Executive Secretary. Two weeks later, Bishop Nobles was released, and George found himself as second counselor to Lee Rasmussen, the new bishop of Denton Second Ward. Numerous callings have followed for both George and Billie.

Billie served as a seminary teacher, then as Stake Relief Society President. She subsequently served as Ward Relief Society President when the Denton Fourth Ward was created. For several months in her stake calling, Billie had to give counsel and direction without the benefit and guidance of a handbook because the General Relief Society organization was changing portions of their programs and revising their handbook. Billie also served approximately five years as Stake Public Affairs Director, and in that capacity, she and Betty Martino initiated Denton's Family of the Year program.

In Denton George has served as a counselor in three bishoprics and on two high councils. George and Billie also served a twelve month Public Affairs mission in 1995-96, and they have been ordinance workers in the Dallas Temple. George served for approximately five years as director of the Stake Family History Center, succeeding Dayonne Work when she and her husband, Pete, left in 2000 for a mission to Nigeria. George still feels that the most rewarding of his callings was as scoutmaster and explorer advisor in the Denton Third and Fourth Wards.

When returning to Denton, George was not mentally prepared for the high degree of spirituality and gospel maturity to be found among the Denton saints. Because there had been no LDS church in Denton during the Hubbards' earlier sojourns here, how could there be anything now to match the gospel environments George and Billie had experienced in their twenty-nine years in Provo, Los Angeles, and San Jose. But instead of finding small, struggling Church units, they found two strong wards and an impressive church building. More importantly, they found Church members who were outstanding in terms of spirituality and capability. It was truly a testimony of the spiritual and enabling powers of the Holy Ghost functioning in all parts of the Lord's vineyard.

Walter and Mae Linnenschmidt

Walter and Mae Linnenschmidt couldn't have been more different from one another. Walter, mild and meek, was a rather thin man weighing perhaps 150 pounds. Mae, on the other hand, was outgoing and forceful. And she was huge, tipping the scale at about 400 pounds. In physics, we are taught that unlikes attract. This was certainly true of Walter and Mae.

The Linnenschmidts, baptized on January 6, 1966, were very much a part of the Church's development in its early years. Mae loved the children, and she spent many happy years teaching in Primary. When she became so large that transportation was difficult, she became a faithful user of the telephone. When reminders needed to be made or when help was needed or when reports were due, Mae was the dependable person for making the needed phone calls. And when reports were late, people quickly learned that it was better to go ahead and get them done rather than to hear a second time from Mae.

Mae's large size was partially, certainly not wholly, due to her love of donuts, pizza, and Dr Pepper. Walter frequently added fuel to the fire by buying day-old bakery products and bringing them home to her. On one occasion, Art Cooper asked Walter why he did this instead of encouraging her to reduce her food consumption.

Walter's reply, given in all seriousness, was, "If she loses weight, she might leave me for someone else."

Additional Contributors

There were many other families who also made significant contributions to the early development of the Church in Denton. Brief mention must be made of Earl and Dorreyce Cochran, who made their horses, wagons, and hay available for outings and who were very generous with their time.

Peter Covino, an outgoing intellectual, never passed an opportunity to plead repentance to those who needed it. He also made outstanding presentations of gospel topics in classes and cottage meetings.

Jose and Yolanda Fernandez made many contributions, and are remembered fondly for Yolanda's sumptuous chicken enchiladas.

Bill and Kathy Biggs and Bill and Linda Barnett must also be mentioned. Joan and Omar Bjelde, Bill and Dorothy Cudd, Ted and Verla Lewis, Bob and Mary Ann McCutcheon, Karen and Kerry Pittman, Jack and Betty Duncan, Chuck and Kay Stephens, Don and Mary Williams and many others all have added strength and character to the Church in Denton.

The Lord truly provided.

Part Four
THE GROWTH YEARS

Introduction

The period from July 20, 1975 to May 3, 1992 characterizes the Growth Years of The Church of Jesus Christ of Latter-day Saints in Denton, Texas. This period opens with the division of the Denton Ward, and culminates with the creation of the Denton Stake.

In just over seven years, the Denton Sunday School had grown into a branch which, in turn, had grown into a ward. Now, the growth years would see the creation of additional wards in Denton and additional stakes encompassing Denton.

In this growth period Denton was served by several new wards and stakes. From the Denton Ward, the Denton First, Second, Third, and Fourth Wards were created. Starting with the Ft. Worth Stake, stake divisions led to the Ft. Worth North Stake, the Lewisville Stake, and the Denton Stake.

To enable this growth, Denton saints would be called upon to fill increasing numbers of local and stake leadership positions. Again, the key to this growth lay in the spirituality and leadership abilities of many of the earlier new converts and move-ins, as well as those now arriving on the scene.

In addition to the creation of new wards and stakes, these Growth Years saw the Denton saints involved in several significant projects and milestones.

The Church Educational System sent John Child, who arrived with his wife, Shanna, in August 1979, to build up the seminary and institute programs in this area.

Wanting to be active participants in the Church's welfare system, the Denton saints purchased a ten acre plot of land in Krugerville, just south of Aubrey, and established an apple orchard that functioned successfully for a number of years.

Growth of the Church throughout Texas and especially in the Metroplex area was such that the First Presidency announced that a Temple would be built in the Dallas area.

And because of the continued membership growth in Denton, the Denton saints were privileged to build a second meeting house. This new building, on Old North Road, was built to function as a stake center. Even though the Lewisville Stake already had a building serving as a stake center, Lewisville began holding stake conferences in the new building in Denton because of its larger seating capacity. Soon, however, the Denton Stake was created, and the Old North Road building became its official stake center.

Some special activities during these growth years were a bi-monthly study group initiated by Sanfred Elieson, a memorable commemoration of America's Bicentennial, and a comprehensive series of preparedness fairs called Granny's Pantry.

The following timeline will show the major events of this development period and their time relationships to one another.

The Growth Years of
The Church of Jesus Christ of Latter-day Saints
in Denton
1975-1992

Denton Events	Year	Area Events
Denton 1ˢᵗ Ward Created 7/20/75 **Denton 2ⁿᵈ Ward Created 7/20/75**	1975	
	1976	Fort Worth North Stake Created 11/14/76
	1977	
	1978	
Child Family Arrives 8/ /79	1979	
Apple Orchard Dedicated 1//6/80 Hubbards Arrive 2/ /80	1980	
	1981	Dallas Temple Announced 4/1/81 Lewisville Stake Created 4/12/81
Denton 3ʳᵈ Ward Created 11/14/82	1982	
	1983	
	1984	Dallas Temple Dedicated 10/19/84
Denton 4ᵗʰ Ward Created 9/15/85	1985	
	1986	
Lewisville Stake Center (in Denton) Ground Breaking 6/13/87	1987	
	1988	
Lewisville Stake Center (in Denton) Dedicated 5/28/89	1989	
	1990	
	1991	
Denton Stake Created 5/3/92	1992	

CHAPTER 19
New Wards in Denton

On July 20, 1975, Fort Worth Stake President Horace Leithead came to Denton and presided over the division of the Denton Ward. Newell Kay Brown became Bishop of Denton First Ward, and Wally Cochran and Al White were called as his First and Second Counselors. Robert H. Nobles became Bishop of the Denton Second Ward, with Art Cooper and David Steiner as his First and Second Counselors. David Steiner, an orthopedic surgeon had recently moved to Denton with his wife, Mary, and their children. It is believed that Denton, at that time, was the smallest city in Texas having more than one ward.

During this growth period the Denton Second Ward was divided on November 14, 1982, to form the Denton Third Ward; and then the Denton Third Ward was divided on September 15, 1985, to form the Denton Fourth Ward. In addition, the Fort Worth Stake was divided on November 14, 1976, to form the Fort Worth North Stake; the Fort Worth North Stake was divided on April 12, 1981, to form the Lewisville Stake; and the Lewisville Stake was divided on May 3, 1992, to form the Denton Stake.

It should come as no surprise that during this Growth Period several LDS families in Denton lived in four different stakes and in four different wards without ever moving their residences.

Some Bishops' Experiences

All bishops have their stories to tell, both of spiritual experiences and of human interest situations. This is especially true during the early stages of a bishop's tenure. As a representative example, three such stories will be included here. (A list of the various bishops in these Denton wards along with the dates of their terms in office is included in Appendix 3.)

Bishop John Child, Denton First Ward

When John Child became bishop of Denton First Ward in 1984, he became a very busy person. President Gordon Watts, Lewisville Stake president at the time, also called Bishop Child to be the agent bishop for the Malone Street building. Then President Watts called Bishop Child to be transient bishop for the stake. Next, Bishop Child became chairman of the Bishops' Council in the stake, then regional welfare bishop, then the stake representative for overseeing the construction of the new stake center on Old North Road.

On the day that John Child was sustained to be Bishop of Denton First Ward, one of the sisters told him she would accept him as bishop provided he never call her to work in the Primary.

"I'll never give you that calling," he assured her. Then he added, "But the Lord might."

The Primary needed teachers, and over the next two or three months, Bishop Child kept getting promptings that this particular sister should be given such a call. Finally, he asked his counselors about it, and they both had received the same promptings. Wanting to be sure that they would be acting according to the mind and will of the Lord, the bishopric took another week to pray about the matter. When they next met, they were convinced that this was the right sister for a particular Primary class.

Bishop Child's *modus operandi* was to have his counselors issue all the callings in the ward, but in this case he told them that he would do this one himself. As the sister took a seat in the Bishop's office, she blurted out, "If you are calling me to the Primary, the answer is NO."

The Bishop then explained to her that he and his counselors had considered and prayed about the calling for some time, and they were convinced that it was a calling from the Lord. Again the sister emphatically said, "NO."

"O.K.," Bishop Child said. "Let's kneel and pray. I want you to be the voice, and you tell the Lord that you won't accept His call."

Sitting for a few minutes without moving, she finally said, "All right. I'll do it. But I won't like it."

After a few weeks, reports began to come in about what a good job this sister was doing with her class. Then the reports became glowing reports from the Primary presidency and from parents. Four or five months later, as this sister passed Bishop Child in the corridor, she said to him, "If you ever release me from this calling, I'll kill you."

We can only conclude that this really is the Lord's church.

Bishop Bob Nobles, Denton Second Ward

For Bishop Nobles, who was relatively new in the Church, being Bishop of Denton Second Ward was a daunting calling, and he earnestly sought the guidance of the Lord. Although blessed with strong and able counselors, Art Cooper and Dave Steiner, the new bishop still felt the need of assurance that the Lord was really in control, and much fasting and prayer ensued.

Two of the tasks the new Bishopric faced were in determining who to call to be Relief Society President and Primary President. Brother Cooper, in his autobiographical book, *Panguitch Professor*, gives a moving account of how this new bishopric approached these tasks as guided by the Spirit.

> Bishop Nobles would say, "Brother Cooper, who do you recommend for Relief Society President?"
>
> I replied, "Maurine Richards."
>
> He then asked, "Brother Steiner, who do you recommend?"
>
> Dave answered, "Maurine Richards."
>
> Then Bishop Nobles said, "The name I have written down here is Maurine Richards."
>
> "Brother Cooper, who do you recommend for Primary President?"
>
> I replied, "Floss Covino."
>
> He then asked, "Brother Steiner, who do you recommend?"
>
> Dave answered, "Floss Covino."
>
> Then Bishop Nobles said, "The name I have written down here is Floss Covino."

The Spirit bore witness that these were the Lord's choices. In like manner, the Bishopric proceeded to organize the ward with the same unity and spiritual promptings. In later years, Brother Nobles, who has very special and sacred memories of that meeting, reminisced simply, "We learned at that time who was really running things. That was something I needed to know."

Bishop Doyle Thompson, Jr., Denton Fourth Ward

As the Church membership continued to grow, it was soon time for another division, and on September 15, 1985, the Denton Fourth Ward was created by dividing the Denton Third

Ward. Doyle Thompson, Jr. became Bishop of the Fourth Ward with Ken Gray and Mark Ragsdale as his First and Second Counselors. This bishopric had an unusual working relationship. Bishop Thompson, who spent winters in his home in Denton, was a wheat farmer. His farm, however, was not in Denton; it was in South Dakota, and he spent his entire summers up there working his farm.

Doyle's call to be bishop came in a somewhat unusual manner. He was in his home on the farm, having barely escaped death that day from an accident with some of his heavy machinery. While his wife was still tending to his cuts and bleeding, the phone rang, and President Watts said, "I want to talk to you and your wife. How soon can you get down here?"

"We are right in the middle of things, but we can be down there on Saturday," Doyle responded. So Doyle and Joyce drove hurriedly down to Denton, and President Watts issued the call to become bishop of the Denton Fourth Ward which was about to be created.

With the source of his livelihood in South Dakota and with his spiritual responsibilities as bishop being in Denton, Doyle found himself in a very unusual situation. However, with very able counselors in Denton, Doyle was equal to the task. By means of innumerable phone conversations and email exchanges, Bishop Thompson essentially led the ward through his counselors during half of each year. This arrangement might be termed "complete delegation." And Satan's efforts to destroy him prior to receiving his call were thwarted.

Some Special Activities

America's Bicentennial

July 4, 1976, was a special date for all Americans, and the two Denton wards went all out to have a bicentennial celebration worthy of the occasion. Combining for a special program and dinner in commemoration of the occasion, the First and Second Wards decorated the cultural hall appropriately, and they organized an evening of music and singing, patriotic messages, and food. It was an occasion for displaying the Mormons' complete loyalty to their nation on the 200th anniversary of its founding. Many of Denton's civic leaders responded to invitations to attend.

Lucile Guess's eyes filled with tears as she later reminisced about the flag ceremony. Lucile's son, Walter, along with Jeff Jones, were in the ROTC during their senior years at Denton High School. The two boys recruited the rest of the ROTC, and at the appointed time they all made a grand entrance into the cultural hall as a uniformed honor guard, marching proudly in full uniform with polished shoes and carrying the American flag. Sarah Davis, at the piano, added her own special touch by playing the marching music for the honor guard. It is reported that the several leaders and dignitaries from the community were visibly impressed with the entire program.

Athletics

Just as Denton's excellence in music and drama continued after dividing the Denton Ward, its athletic heritage also continued, and it reached its climax with the 1976 softball team.

Combining the two Denton wards to field a softball team that included Vaughn Andrus, Jim and David Martino, John R. Porter, Wally Cochran, Glen Davis, Dave Christenson, A.L. Payne,

Jimmie Jones, and Rick Riddle, the team won the stake championship, the district championship, and the region championship. They then went to Bossier City, Louisiana, where they won the area championship, which was as high as they could go in those years. For three years in a row, beginning with their championship year of 1976, Denton's team defeated the same Dallas team to win the regional tournament. As regional champions, the Dentonites then played in three consecutive area tournaments, winning the first one in which they participated. The regional and area tournaments were then discontinued after 1978.

1976 Softball Team
Stake, District, Regional and Area Champions
Front Row: Jimmie Jones, Jim Martino,
David Martino, Rick Riddle, Vaughn Andrus.
Back Row: Glen Davis, Wally Cochran,
John R. Porter, Dave Christenson, A. L. Payne.

According to Vaughn Andrus, the best player on the Dallas softball team in the regionals was Larry Gibbons. Years later, Brother Gibbons, as an area authority, presided over a Denton stake conference in which Brother Andrus was stake president. During the tournaments, however, Brother Andrus never dreamed that he and Brother Gibbons would have such a relationship in the future.

In basketball, the Denton Ward teams, with former college players such as Tony Wright and Wally Cochran, were frequent stake champions. Their major competition came from the Gainesville Branch that fielded teams composed of the McCage brothers plus one or two non-member recruits. In 1979, Gainesville dethroned Denton as basketball champions of the Fort Worth North Stake. It was a proud moment for Gainesville.

Twentieth Year Reunion

The month of November 1979 marked the twentieth anniversary of the founding of the church in Denton. It was on November 1, 1959, that twenty-three people met in the Porters's home in Denton and organized the second Sunday School which endured and grew into three wards and two branches. It was an occasion to be celebrated.

The reunion began at 2:00pm Saturday, November 24, 1979, with an afternoon testimony meeting that continued for about two hours in the Malone Street chapel. After the testimony meeting in which the chapel was filled to capacity, the attendees used the free time to visit and become reacquainted. Then at 6:00 they seated themselves for a lovely dinner followed by entertainment consisting of a roadshow titled "Now He Does," history highlights, and favorite entertainment of the past. It was an occasion of spiritual enjoyment which brought back many fond memories of Church involvement during the past two decades.

DENTON WARD REUNION

CELEBRATING 20 YEARS OF THE CHURCH IN DENTON
Saturday, November 24, 1979
LDS Chapel - 1801 Malone Street

o 1:00 P.M.   **REGISTRATION AND BROWSING**
HISTORY DISPLAY - North Foyer

o 2:00 P.M.   **TESTIMONY MEETING** in the Chapel

•• ••

•• ••   **FREE TIME FOR VISITING**   •• ••

•• ••

o 6:00 P.M. **SEATED DINNER** in the Cultural Hall
Admittance by ticket - advance sales.
Children under 12 - 75¢ Adults - $1.50
Ticket sales close Sunday, November 18

o 7:30 P.M.   **REUNION REVUE**
ROADSHOWS - Denton I and II Wards
History Highlights and Favorite Entertainment
of the Past

1979 Ward Reunion
Above, the reunion program.
At left, Jim Richards bears his testimony.

Denton's First Senior Missionaries

Toward the end of 1979, Maurice and Edleweis Arrington received a call to serve a full-time mission for the Church. They were the first senior couple to be called on a mission from Denton.

The call, issued on a Sunday by Bishop Nobles, came as a complete surprise to the Arringtons, and they didn't know quite how to respond. They wanted to go, but they were not sure that they could afford it.

"To be able to afford a mission, we would have to sell our home," they said. "We live next door to Art Cooper, and his home has been on the market for six years without being sold."

"The Lord will open the way," Bishop Nobles counseled. "Go home and pray about it, and then let me know."

Maurice and Edleweis did pray about it, and they felt that if the Lord really wanted them to go, they could find a way to do it. So the next day, on a Monday morning, they put a "For Sale" sign in front of their house. By noon of that same day, a buyer had come forth, and the sale was consummated. They left in January 1980 for an eighteen-month proselyting mission in Colorado. A proselyting mission was the preference they requested.

The Arringtons put their usual full efforts into being good missionaries, and at one point their mission president honored them with a special award for the hours they gave and for the efforts they made. On one occasion, while serving in Colby, Kansas, they were featured on a local radio station in a series of ten-minute segments discussing the role of missionaries in this golden age of the gospel and surveying various gospel themes.

It turned out that the Arringtons were involved in other activities in addition to proselyting. While serving in Denver, they became involved with the new cannery the Church was establishing, and they took pride in their roles in getting the cannery ready to open. Upon their return home, the Arringtons reported having had some grand spiritual experiences.

Bi-Monthly Study Group

One of the practices affected by the division of the Denton Ward was the bi-monthly study group organized earlier by Sanfred Elieson. Because the Eliesons lived in the newly designated Denton First Ward, that ward became the unofficial sponsor of the study group with the Ragsdale, Martino, and Child families being principle supporters. Brother Child eventually became the instructor when Brother Elieson's health and other commitments prevented his continuing. This study group, which concentrates on the scriptures and doctrines of the Church, still meets on a bi-monthly basis.

In the Denton Second Ward, Bishop Nobles felt that a separate study group in his ward would be appropriate, and he asked Art Cooper to be the instructor. Using B. H. Roberts' *Documentary History of the Church*, Brother Cooper taught the history of the Church. Participation was good for three to four years, but the group finally disbanded as participation began to wane.

Granny's Pantry

The Church has always put an emphasis on self-reliance, on prudent living, and on being prepared for possible disasters of all kinds. On three occasions, in 1979, 1980, and 1981, the Denton First and Second Wards sponsored a family preparedness fair called Granny's Pantry.

Under the direction of Lucile Guess and Phyllis Bates, the two wards turned the Malone Street building into a living, working museum with displays, exhibits, demonstrations, and instruction on all phases of personal health; growing, preparation and storage of food; family budgeting and economic purchasing; and other related topics. It was a complete presentation which included aerobic dancing demonstrations, amateur radio operation, home manufacture, care for the elderly, personal and family finance, and many other aspects of self-reliance. Local participation included exhibits and demonstrations from civil defense, fire fighters, and law enforcement agencies.

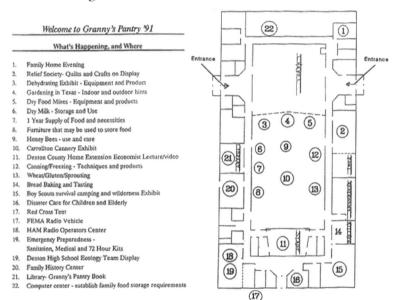

Welcome to Granny's Pantry '91

What's Happening, and Where

1. Family Home Evening
2. Relief Society- Quilts and Crafts on Display
3. Dehydrating Exhibit - Equipment and Product
4. Gardening in Texas - Indoor and outdoor hints
5. Dry Food Mixes - Equipment and products
6. Dry Milk - Storage and Use
7. 1 Year Supply of Food and necessities
8. Furniture that may be used to store food
9. Honey Bees - use and care
10. Carrollton Cannery Exhibit
11. Denton County Home Extension Economist Lecture/video
12. Canning/Freezing - Techniques and products
13. Wheat/Gluten/Sprouting
14. Bread Baking and Tasting
15. Boy Scouts survival camping and wilderness Exhibit
16. Disaster Care for Children and Elderly
17. Red Cross Tent
17. FEMA Radio Vehicle
18. HAM Radio Operators Center
19. Emergency Preparedness -
    Sanitation, Medical and 72 Hour Kits
19. Denton High School Ecology Team Display
20. Family History Center
21. Library- Granny's Pantry Book
22. Computer center - establish family food storage requirements

Granny's Pantry, 1991
The Denton public was invited
to this preparedness fair.

The townspeople were invited to attend, and the townspeople came. And they were impressed. When community members learned that a fourth presentation was not planned for 1982, many of them praised the first three presentations and voiced their regrets at not having another. It is believed by many that Granny's Pantry did more to bring the LDS members and the townspeople together than any other single set of activities.

In 1991, at President Jim Martino's request, Lucile Guess and Karen Pittman coordinated a fourth Granny's Pantry, this time in the Denton Stake Center. A fifth presentation was held the following year in the Denton Civic Center. The interest level of these last two presentations, however, did not match that of the first three presentations.

Music and Drama

The tradition established in the earlier years by the Denton saints continued into the period of the growth years

When Denton's Festival of Carols was discontinued upon Carol Lynn Mizell's retirement as its director, Kevin Dartt and Margaret Porter combined to lead the Denton saints in instituting their own Christmas musical celebration, "An Evening of Christmas Joys." This event began in 1987 with musical numbers by a stake choir and orchestra interspersed with narrations by Sanfred Elieson of Joseph Smith's vision and the Christmas story. "An Evening of Christmas Joys" has become an annual tradition as a contribution to the community of Denton. And the black and white dress standards instituted by Margaret Porter still prevail.

In addition to choral presentations, the Denton Stake has continued to produce outstanding roadshows and musical plays. Their 1977 roadshow, "Olivia Ostrich" continued the tradition

Denton's 1977 Roadshow: "Oops–Olivia Ostrich"
Costuming and dramatics were again at their usual best.

of excellence in song, choreography, and costuming.

With Tom Dartt's conversion in 1977, additional artistic and creative talents became available. Tom became the master builder of scenery and props for the productions. In one stake social, Polynesian dancers danced in front of a "live" volcano spouting "fire." For a production of *Showboat*, Tom built a model of a river boat complete with steam coming out of its stacks. For the backdrop for a New Year's dance, he built a large scale model of a castle.

Whatever they did, the church members did it with enthusiasm and with excellence.

Special Youth Activities

Special Trips

The Denton youth in the Lewisville Stake (and in the subsequent Denton Stake) have participated in several trips of a special nature. Destinations have been Church history locations in and around Jackson County, Missouri, and to Nauvoo, Illinois. Baptismal excursions have been made to the Mesa, Washington, and Nauvoo Temples.

Youth from the two Denton Wards at the Washington, D.C. Temple
Summer 1981

Dance Festival

Every other year, thousands of LDS youth gathered in the spring for dance festivals in various areas of the Church. For the MIA "June Conference," an all-Church dance festival was then held in Salt Lake City. Several youths from Denton participated with the Dallas Stake group who went to Salt Lake City in June of 1963 or 1964 where they danced in the festival held at the University of Utah. When June Conference was discontinued, dance festivals continued on a more local regional or area basis.

In 1986 about fourteen hundred LDS youth in the North Texas area participated in a Bi-Regional dance festival staged in the Dallas Convention Center. Known as Dance Fest '86, the festival participants included stakes from Fort Worth eastward to Longview. The event, along with many other events throughout Texas at that time, commemorated the Texas Sesquicentennial celebration. Church dance festivals in those days were gala displays of large group choreography and costuming. In addition to the youth participating as dancers, leadership from Denton included Wendy Guess, who choreographed the event, Adrian Work and Jo Ann Baria, who designed the costumes, and Russell-Newman, which furnished the costume material. Denton's Jim Martino served as the overall chairman.

Dance Festival at University of Utah
Dance Festivals were a highlight for many of the Denton youth.

Walk in the Light

On November 28, 1992, the cover of the *Church News* featured seven young women from the Denton Stake. The girls were Andrea Child, Karina Martino, Angela Stephens, Elka Pennington, Kellie Cudd, Tonya Brown, and Sara Jane Barnes. Along with other stakes throughout the Church, these, and additional girls in the Denton Stake, were participating in the Young Women Worldwide Celebration: "Walk in the Light."

As part of their participation, the girls of the Denton Stake made a seven-foot replica of the Young Women logo. Using the replica to feature seven values every girl should have, the featured girls made short talks on each value and how it had helped her walk in the light. Associated service projects in the stake included singing at an old folks home, cleaning a city park, tending children, making stuffed toys for a local children's hospital, making a baby quilt, and having a baby shower for one of the members.

Denton Young Women on the cover of *Church News*,
November 28, 1992
Left, top to bottom: Karina Martino, Amanda Child, Angela Stephens
Right, top to bottom: Sara Jane Barnes, Kellie Cudd, Tonya Brown, Elka Pennington

CHAPTER 20

The Church Education System

*W*hen John Child of the Church Education System arrived in 1979 to supervise the Institute and Seminary programs in the Fort Worth North Stake and Region, there was much to be done. Rand Packer, Institute Director at the University of Texas at Arlington, had been reassigned a year before John's arrival, and he was no longer supervising CES programs in the Fort Worth North Stake. Thus, things were at a virtual standstill when Brother Child arrived.

Institute

Art Cooper was the first Institute teacher in Denton. Art had given assistance to the institute director at the University of Arizona, and he had also been a branch president there. When Dale Tingey of the Church Educational System learned of Art's planned move to Denton, he contacted Richard S. Williams, the CES director in San Antonio (who at that time handled all of Texas except El Paso), and made arrangements for Art to teach Institute classes for NTSU and TWU students. Starting in 1966, Art taught Institute for two years, and he used Lowell Bennion's *The Religion of the Latter-day Saints* as the text for Denton's first Institute class.

Each year the opening social for the Institute in Denton was a gala affair with lavish decorations. On one occasion crepe paper streamers adorned the walls and ceiling, both inside the Primary room and in the corridor leading to the Primary room. Gaily painted welcoming signs were posted. But what to do

with the baptism font?
Could it be made into a
showpiece? The decorations
committee put green
floating foam into the water
and added lengths of green
ivy. Then they put a pump
into the water and used it to
send a spray of water into the
air. It was a spectacular
display and appreciated by
all, — until, that is, one of
the more influential

Institute of Religion
Opening Social, September 1967

priesthood leaders arrived and disapproved of the use being
made of the font where sacred baptisms were performed.
Everything was removed from the water, the sliding doors were
closed, but the rest of the social proceeded as planned.

When Robert Cummings arrived at the University of Texas
at Arlington in 1968 to be CES director for the Greater Fort
Worth region, he replaced Brother Cooper as the Denton
Institute teacher. Assuming the teaching responsibility for

John and Shanna Child

Denton, Brother Cummings taught an
Institute class in Denton once a week.
Rand Packer, who succeeded Brother
Cummings in 1973, continued that
pattern. Brother Packer, however, was
transferred elsewhere in 1978, and for
the next year, the program had no one
in charge until John Child's arrival in
1979 with his wife, Shanna, and family.
Starting with 25-30 students,
Brother Child held evening classes in

Denton at the Malone Street building. He also taught a class in Hurst for 35-40 students at the Fort Worth North Stake Center. Recognizing the large potential student base in the two universities in Denton, Brother Child decided to concentrate his efforts in Denton, and he made Denton his home.

Because Brother Child had a Ph.D. degree in history, he was accepted as an adjunct faculty member in NTSU's Department of Religion. This meant that the LDS Institute classes could now be taught on campus in the regular classrooms. It also meant that students taking the non-denominational Institute classes (Old Testament, New Testament, History of Religious Thought, etc.) could receive up to six hours college credit toward graduation. It was a very desirable situation. Brother Child taught non-denominational classes on campus in the day time, and church-oriented classes (*Book of Mormon*, Church History, etc.) in the evening at the Malone Street building.

This on-campus arrangement ended when one of Denton's Protestant ministers, Ted Karff, went to Austin and campaigned that the Departments of Religion in the various state colleges be turned into seminaries for producing candidates for the ministry. Not only was his idea rejected, but the end result was that the Departments of Religion in every state supported college in Texas were dissolved. Thus, Brother Child found himself again having to function off campus and having to rent classroom space. Omar Bjelde, Joe McWilliams, and Patricia McWilliams are among those who owned facilities that the Institute rented.

At this point, the Martino family stepped forward. Foreseeing the positive benefits if the Institute had its own building, the Martinos felt that the one block stretch of Mulberry Street between Welch Street and Avenue A would be the right location. It was just a block off the UNT campus, and it would be easily accessible to students with tight schedules. So, unknown to John Child, the Martinos bought properties containing four houses on the north side of Mulberry Street in the block immediately to the west of Welch. They felt, however, that one more adjacent piece of property, facing on Welch, was necessary to have the right amount of space for an Institute building and parking. But that fifth property was not available.

As a result of the four purchases already made, the Institute began in 1995 to hold classes and social functions in an old two-story frame house at the northwest corner of the intersection of Welch and Mulberry Streets. Institute students along with LDS faculty members worked together to renovate the house which had been a boarding house for UNT students. They painted the walls, mounted black boards, and installed new carpeting. Quickly, they had a facility that served well for classes and for social activities.

With Institute now functioning in its own facility, stake and CES leaders again turned their thoughts to a new building specifically designed and constructed for the Institute programs.

Impetus for these thoughts came from the emphasis the Church was now placing on encouraging LDS students to attend college and Institute in their local areas. Brigham Young University could not possibly accommodate all the LDS students who wanted to attend there, and when Apostle Boyd K. Packer suggested that students plan to spend their first two years of college on local campuses, the Martinos felt that the time had now arrived for an Institute building in Denton. It just so happened that the fifth piece of needed property became available at that time, and David Martino quickly arranged for the Church to purchase it.

Each year, under Brother Child's leadership, the Institute

enrollment increased in Denton, and the missionary-minded students were bringing in ten to twenty converts each year. An enrollment of 100 students was needed in order for the Church to justify constructing a new Institute building. By 1990 the needed enrollment of 100 students had been attained and even exceeded. Denton would get its Institute building, although construction would not start for another five years.

In 1995, the Church gave clearance to proceed with the construction of the Institute building. It would be located at the intersection of Welch and Mulberry Streets on property already purchased by the Martinos. All five lots would be needed for the building and its parking lot, so to clear the lots, one house was moved to property owned by another Church member, and the other houses were razed and the lumber taken to the stake's apple orchard and burned. During the construction period, Institute classes were held in one of the other Martino-owned houses across the street.

The new Institute building was completed, and Stake President James Martino dedicated it on October 18, 1998. The Denton Fifth Ward, intended to accommodate single

New Institute of Religion Building
Dedicated October 18, 1996

adults under the age of 31, now had a new place to meet. This church unit began as the Denton Fifth Branch in 1993 with Paul Fisher, chairman of UNT's Computer Science department, as Branch President. Beginning as a unit for singles 30 years of age and under, and also for married students, the branch grew, and in 1995 it became a ward, but only for single young adults. Brother Fisher became the first bishop of the ward. The new ward and its new building provided a much improved environment for spiritual gatherings and activities throughout each week. And the Institute students now had a home of their own.

Dean Garner replaced John Child as Institute Director in 1998, a change that enabled Brother Child to concentrate his efforts on the Dallas and Fort Worth regions while Brother Garner took care of the Denton area. Brother Garner directed the Institute for five years before departing in 2003 to join the Institute faculty at the Southern Utah University in Cedar City, Utah. Successive Institute Directors have been Keith Burkhard (2003 – 2005) and Juan Henderson (2005 – Present).

Paul Fisher served as Fifth Ward bishop (and branch president) from 1993 until 1996. His successors have been Steve Peterson (1996 - 2001), Bryan Galloway (2001 - 2005), David Martino (2005 – 2008), and Kurt Hansen (2008 - Present).

Seminary

With regard to seminary, both of Denton's wards had been holding seminary, but neither ward was organized for the coming school year at the time of Brother Child's arrival in August of 1979. A fast reorganizing process was in order, and Brother Child had only three or four days before the start of school to accomplish the task. Going to work with stake and ward leaders, he succeeded in having teachers called: Betty Martino for Denton First Ward and Pat Ragsdale for Denton Second Ward. With these two sisters leading the way, momentum accumulated, and the Denton First and Second Wards quickly became the top two wards in the stake in terms of Seminary enrollment and attendance. With Betty Martino as teacher, the Denton First Ward seminary led the stake in scripture mastery competitions for several years. Combined Seminary attendance in the two Denton wards and the two Lewisville wards soon reached 90%, and the completion percentages were in the high 80s. Subsequently, after the Denton and Lewisville Stakes came into existence, the seminary programs in these two stakes led the entire U. S. Southern Plains area in all seminary categories for several years.

CHAPTER 21
The Dallas Temple

With the First Presidency's announcement on April 1, 1981, of nine sites for new temples, Church members throughout Texas, and especially in the Metroplex area, were overjoyed to learn that the Dallas area was one of those sites. Already, in anticipation of such an announcement, a committee had been unofficially searching for candidate sites. One of the proposed sites was a gently sloping hill owned by Newton Rayzor. Situated at the intersection of University Avenue and Interstate 35 in Denton, it was a lovely location. But it was not to be. A score of other sites were also considered, with the final choice being the site on Willow Lane in north Dallas behind the Cooper Aerobics Center.

Almost immediately, opposition arose from local churches and from residents living the general area of the selected site on Willow Lane. The opposition came in different forms, such as negative publicity in the press. Before the announcement of the Dallas Temple, local newspapers generally ignored the Mormons. The LDS Public Affairs representatives were rarely successful in their attempts to have notices and news of the Church included in the Dallas and Denton newspapers. But after the announcement, items (mostly negative) on Mormonism appeared frequently in the pages of the *Dallas Morning News* and the *Dallas Times Herald*. As one example, a front page headline in the *Dallas Morning News* of March 8, 1982, read: "Southern Baptists Brace for Invasion of Mormons." In this article, Dr. Edmund Poole of the First Baptist Church in Dallas, bemoaned the supposed fact that 231

Baptists are converted to Mormonism each day. Occasionally
an article rebutting the prevailing anti-Mormon sentiment
would also be printed. A week following the Poole article, the
Dallas Times Herald, printed a Letter to the Editor in which a
non-Mormon writer offered some tongue-in-cheek
suggestions to Dr. Poole, one of which was "Dr. Poole should
try to discover what is lacking in Baptist teachings that causes
231 Baptists per day to turn to Mormonism."

The opposition also manifested itself in a variety of other
ways. Neighborhood groups voiced opposition, even offering
to buy the property from the Church. A Mr. Ed Decker came
to Dallas for the specific purpose of teaching non-Mormons
how to ask embarrassing questions about the Church. Picketing
with public displays of temple ordinance clothing occurred on
many occasions.

General misunderstandings about the Church in general
and the temple in particular added to the apprehensions of the
residents. For example, some wanted to know what times of
the day and night would Moroni be blowing his horn. Others
were concerned that the lights of the temple would be a
distraction to the neighboring homes.

Still, plans to build the House of the Lord on Willow Lane
proceeded.

Groundbreaking

Groundbreaking for the Temple took place on January
22, 1983, with President Hinckley and other General
Authorities present. It was a cold, blustery day, and visible
opposition from opponents did not materialize. President
Hinkley amused those in attendance by commenting that the
absence of anti-temple demonstrators was probably due to

the weather and the fact that the Dallas Cowboys were playing in a playoff game that day.

In addition to the Temple groundbreaking, the new Welfare Center in Carrolton was dedicated in the afternoon of that same day. To keep the groundbreaking ceremony at a low key, only stake leaders were invited to attend. Ward and branch leaders were invited to the Welfare Center dedication. When Gainesville Branch President Ken Fette and his wife, Kathleen, arrived at the Welfare Center, they parked on the east side of the building close to the east door. This was not the entrance the visitors were expected to use, but the weather was so disagreeable that the Fettes wanted to minimize their exposure. Upon entering through the east door, they found themselves in a room with President Hinckley, H. Burke Peterson, and Jacob de Jager. Although the Fettes had made an unexpected entry, they were warmly welcomed and made to feel quite comfortable, another example of the love and human feelings the Church leaders have for all.

Public Viewing

Construction of the Temple started shortly after the groundbreaking. It is interesting to note that overt opposition to the temple proceeded to wane as construction progressed. Near the end of the construction period, newspaper attention had become more positive than negative.

Finally, from September 7 through 26 in 1984, the completed temple was opened for viewing by the general public. Despite the fact that some picketing and demonstrations again occurred in front of the temple property, there were no serious incidents, and at the viewing, the public seemed not to be unduly affected.

Dr. W. A. Criswell, senior pastor of the 23,000 member First Baptist Church in Dallas, and one who had been very vocal in opposing the construction of the temple, was one of the viewers. Denton's Sanfred Elieson personally conducted Dr. Criswell and three of his associates through the facility. Sanfred moved at a deliberately slow pace, pointing out the many paintings featuring Christ, showing the King James version of the Bible on the temple altars, and explaining the significance of the various areas through which they toured. Following the tour, Sanfred led the Criswell group into one of the temple's office rooms where President and Sister Hobson joined them for a discussion. Dr. Criswell asked many things including questions about doctrine, about administration, and of course, about polygamy. After Sanfred gave what appeared to be very satisfying responses, an impressed Dr. Criswell said, "Mr. Elieson, you would make a good Baptist." Responding in his unique, thoughtful style, Sanfred replied, "Dr. Criswell, with a little study you would make a good Mormon." They parted on amiable terms.

Dedication and Beginning of Ordinance Work

Dedication of the Dallas Temple took place on October 19, 1984, with additional dedicatory services held on the following two days. President Gordon B. Hinckley presided. The initial temple presidency consisted of Ivan L. Hobson, President; Richard Ragsdale, First Counselor; and Alfred White, Jr., Second Counselor. (Alfred White, Jr. was the father of Denton's Alfred White, III. He and his wife came from their home in Utah in response to a mission call to serve in the Temple presidency.) Following the dedication, a three-week period was needed for cleaning and for training the temple workers. So in November 1984, the temple was opened for sacred ordinances to be performed within.

In order for temple ordinance work for the dead to be done, names of the dead must be available. For the Dallas Temple, the Church had promised to provide 10,000 name cards to get things started; however, when the temple opened, the name cards were not forthcoming. So a call went out to local seminary students to spend two or more hours a week preparing name cards. Within two weeks, these youths had 10,000 name cards prepared, and baptisms for the dead began on November 10. The other ordinances for the dead began a few days later.

The Dallas Temple

Temple Building Fund

As a prerequisite to constructing the temple, each stake in the proposed temple district accepted the challenge to raise a certain amount of money to be applied to construction costs. These quotas were eagerly received, and the stakes not only raised the requested amounts, many of them raised more. Therefore, when the final costs of the temple were determined, it turned out that the Temple Building Fund had a $60,000 surplus. President Hobson, President Ragsdale, and President Davidson (who succeeded President White on March 2, 1986) all felt that this surplus could be put to good use over the future years in providing for various needs that were likely to arise. But when the Temple Department in Salt Lake City learned about the surplus, they insisted that it be turned over to them.

"Obedience is the first law of heaven," so President Hobsen and President Ragsdale obediently, but reluctantly, wrote a check for $60,00 and sent it to Salt Lake. But they included a specially worded letter with the check. They strongly suggested that the Temple Department send a letter to every bishop and every stake president in the Dallas Temple District explaining why they had demanded the money that had been raised locally with the understanding that it would be used locally. That would mean a lot of explanatory letters because the Dallas Temple District included all of Texas except El Paso, all of Oklahoma, and parts of Louisiana, Arkansas, Missouri, Kansas, and New Mexico. The following week, the Temple Department returned the $60,000 check.

Expansion and Rededication

Initially the Dallas Temple served a district of 67 stakes. As other temples were constructed in Houston, St. Louis,

Albuquerque, Lubbock, Oklahoma City, San Antonio, and Baton Rouge, the Dallas Temple district shrank in geographical size to 15 stakes in 2001. (Stake divisions and realignments, however, brought this number up to 19 by early 2008.) But as Church membership continued to grow, it became apparent that certain alterations and expansions of the physical temple would greatly enhance its serviceability to patrons. A larger sealing room was needed as well as a cafeteria. Additional dressing and study rooms for temple workers were needed. Larger and more private places for youth to wait when not doing baptisms or when waiting to be sealed to parents would enhance the spirituality within the temple. So on April 15, 1988, the Dallas Temple closed for eleven months for these changes to be made. On Sunday, March 5, 1989, the temple was rededicated with President Hinckley again presiding.

Spiritual Experiences

Spiritual experiences occur in all temples of the Church, and while it can be very faith-promoting to hear of these experiences, it is rare that they are related outside of the temples because of their sacred and holy nature. The following two experiences, both involving temple workers from Denton, are included in this book because they have already appeared elsewhere in print. These accounts by Richard Ragsdale and Doyle Thompson are given in their own words.

Richard Ragsdale

After an endowment session on December 5, 1985, a brother asked if it would be possible to go and see a sealing room. I took him to one of the sealing rooms. He walked over to the altar, looked all around, tears came to his eyes, and he said, "Are all the sealing rooms in the temple like this? Are they all the same size and same color?" I said, "No. Are you looking for any particular color?" He replied, "Yes, I am looking for a blue pastel room." "Come with me," was my reply.

We then walked to another sealing room. He walked over to the altar, looked around, and tears again started streaming from his eyes. He said, "President Ragsdale, three months before the temple was opened I had a dream, and I saw my mother and father. Now, my father is a member of another church. All of his sons have gone on missions, all of his sons and daughters have been married in temples, and my mother is a member of the Church. Yet, our father just won't have anything to do with the Church. But in my dream, I saw my father and my mother kneeling at this altar in this sealing room with the exact same colors, same size and exactly the way it looks right now. They were being sealed at the altar for eternity." The brother relating the experience now feels a surety that his father will join the Church sooner or later.

Doyle Thompson

I was working in the temple as an ordinance worker on January 8, 1987. Having been assigned as session officiator for the 10:00 a.m. session, I was in an ordinance room. As the room was filling with patrons, I noticed an older gentleman looking at me and smiling. There was a very special feeling in the room all during the session. I knew not why I felt a strong kindred spirit to this particular gentleman. After the session was over he came up to me and touched me on my shoulder and said, "Don't go away yet. I need to talk to you. You don't recognize me, do you?" I said, "No, but I feel a close kinship and brotherhood to you." He said, "You should, for we knew each other many, many years ago" (meaning our pre-mortal life). With his final statement he hugged me and with tears in his eyes said I had been his best friend. He then walked away. I am sure from the strong attachment we felt for one another in the Lord's house that we did indeed know one another on the other side of the veil. This was a special experience for me in the Lord's Holy Temple.

Denton Temple Workers

Many of the Church members in Denton have served in various capacities in the Dallas Temple. In addition to those who have served as ordinance workers or as volunteer workers, a small number have also served in special leadership capacities. For example, several brothers and sisters from the Denton area have served as Shift Coordinators. As has already been mentioned in an earlier chapter, Richard Ragsdale and Sanfred Elieson were called as Sealers when the temple first opened. Both these brothers also served in the temple presidency – Brother Ragsdale as First Counselor to Ivan Hobson, the Temple's first president, and Sanfred Elieson as First Counselor to Robert McCook, the Temple's second president.

Maurice Arrington was also called as one of the Temple's first sealers. Brother Arrington speaks of a rather unusual interview with President Hinckley on that occasion. Rather than interrogating Brother Arrington to verify his worthiness, President Hinckley simply said, "Brother Arrington, because you are worthy, you are called to be a sealer." Maurice served as a sealer from 1985 to 2000. He once confided to his son, Kenneth, that among his greatest joys were the times couples returned and thanked him for sealing them and for the wise counsel he had given them at the time. Brother Arrington also commented to his family on several occasions that "you can't believe how thin the veil is in the Temple."

Frank Martino was called as a Sealer in 1994, and then in October 1999, President Monson called Brother Martino to be First Counselor to Owen Jacobsen, the Temple's sixth president. When President Jacobsen had to be released early (August 2000) because of his wife's ill health, President Hinckley called Brother Martino to be the Temple's seventh president, filling the remaining portion of President Jacobsen's term. In June 2001, Robert Nobles was called as the fifth Sealer from Denton.

Sam Briggs's Wood Carving

One further story is appropriate before closing this chapter on the Dallas Temple. Patrons to the Dallas Temple should spend a few moments in the visitors' waiting room and observe a wood carving of a family of seven kneeling in prayer with the Savior standing behind them with outstretched arms offering love and protection. Sam Briggs, a member of Denton Second Ward but now deceased, designed and carved the beautiful work. Sam, who had been relatively inactive for some time, was a barber in Krum by profession and an excellent wood carver by avocation.

With the announcement that a temple would be built in Dallas, Sam "woke up" spiritually, and he wanted to make some kind of contribution to the Temple. Richard Ragsdale suggested a wood carving of some kind, and he arranged for Sam to have an interview with President Hobson to discuss the matter. As the three men discussed various possible themes, they soon found themselves agreeing on a wood carving that somehow would depict a family in a spiritual setting. Sam's wife, Carol, tells the story from this point.

When Sam was asked to do a carving for the temple he felt surprised, as he hadn't been active in the Church for some time. However, he was very proud and honored to be asked. Little did he know what a spiritual experience it was going to be. It had earlier been decided by Sam and President Hobson that the carving should represent Christ and a family. Sam began to carve about the last part of 1983. He couldn't seem to get the figures to come out right. He started several figures but couldn't complete them. He fasted and prayed until he began to feel the spirit and inspiration he needed. It seemed like a miracle was happening. He was so excited and couldn't seem to work fast enough.

A barber by trade, he didn't open his barber shop until 11:00 a.m., but he would leave the house sometimes at 8:00 a.m. so he could go to the shop and whittle. He would whittle six to eight hours a day and loved every minute. I saw this wonderful man who had once lost the spirit, receive it again as he worked on the project for the Lord's House. What a rare and wonderful opportunity he had. When it was completed he stood back and said, "This is my best work." Sam and I both knew that he had a God-given talent but found out that in being able to do something for the Lord you have to have the Holy Spirit to guide you or your talent is of little worth.

Sam had put his spiritual life back together, and he looked upon this carving as his ultimate achievement. Apparently it was, for two weeks later while out jogging, Sam was hit by a truck and killed instantly.

Sam Briggs's Wood Carving
created for the Dallas Temple

CHAPTER 22

The Apple Orchard

*I*n the late 1970s the priesthood leadership in the Fort Worth North Stake set out to comply with the Church's policy of having each stake produce a crop or product for the Church's welfare program. Partly because the stake president, Richard Ragsdale, was a Dentonite, and largely because the two Denton wards at that time were in a more rural setting than the other wards in the stake, the Denton First and Second Wards took the lead in launching the project.

Several types of crops were considered, such as pinto beans, peaches, tomatoes, and onions. After considering these various options, a steering committee composed of President Ragsdale, Frank Martino, and John Child, decided that the project should be a grape orchard. The brethren, however, had no real experience with regard to the kind of grapes to plant nor of how to grow them. To determine what might grow best in the Denton area, Brother Child planted 30 – 40 varieties of grapes along the side of his own house. The steering committee gathered information and understanding by visiting vineyards and wineries in De Leon, Aledo, Bowie, and Weatherford; and they contacted Texas A&M for additional information and advice. Possible sites were considered in the southwest portion of Denton County, and the stake even made an escrow deposit on a 15-acre plot near Argyle.

Everything looked good, and the stake leaders were all set to proceed when two things happened. Soil and water tests on the lands being considered showed too much salt for successful irrigation. At about the same time, the Church Welfare Department announced in the summer of 1979 that they wanted the Fort Worth North Stake to grow apples instead of grapes. So it was back to square one.

President Ragsdale gave the apple orchard assignment to the Denton Second Ward, and Bishop Nobles organized a new orchard committee composed of himself, Earl Cochran, Doyle Thompson, Sr., Doyle Thompson, Jr., Clarence Sunding, and Maurice Arrington. Although Clarence Sunding, father of Joyce Thompson, Doyle, Jr's wife, was a non-member, he was very interested in the project, and he gave significant help. This new committee began gathering information and consulting experts at Texas A&M with regard to apples. Despite much local skepticism, apple growers in Montague County and experts at Texas A&M agreed that apples could be grown in the Denton area. A certain kind of soil and an adequate water supply would be needed.

With President Ragsdale's approval, a twelve acre plot that fit the requirements was located and purchased in Krugerville, just south of Aubrey. Ten acres would be used for trees, and two acres would contain buildings, a well, and access roads. Church welfare representatives from Salt Lake, A&M experts, and local agricultural experts all agreed with the land selection. Each ward in the stake was assessed a specific amount of money for the purchase, and within a short period of time, the Church owned the land free and clear. Following their fast and testimony meeting on January 6, 1980, members of the Denton Second Ward gathered at the orchard site, and President Ragsdale dedicated the land.

"Bless this land that it will produce apples … to fulfill our welfare assignment. Bless this ward. Help us each as we grow in brotherhood. Help us to live in the light."

After clearing and leveling the land, three wells were dug, a storage and tool barn was built, a fence was built around the property, and Arizona Cypress trees were planted as wind breaks. The plan called for planting 1,500 apple trees of various varieties and for being able to deliver up to 30 to 40 gallons of water per day to each tree. The anticipated yield would start small and build up to 700 bushels of apples per acre by the seventh year.

Before any planting could be attempted, tree rows had to be laid out and the exact location of each tree plotted on a master plan. This was necessary in order to plan and install an irrigation system that would deliver water to each tree. The plan called for a grid layout of 36 rows with 40 to 42 trees in each row. With R. B. Pennington driving a tractor and plow and Earl Cochran giving directions, an initial grid was created in the surface of the soil. Later, with Earl Cochran sighting through a surveyor's transit and Doyle Thompson, Jr. driving the tractor and plow, a more precise grid was laid out. The orchard committee was now ready to order trees.

Along with trees, machinery and other equipment were needed. Upon learning that the Moab (Utah) Stake had and was trying to sell the kinds of equipment needed at the apple orchard, arrangements were made for the purchase of several items. R. B. Pennington drove his semi trailer to Moab, loaded the purchased equipment on it, and drove it back to Denton. R. B. also proved quite helpful in another way. As the owner of a gas station and tire shop in Aubrey and also as a welder, he was invaluable in repairing the orchard equipment and keeping it in working order.

Beginning as early as October 1979, the search was on for apple trees. Because of a hard freeze that had killed 80% of the apple trees in the state of Washington, the nurseries being contacted had no trees available to send to Denton. An apple orchard with no trees cannot produce fruit, so Bishop Nobles called for a day of fasting and prayer in the Denton Second Ward. Almost immediately, the Blue Ridge nursery in Princes Anne, Maryland, called saying they had enough trees to take care of Denton's needs, and the trees were on their way. The stake had requested 750 trees to be shipped in January 1980, with the balance to be shipped the following year. When the first trees arrived, the weather was cold and the ground was frozen. Work parties were organized, however, and the planting was accomplished.

Earl Cochran was the first orchard supervisor with Jan Martin and Doyle Thompson, Jr. as counselors. Later, Jim Matheson was hired on a part-time basis to assist Brother Cochran. When Jim was set apart, he was promised that he would never work alone, and Jim bears testimony of having been guided by the Holy Spirit on many occasions.

After getting the trees planted, watering had to be provided. Because the wells and a drip system to each tree had not yet been completed, Earl and his assistants put 55-gallon drums of water in the back of a pickup truck and drove around to each tree. Watering every tree in the morning and again in the evening six days a week, they kept the trees nourished until the automated watering system was ready to assume the task.

At this time it was decided to assign specific rows of trees to each ward and branch in the stake. Each unit would do weeding, pruning, and picking, while the orchard personnel would continue fertilizing and watering. In some cases, this worked well; in other cases, it didn't. With regard to pruning, for example, Brother Matheson reports that in some rows trees were pruned well, in other rows they were insufficiently pruned, and in a few rows the tree limbs were simply amputated.

In addition, some wards were much more responsive than others in providing work crews at times when they were needed for weeding and picking. Still, apples, in large quantities, were produced.

Gainesville's Norma Harper had an experience at the orchard one Saturday morning that shows true brotherhood in action. Responding to a call to all the wards to come now and prune their assigned trees, Norma arrived early at the orchard. No one else from Gainesville was there, so Norma set about pruning trees in the row she thought was assigned to Gainesville. After a while, some men unknown to Norma arrived and began pruning on the same row where Norma was working. They were from The Colony Ward. It soon became understood by all that Norma was working on the wrong row, and when Gainesville's row was pointed out to her, she went there and began again to prune by herself. It all became a special experience for Norma when the brethren from The Colony finished their rows, for they then joined her and helped her finish her row. For Norma, it was a heart-warming and faith-promoting experience.

Earl Cochran, a rather elderly person, eventually, died, and Brother Matheson became the orchard supervisor. Brother Matheson reports another occasion where divine help was sought through fasting and prayer. Pollination at blossom times was being provided by bees from beehives placed in the orchard by Tom Thompson. In the spring of one year the bees were decimated by mites and wax-moth larvae, and when the blossoms came, there were too few bees available for pollination. Bishop Nobles called for another day of fasting and prayer. After the Church meetings that Sunday, Brother Matheson drove out to the orchard and found the trees covered with migrating Monarch butterflies. He described it as an eerie, yet beautiful sight, and the pollination was accomplished.

"You can't grow apples in the Denton area," local Church leaders were repeatedly told by those who "knew." But the apples did grow. In its peak year, the apple orchard, with over 1,600 trees, produced over 200,000 pounds of apples. During each year of orchard operation, the apples were trucked to the Church cannery in Carrolton where they were processed into apple sauce as part of the Church Welfare program for this area.

Transporting the apples to the cannery in Carrolton was a major task. In the latter stages of the project, an eighteen wheel refrigerated "reefer" was made available, but before that, the apples were transported in pickup trucks and trailers. During times when the cannery could not take any more, temporary cold storage facilities had to be rented.

On one of Brother Jim Matheson's trips to the cannery, he picked up a food order from the adjacent bishop's storehouse in response to a request by Bishop Child. While driving through Lewisville on I-35E on his return trip, Jim noticed greenish papers fluttering in the air. Stopping his truck to investigate, he found that it was money, and he picked up three one-dollar bills and one one-hundred-dollar bill. Having no idea where the money came from, Jim wondered for a moment about what to do with it. Then the prompting came to him to put the money into one of the grocery sacks for the needy family that was to receive the food. Later when talking to Bishop Child about the incident, the bishop told him, "This family made a choice to pay a full tithing, even though they needed $102.00 for a Texas vehicle inspection and car repairs." They made what many would consider to be a very difficult decision, and their faith was rewarded.

During the life of the orchard, the Lewisville Stake was created in 1981 from a division of the Fort Worth North Stake, and the Denton Stake was created in 1992 from a division of the Lewisville Stake. In both of these divisions, responsibility for the apple orchard was assumed by the stake containing the Denton wards. John Child, who for five years had the High Council assignment of getting the project started and of overseeing its entire operation, provided needed consistency, and he deserves much of the credit for the success of the project.

In 1995, the Church cannery in Carrollton ceased doing wet-pack canning, which meant, among other things, that no more apple sauce would be produced. The Church's Welfare Department in Salt Lake decided that the apple orchard should be discontinued and sold, so it was put up for bid. Neighbors of the orchard collaborated in a successful bid of $47,200. For two more years, the apple orchard continued to produce, then because of neglect, a decline set in. Army worms and locusts destroyed most of the trees, and the three wells collapsed after lightning strikes. By 2002, only two live trees remained.

Bob Nobles, as bishop of the Denton Second Ward and as an active leader in the orchard project, feels that the project produced benefits far beyond the production of apples. As a result of their participation, several Church members came out of inactivity. They became involved again in Church service and attendance, and they rejuvenated and strengthened their testimonies. Jim Matheson is a prime example of this type of benefit. Jim, who eventually became orchard supervisor, became a spiritual giant as well as an expert in growing apples.

Earl Cochran, the first orchard supervisor, gained a new focus in the latter part of his life. Retired as director of the Argyle Water Works, Earl needed new challenges and responsibilities, and the orchard provided just that. Earl was there working almost every day.

Bishop Nobles has also cited the *esprit de corps* generated by the orchard project. It served to mold the participants into a unified team, and personal relationships were established that have endured over the ensuing years.

CHAPTER 23
Building the Stake Center

$\mathcal{A}$s the Church continued to grow in Denton, it became obvious by 1984 that a second meeting house was needed. It was also obvious that if the growth continued (and the projections strongly indicated that it would continue), a stake center would be needed in Denton in the not too distant future.

Blending these two needs into one project, Church leaders in Denton went to work searching out an appropriate building site and securing approval from Salt Lake City. They selected the site on Old North Road, and groundbreaking occurred on June 13, 1987. As has already been mentioned, the site had formerly been owned by the grandparents of Doyle Thompson, Jr. Today, Doyle, Jr. still has many fond memories of spending time on that property during the summers and doing all the things (work and play) that boys did on farms in those years.

The Denton wards were a part of the Lewisville Stake which had improvised a stake center by building an addition onto the rear of the only LDS chapel in Lewisville at that time. The rapidly growing stake membership made it apparent, however, that a larger facility was needed for stake functions. Therefore, the new building to be built in Denton would be known as the Lewisville Stake Center. Dentonites nevertheless referred to the anticipated building as their "future stake center," and when the Denton Stake was created in 1992 from a division of the Lewisville Stake, the building officially became the Denton Stake Center.

Groundbreaking for the Denton Stake Center, June 13, 1987
Left to Right: Richard Ragsdale, Bob Nobles, Lewisville Stake President
Gordon T. Watts, Jack Semones, John W. Porter, Margaret Porter.

It is not at all unusual for delays and unanticipated situations to occur in large-scale building projects. The new stake center was no exception. The first delay occurred at the inception of the project when the Church raised the stake membership requirement to 6,000 members before it would approve the construction of a stake center. The Lewisville Stake had qualified under the old limitation, but the requirement changed before approval had been granted. About a year and a half passed before the Lewisville Stake membership reached the 6,000 level. In the meantime, the Stake rented the main auditorium at NTSU for their stake conferences.

It is appropriate at this point to recount the experiences of David Martino and John Child, two of the prime movers in making the Stake Center a reality. Brother Martino, a member of the Lewisville Stake High Council at that time, was the stake physical facilities representative. John Child, Bishop of the Denton First Ward, represented the Bishop's Council in overseeing the construction of the building. These experiences are given in their own words.

David Martino's Experience

In 1984 and 1985 my call as physical facilities representative on the stake high council encompassed the duty to project future land and building needs for the saints as the kingdom grows.

After establishing the need for a 3.0-acre stake center site in Denton, I met with Presidents Ragsdale, Watts, and Nobles to determine the ideal area. We mapped out the future growth area of the stake, (and realizing there was already a Chapel located in the west part of Denton), we decided that east or northeast Denton would be the best location; somewhere inside the future extension of Loop 288.

Following much prayerful deliberation, I contacted Church headquarters in Salt Lake City requesting that someone come down to review three sites that were candidates for the Church site: 1) Ginnings property on the northwest corner of Sherman and Hercules, 2) Morris and Williams properties on Sherman Drive and Kings Row, and 3) Doyle Conine property (Checkmate Development) south of Windsor and east of Old North Road. Consideration was also being given to the possibility of a recreational field adjacent to the stake center. At that time developed land was going for approximately $1.00 per square foot.

When the representative of the Church from Salt Lake City came, it was concluded that the third site, owned by Doyle Conine, would be the one to pursue. While the first two sites were already totally developed, the third site was just an open field, but in the process of going through zoning changes to prepare for development.

In beginning discussions with Doyle Conine, we were discussing a piece of raw land with literally no road access to the property except by a pickup truck or a four wheel drive vehicle. After much bargaining (which I thoroughly enjoyed), we came to a sales price of $.65 per square foot or $85,000 for three acres. (See Tract 1 on Exhibit A) The price and closing of the property were subject to 1) platting the land, 2) having a road to the property, 3) all utilities to the property, 4) all old easements being removed from the property, & 5) the property level must be above the 500-year flood plain.

We were in contract quite some time before the closing of the three acres, and there were a couple of times that President Watts questioned whether or not we should look for another site. Finally all prerequisites were completed by the seller, and we were able to close on the property and take possession.

Some local members were concerned that three acres were not enough for the parking requirements, so they purchased an additional 1.2 acres and donated it to the Church. (See Tract 2 on Exhibit A)

One goal still had not been met—the recreational field. Many local Church leaders expressed a desire for a ball field, but there was not a lot of financial support. Bishop Child requested that I still look into it, so after studying the property on all sides of the Church site, it was decided that a 2.8-acre tract east of the Church would be ideal. (See Tract 3 on Exhibit A). The only problem is that another 2.2 acre tract of flood plain (See Tract 4 on Exhibit A) was between the Church site and the proposed ball field.

A certain family agreed to purchase the 2.8 acres for the

ball field and donate it to the Church if the developer would donate the 2.2-acre tract of flood plain. The purchase of the ball field was also subject to the City of Denton granting a specific use permit. Doyle Conine, the developer, agreed to the deal.

The nine-plus acres is designed so that the saints can play baseball, football, soccer, volleyball, badminton, horse-shoes, etc., have a picnic area, and even have one half to one acre of land for gardening if the need arises.

Building the Kingdom of God is magnificent. The Lord orchestrates our lives to help us see the vision of what the saints can do to build a Zion people. May the youth of Zion use this land and its facilities to share the gospel with their friends and loved ones.

Bishop John Child's Experience

Following the creation of the Lewisville Texas Stake, President Richard W. Ragsdale appointed David Martino as the Stake Building Agent, and he proceeded to locate and get approval to purchase the property for this Stake Center. It was at that time a wilderness with no roads, no bridge, no access to the property which now sits in one of the most desirable housing developments in the city of Denton.

The stake made a big push to raise the level of tithing so that permission could be attained to build on the property. In the fall of 1984 President Richard W. Ragsdale was called into the Presidency of the Dallas Texas Temple, and in December, 1984, Gordon T. Watts was called as President of the Lewisville Texas Stake. The balance of the project was under President Watts' direction.

In the spring of 1986 approval was received to build. Brother

Harold Powell of the Church Building Committee, Bill Fowkes (the area Physical Facilities Representative), the Stake Presidency (President Gordon T. Watts, Robert H. Nobles, and Jack Semones), and the two Bishops of the Wards who were to occupy the building (Bishop John Child - Denton First Ward, and Bishop Doyle Thompson - Denton Fourth Ward) met and selected the Cody plan and the color scheme, called Rio. Bishop Frank Martino and his wife, Betty, and I and my wife, Shanna, made visits to the Dallas and Richardson Stake buildings, and spoke to many people and procured many ideas and suggested changes.

John R. Horton was hired as architect and began drawings. I wrote up the changes wanted and submitted them to the architect and Harold Powell in Salt Lake City. Between July 1986 and July 1987 many preparations were made, and plans and bids were procured. Several meetings were held with the architect and city officials to review needs, permits, and building changes.

Bids were let out, and seven companies met in a pre-bid meeting and took plans. Two weeks later Pack & Peterson gave the low bid of approximately $1.65 million.

Groundbreaking was held on June 13, 1987, under the direction of the Stake President, Gordon T. Watts, and construction began in August. It took 2½ months to get the ground ready, only to have the city require more off street parking. Additional land was donated to bring the parking spaces up from 130 to 340. The construction was delayed while this new land was prepared, the plans changed, and then the rains came. Further delays!

By late fall 1987 the ground was ready and the plumbing, electrical, and cement work began. Foundation pillars were sunk 16 feet deep and the footings and floors were poured.

Vic Fennel was the project foreman. There were many problems to delay the work during construction, including bad weather. Each month there was a meeting to review the progress, and selections made of paint, tile, carpet, flooring, facia, etc. Finally by summer the roof was on, and the brick work and the landscaping were done.

The interior work was done from June through August 1968, after Vic Fennel departed. Flores Copier was assigned as project foreman to get any existing problems corrected and the building in working order.

The Denton First and Fourth Wards began moving into the building in late September, and the first meetings of the wards there were on Sunday, October 23, 1988. Overall, we have a good building, and it should last us for several decades. My hope is that it will be treated with respect. It is great to have it finished and to be using it!

Going the Extra Mile

People parking on the north side of the building can't help noticing the the well-built tool shed at the edge of the parking lot. It was to have a stucco exterior and a shingled roof. Bishop Child, seeing that there would be bricks left over from the main building, asked the brick contractor about the possibility of brick walls instead of stucco on the tool shed. The next day when Bishop Child arrived at the site, the tool shed was already encased in brick – at no extra charge. Then seeing that there would be some tiles left over from the stake center's roof, Bishop Child asked about having tile on the tool shed roof. Again, the next day it was done – at no extra charge.

Completion of the Stake Center

Actual construction of the Stake Center began in August 1987, and fourteen months later, as reported by Bishop Child, the Denton First and Denton Fourth Wards moved in on October 23, 1988. The Denton Second and Denton Third Wards stayed in the Malone Street building.

Dentonites were honored on December 4, 1988, when the Lewisville Stake held its Stake Conference in the new Denton "Stake Center." The new building marked a giant step forward in the growth in the Church in Denton, and the local saints were understandably proud of their accomplishment. But there was one more problem of a major nature yet to be encountered.

Christmas Day, which occurred on a Sunday that year of 1988, was a memorable occasion for the new building. When Bishop Child arrived early in the morning to unlock the building, he found about two-thirds of the floor area was flooded. It seems that after the insulation had been laid above the ceiling of the building, unwrapped water pipes were laid on top of the insulation. During a hard freeze a few days before

The Denton Stake Center
Dedicated May 28, 1989

Christmas, one of the pipes burst, and when the weather sufficiently thawed on the day before Christmas, flooding of the building began. So instead of holding the normal church meetings on that first Christmas Sunday, the members of the Denton First and Fourth Wards spent the greater part of the day removing pews, ripping up a floor boards in the cultural hall, and bringing in shop vacs to dry up a flooded interior. Meetings for that day had to be set aside, but on the following Sunday, the saints were back in the building for their regular services. The final repair bill for the water damage amounted to about $20,000, a consequence of the design specifications made by the Building Department in Salt Lake City who were sure that "the weather would never freeze in Denton."

Dedicatory Services

Dedicatory services for the new building were held on May 28, 1989, only two years after the groundbreaking. Gordon T. Watts, President of the Lewisville Stake, offered the dedicatory prayer.

Shortly after the dedication, a softball field was established on the recreational property, just east of the creek, complete with a large and sturdy backstop erected under the direction of Roy Pennington (son of R. B. and Mabel) as an Eagle Scout project.

Part Five
THE EXPANSION YEARS

Introduction

*T*he Expansion Years begin with the creation of the Denton Stake in May 1992, thirty-two and a half years having passed since the Porters organized a Sunday School in November 1959. This Sunday School grew into the Denton Branch which in turn evolved into the Denton Ward. The Denton Branch also spawned Sunday Schools that grew into branches and then into wards in Decatur, Gainesville and Lewisville.

The Denton Stake, which initially consisted of eight units, stands now (in 2008) at ten units, even though three units have since been transferred to other stakes. As population growth continues, especially south and east of Denton, membership in the Denton Stake continues to grow, and further ward and stake divisions are quite likely in the near future.

When the Denton Stake was organized in 1992, Denton was well positioned for the expansion to come. Denton already had a stake center which could now correctly be called the Denton Stake Center. In addition, the Church had refurbished the Malone Street building, giving it a more modern look. Denton also had its own Institute of Religion building which had been erected adjacent to the University of North Texas campus.

On a regional basis, a Welfare Center had been established in Carrollton, housing social services, an employment center, a cannery, and a bishop's storehouse. And the Dallas Temple had been in operation since 1984.

The physical facilities were in place to accommodate the continuing expansion—which is still continuing. The Expansion Years were well under way.

The following timeline will show the major events of this development period and their time relationships to one another.

The Expansion Years of
The Church of Jesus Christ
of Latter-day Saints in Denton
1992-2008

Denton Events	Year	Area Events
Denton Stake Created 5/3/92	1992	
Denton 5th Ward Created 1/17/93	1993	
	1994	
Spanish Branch Created 7/9/95 Apple Orchard Sold	1995	
Spanish Branch Discontinued	1996	Regional Conference with President Hinckley 3/17/96
Lake Cities Ward Created 2/18/97	1997	
Institute Building Dedicated 10/18/98	1998	
	1999	
	2000	
	2001	Carrollton Stake Created 12/9/01
Lake Cities 1st Ward Created 10/13/02 Lake Cities 2nd Ward Created 10/13/02	2002	
Denton 6th (Spanish) Branch Created 12/14/03	2003	
	2004	
	2005	
	2006	
Justin Ward Created 1/1/07 General Realignment of Denton Stake 1/1/07	2007	
	2008	Frisco Stake Created 5/4/08 Lake Cities 2nd Ward Transferred to Lewisville Stake 5/4/08

CHAPTER 24

Creating the Denton Stake

*O*n Sunday, May 3, 1992, members of the Lewisville Stake gathered in the coliseum at the University of North Texas for a stake conference. It was a momentous occasion for the saints in Denton, for it was at this stake conference that the Lewisville Stake was divided and the Denton Stake created. The division came as no surprise, however, because Denton had been a focal point of the Church in north Texas and the "stake center" for the Lewisville Stake had been in Denton for four years.

Elder Cree-L Kofford of the First Quorum of Seventy was the presiding authority at the conference. Assisting Elder Kofford was Owen Jacobsen, a regional representative and later a president of the Dallas Temple. On Saturday, May 2, Elders

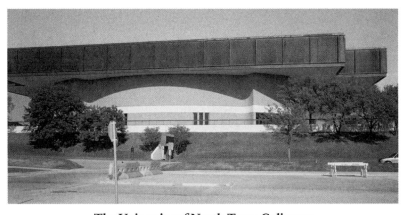

The University of North Texas Coliseum
The UNT Coliseum was where the Denton Stake was created May 3, 1992,
and where the Regional Conference with President Hinckley was held
March 17, 1996.

Kofford and Jacobsen interviewed all the Lewisville Stake presidency, the high council, and all the bishops. At the end of the day, they felt they knew the will of the Lord, and they called James Martino, son of Frank and Betty Martino, to be the president of the new Denton Stake.

Martino , Andrus

New stake formed by Mormons

The Church of Jesus Christ of Latter-day Saints recently announced the formation of a new stake in the Denton area.

The stake, the second level of organization, is made up of "wards" or local congregations. The new stake was formed from the Lewisville Warner

Texas Stake which has increased its membership from 1,200 members in 1981 to 6,000 currently.

Those included in the Denton Texas Stake will be the four Denton wards, two wards in The Colony, and Gainesville and Decatur wards also. The Denton Texas Stake makes the 11th stake in the Dallas-Fort Worth region.

James B. Martino, president of Russell-Newman Manufacturing Co. of Denton, will be president of the Denton Texas Stake. Vaughn A. Andrus, president of the Farmers & Merchants State Bank of Krum, will serve as first

James Martino becomes first Stake President of Denton Stake
Denton Record-Chronicle, May 1992

Brother Martino had received a spiritual prompting that weekend that he would be called as the stake president. In response to this prompting, he walked from the stake center in Denton to the adjoining softball field across the creek, and there he had prayer and meditation. If the call should come, who should be his counselors? The answers came. Vaughn Andrus should be called as First Counselor and Mark Warner as Second Counselor.

All three members of the new stake presidency were currently serving as bishops of their respective wards; Brother Martino was bishop of Denton First Ward, Brother Andrus was bishop of Denton Third Ward, and Brother Warner was bishop of The Colony Ward. The first order of business for the new stake presidency, therefore, was to call three new bishops. So for the first week in their new callings, they served both as a stake presidency and as bishops, a situation that posed a few scheduling challenges.

It was a young stake presidency, and together, they had 18 children living at home. Sensing the need for some cautionary counsel, Elder Kofford advised, "It doesn't make any difference how long or how late your meetings go. Your children will be in bed asleep when you get home. But you must make it a point to be with your families while they are awake. Always plan to have supper with your families." Heeding this advice, the stake presidency made it a point to begin their evening meetings at 8:00.

Elder Kofford also counseled the new stake presidency to establish a few priorities which they felt impressed that the Lord would want accomplished. Seeking a theme on which to base these priorities, the stake presidency soon focused on a theme of "personal spiritual development," with an emphasis on personal and family scripture study and prayer.

Almost every ward and stake conference would have some kind of emphasis on this theme. President Martino states: "We realized that if we could strengthen the members as they became more sensitive to the Spirit, then we would in turn strengthen the family." Letters were written to all members, goals were made, and challenges were issued, all with the intent of helping the membership establish habits of daily personal and family prayer and scripture study. The Denton Stake has functioned with a yearly theme ever since.

President Martino received testimonies from many families expressing gratitude for the help they received by trying to adhere to this theme. He gives one example.

One family came to me concerned because there was a constant feeling of negativity in their home. Their day seemed to be a routine of going through life's motions. They were stagnant in a world that was rushing by them. Bickering and a lack of joy and happiness characterized the home. Changing their daily patterns was not easy, but as they gradually migrated to a kneeling family prayer twice a day, marvelous things began to happen.

How special an experience to let the children hear their father pray that one son would be able to cope with the pressures of some peers at school; to hear the mother pray that a daughter would be able to make wise decisions concerning a specific friend; or to hear a child pray that parents would express appreciation for the amount of good that happened in the home.

After only a short amount of time, the entire family began to be more in tune with the promptings that come from the Holy Spirit. They began to have more empathy for each other's feelings, and the spirit of love and peace grew in the home.

In a subsequent interview with President Martino, the parents mused about how something as simple as prayer and scripture study can make such a difference in a home. President Martino's response was that "our Father in Heaven is waiting at the door to bless us if we will but ask. When we go to Him in prayer, opening up with true desire and sincerity, then we are prepared to be taught by the Spirit. This brings about greater faith in the Lord Jesus Christ, and gives each of us hope for things to come."

President Martino served seven and a half years as president of the Denton Stake, until being called in 1999 to serve as president of the Venezuela Maracaibo Mission.

CHAPTER 25

Regional Conference
with President Hinckley

*O*n 1959, John and Margaret Porter planted a gospel seed in Denton. They nourished it and cared for it as only they could have done. The seed sprouted and developed roots. And it grew. The Lord gathered additional helpers, and the seed continued to grow. It grew and developed into a stake of Zion large enough and strong enough to be chosen to host a bi-regional conference personally presided over by President Gordon B. Hinckley. On March 16-17, 1996, the Church's prophet, seer, and revelator came to Denton as a crowning recognition of the strength of the Denton Stake in this portion of the Lord's vineyard.

One can only imagine the feelings of John and Margaret Porter on this occasion. The Porters, who, as servants of the Lord, were prime movers in starting the Church in Denton in 1959 and who were so instrumental in its early growth, were now seeing the culminating fruits of their labors — from organizing a small Sunday School to hosting a Prophet of the Lord.

With true humility, Margaret refuses to take credit for what she and John accomplished in Denton. "We didn't do it," she insists, "the Lord did it." But the Lord needed the right people through whom to work.

On Saturday, March 16, President Hinckley presided at a priesthood leadership meeting in the Denton Stake Center. The following day, Sunday, the bi-regional conference session was held in the Coliseum of the University of North Texas.

President Gordon B. Hinckley
Denton Record-Chronicle, March 18, 1996

Prior to the priesthood leadership meeting on Saturday, a group of five or six brethren who had just finished applying clean-up touches to the stake center were standing in the north foyer of the building when a white car drove up to the entrance. As they watched, President Hinckley stepped out of the car and strode by himself into the building. Being awestruck, the local brethren stood there unable to say anything. Carl Stocker remembers that it was President Hinckley who broke the ice.

"Breathe, brethren. Breathe," he said. Then they all relaxed and shook hands with the prophet.

James Martino was president of the hosting Denton Stake at that time, and he has written a beautiful account of the conference and of the special feelings he experienced. President Martino's account follows just as he wrote it.

An Incredible Weekend with the Prophet

Saturday, March 16, 1996, began with the sun rising as any other beautiful spring day in Texas, but this day would prove to be one that was very special. To my knowledge, the Prophet of the Church had never preached in Denton, Texas, before this day, but on this Saturday, the Saints in the area were to receive a spiritual feast.

We had known for several months that Denton would be the host for a bi-regional conference. There would be two sessions on Sunday (one for the Fort Worth region and one for the Plano region) and both would be held in the coliseum at the University of North Texas, but the Saturday afternoon priesthood leadership session was to be held at the Denton Stake Center. The General Authorities that attended the conference were President Gordon B. Hinckley, president and prophet of the Church, along with Elders Robert D. Hales and L. Tom Perry of the Quorum of the Twelve. We also had Elder Lynn L. Mickelson and W. Mack Lawrence of the Seventy, and Larry Gibbons and David Bednar, who were (at the time) regional representatives. I am certain that never before has the Denton Stake Center been filled with such a powerful group of Church leaders.

We worked the entire week cleaning and scrubbing the chapel. The physical facilities department, along with much member support, all helped us to prepare for this special weekend. We had individuals in charge of ushering, security, music, parking, facilities, etc. for both Saturday and Sunday. For many of our members, it was the first time for them to even be in the same facility as the Prophet.

The weekend began with an intimate and special luncheon for the eight stake presidents involved in the conference and each of the General Authorities listed above. President Hinckley asked us many questions and attempted to get to know us, and then he spent some time teaching us about the role of stake presidents. He encouraged us to stay close to the Spirit that we might receive revelation to know what the Lord wanted us to do, and to love the people with all of our hearts. He explained that love meant calling to repentance when necessary, but to do it with charitable hearts and loving concern. He cautioned us of our responsibility to our families and make sure we were placing them as our most important priority.

The next meeting was a four hour priesthood leadership meeting where each one of the General Authorities and regional representatives spoke. I was asked to sit on the stand at the opening and then we all moved to the congregational area to listen to the Brethren. It was amazing to look up at the prophet at the pulpit of the Denton Stake Center and listen to him speak. I do not think that any of us in attendance thought that we would ever see that happen. The words that were taught all centered on priesthood stewardship and basic priesthood organization, including effective use of meetings, prayer and direction by the Spirit. President Hinckley blessed the priesthood leaders to be admirable and worthy fathers and husbands, while at the same time fulfilling their priesthood assignments. President Hinckley is an older man, in the eyes of the world, and there were times we could see his true age, but whenever he stepped up to the podium to speak, it was as if the Spirit would envelope him. He would teach with power and strength. He was bold and yet encouraging. I do not believe I have ever felt such a positive witness of his calling as a prophet. I have always enjoyed being at the feet of a General Authority, but I must admit that there is a difference in the Spirit of one that is a prophet, seer, and revelator versus one that is not. We were richly blessed in this priesthood session. These are special times, when on one hand you recognize that these prophets are regular people like you and me in one way, but in another special way, your heart burns to confirm that there sits a prophet of God. I do not know that President Hinckley taught me anything new, but I did come away with a desire to become more committed than ever before, and that there is a greater urgency than I have felt in the past. I realize that Denton needs to develop more leadership, both among the members we have now, as well as among those that do not yet know of the restoration of the gospel. I realize that I must do more to lead in that way. The gospel is true, and it must be shared with others with more urgency and haste. Denton is going to grow and we must be prepared for that growth.

Following the Priesthood Leadership meeting, the stake presidents, along with our wives, were invited to a dinner in Plano with all of the General Authorities that were visiting. We were able to sit informally and talk about families and our lives, and feel a special love and concern that the Church has for all of its members. During the day I was touched at the way that even members of the Twelve respect and honor the Prophet and other members. There was a lesson in that alone for us all to learn.

Once the dinner was over, we were invited to attend a special meeting with the full-time missionaries in the Dallas and Fort Worth areas. What a joyful time to look at the faces of these young men and women and see their testimonies and the uplift it was for them to be in the presence of the Prophet. One of the first things that President Hinckley emphasized to the missionaries was the importance of a smile. He told them that before anyone hears a word they say, they will look at the missionaries in their faces and they need to see the joy of our hearts radiated in the expression on our faces. He taught them to be bold and to remain positive. He taught them that missionary work is hard work, but it is worth it. Then he bore a sweet, powerful testimony of the truthfulness and importance of the work that these missionaries were doing.

On Sunday morning, my son Ben and I arrived at the coliseum at the University of North Texas at 6:20 AM for the conference that was to begin at 9:00 AM. We verified that everything was ready and working, including the organization of chairs on the stand, the sound system, the lighting, etc. We reviewed with the group in charge of ushering, security, and emergency medical help. Not too much later, Jennie, Emily, Lauren, Kimberly, and Jason arrived (Karina was at BYU); and before long we had 7,910 people from the four stakes that were invited to participate in this conference. We had arranged a special gathering area below the coliseum where we could drive President and Sister Hinckley directly into this secure and quiet area.

Before they arrived we were able to meet in this intimate setting with the other General Authorities and as the stake president hosting the conference, I was invited to bring my family to this area as well. President and Sister Hinckley arrived at around 8:15 AM. My children had wondered and we had discussed what it would be like to meet the Prophet. Before President Hinckley arrived, Lauren was so anxious about it that she went to the door to look out and only a few feet away, President and Sister Hinckley were walking in to our room. Lauren became very emotional and teary as she was able to meet President Hinckley and then Sister Hinckley reached over and gave her a hug and a kiss on the cheek. I know that none of us will ever forget this experience. They saw, heard, and felt the testimony of a prophet of God. Our hearts burned with joy and excitement as the Spirit would continually bear witness of the calling of this man. I know that we are now accountable to be witnesses of this work to others because of the powerful testimony of the Spirit that was granted to us. Elder Robert D. Hales was there when Lauren had her

special experience and following the conference he spoke to
Lauren and said that the feeling she had when she saw President
Hinckley was the same feeling that she would have when she
knew she had found the right man to marry. He was so sweet to
all of our children. Elder Lynn Mickelson challenged Ben to be
a missionary and stay committed to the gospel. When Ben
accepted the challenge, he gave Ben a tie tack with a star and a
"C" (for commitment) that was a reminder of this commitment
he had made.

I was so impressed by being in the presence of the Prophet.
I could see him begin his talks a little slow and then gain
inspiration as to what we needed; he would then get stronger
and stronger. He took time to greet and shake hands with many
of the saints and he talked to many of us individually. I was
impressed how quick his memory and mind are, how in tune
he is with the needs of the saints. But you know, why should I
be surprised—he is a prophet, seer, and revelator. He is the
Lord's servant to lead and guide us here on earth today.

The conference was a treat. Never before had so many
members of the Church been gathered together in Denton,
Texas! Never before had the Prophet of God addressed a
gathering in our city! All of those in attendance were blessed. I
have sung the hymn, "We Thank Thee, O God, for a Prophet"
many times, but when you realize that the man to whom we
are referring is sitting next to you, the words of the hymn take
on a totally different meaning. Sister Hinckley spoke to us and
I will never forget her down-to-earth words that reminded us
that her husband is a man, but one with a special calling. She
told us that many will ask her what it is like to be married to
the president of the Church. Her response was sweet,
humorous, and truthful, when she responded, "some days are
better than others." President Hinckley spoke to us about being

smart (getting a good education), being true to covenants and commandments, being kind, and other counsel that if we will just hearken to we will have joy in our lives.

Following the morning conference, we had a lunch for all of the guests in a secluded room below the coliseum. One final, intimate setting to enjoy the incredible and unique weekend we had just concluded. Following the meal, the Plano session of the Regional Conference began and this 86 year old man continued his pace of using all of his power to testify of the work in which we are all involved.

I am so grateful to have a testimony of the gospel of Jesus Christ. I do not know where my life would be without it. I know that it provides the basis for our entire family and it is the bond that brings us such great joy. I know that this conference has made me feel more committed and my dedication has been strengthened. The Denton community was told of the proceedings of the conference through a wonderful article that appeared in the *Denton Record-Chronicle* the day after the conference. There were many less actives in attendance and many that are not yet members. I do understand with greater clarity that I serve as stake president to all those that live within our stake boundaries. It does not matter if they are members or not, and we must find ways to reach out to others that they might know the glorious news that we know—that the gospel of Jesus Christ, in its fulness, has been restored to the earth today, with all of its power and authority. The conference made me realize that I must be a better father, husband, and leader. I must become more sensitive to the Spirit. What an uplifting and enriching weekend. May I learn to be a better instrument in the hands of the Lord to lead and motivate in a small degree like President Gordon B. Hinckley.

CHAPTER 26

Expanding Membership and New Wards and Stakes

With the continued population growth in the Metroplex area, and particularly in and around Denton, considerable expansion in the Denton Stake and in its neighboring stakes has occurred in recent years. And the expansion seems not to be slowing. With regard to the Denton Stake, which now is enjoying its third stake president, the following is merely a brief summary of the expansion that has taken place.

James Martino
First Stake President of the Denton Stake

At the time of its creation in May 1992, the Denton Stake consisted of seven wards and one branch as follows:

Decatur Ward	Denton Fourth Ward
Denton First Ward	Gainesville Branch
Denton Second Ward	The Colony First Ward
Denton Third Ward	The Colony Second Ward

During President Martino's tenure, the Denton Fifth Branch (now the Denton Fifth Ward) was organized in January 1993. Seeing the potential of college students as today's missionaries and tomorrow's leaders, President Martino felt they would thrive much better if organized into their own church unit. The stake also began petitioning for an Institute building, a goal that was fulfilled in 1996 when an Institute

**President
James Martino**

building was completed and dedicated. Initially, the Denton Fifth Branch served both single and married students at Denton's two universities, but it later was changed to serve singles in the age range of 19 to 30, whether students or not. Married students were to be integrated into the wards in which they lived.

Feeling that the Spanish speaking members would benefit by being a unit unto themselves, President Martino organized a Spanish Branch in July 1995, with Leonardo Osorio as Branch President. George and Lorna Strasser were called from the Denton First Ward to add leadership support. Because the expected growth did not materialize and because the Hispanic members also spoke English, the branch was discontinued in 1997 with the members being re-integrated into the wards in which they lived.

During these years, membership in the Denton Stake continued to expand, with the heaviest area of population growth being along the I-35E corridor between Denton and Lake Dallas. Church membership in that area grew accordingly. In February 1997, the Denton Fourth Ward was divided to form the Lake Cities Ward. Richard Blanco, bishop of Denton Fourth Ward at the time of its division, continued as its bishop, and Dean Garner, LDS Institute Director, became bishop of the Lake Cities Ward. In 1993 James Gwilliam replaced Bishop Blanco in Denton Fourth Ward, and in 1997 David Harris replaced Bishop Gwilliam.

During this same period of time, expansion was also occurring in Decatur and Gainesville through conversions and move-ins. The Decatur Branch had earlier become a ward on March 1, 1987, and President Jack Cannon was now Bishop Jack Cannon. In Gainesville, the branch became a ward on March 26, 1995, and President Max Chartrand became Bishop Max Chartrand. Growth in Gainesville required an expansion of their building which was completed and rededicated on February 21, 1999.

Vaughn Andrus
Second President of the Denton Stake

In 1999, the mantle of leadership fell upon Vaughn Andrus who followed Brother Martino as stake president. In December 1999, Elder Lance B. Wickman of the First Quorum of the Seventy set Brother Andrus apart as the second president of the Denton Stake. One of President Andrus' first functions was to ordain the highly respected Bob Nobles to the office of Patriarch.

The Denton Stake at that time had expanded into the following ten units.

Decatur Ward	Denton Fifth Ward
Denton First Ward	Gainesville Ward
Denton Second Ward	Lake Cities Ward
Denton Third Ward	The Colony First Ward
Denton Fourth Ward	The Colony Second Ward

Before becoming Denton's second stake president, Brother Andrus' church callings included serving as a stake financial clerk, a stake clerk, a High Counselor, a bishop's counselor, and a bishop. In the years when Denton was a part of the Fort Worth Stake and then the Fort Worth North Stake, Brother Andrus spent countless hours in company with Dick Ragsdale and Frank Martino as they traveled to meetings in Fort Worth and to outlying portions of the stake. He refers to those trips as "spiritually growing and maturing experiences." He also speaks of the joy and growth he received in earlier years from associations with Horace Leithead, president of the Ft. Worth Stake and with Gordon Watts, president of the Lewisville Stake.

**President
Vaughn Andrus**

As president of the Denton Stake, President Andrus selected Mark Warner to be First Counselor and David Passey, bishop of Denton Third Ward as Second Counselor. On December 9, 2001, President Warner had to be released when the two Colony wards were transferred to the newly created Carrollton Stake. David Passey became First Counselor to President Andrus, and Jack Cannon, bishop of the Decatur Ward became Second Counselor. President Passey served until 2007 when he accepted a position with NATO in Brussels, Belgium. Brother Cannon then became First Counselor to President Andrus, and Steve Petersen, former bishop of Denton Fifth Ward, became Second Counselor.

Under President Andrus' leadership, the Denton Stake continued to focus each year on a specific theme of spiritual development. In 2005, the theme focused on improving one's ability to receive and recognize personal revelation. In 2006, the theme was to stand in holy places. Three types of holy places were specifically emphasized: the home, the chapel, and the temple. Not only should we choose to be in holy places, but we should live so that the holiness of those places is enhanced, not compromised, by our presence. In 2007, the theme of the previous year was continued, but with the added challenge of reading the *Book of Mormon* in the first six months of the year as a means of increasing our understanding and appreciation of Christ's atonement. Reading the entire New Testament, as a complement to the Sunday School curriculum for 2007, was the stake challenge for the last half of the year.

Also under President Andrus' leadership, expansion within the Denton Stake has continued. During this period, boundaries remained fairly stable among the Denton First and Second Wards. But as residential development continued to increase in Corinth, a ward division became necessary. The Lake Cities Ward was divided on October 13, 2002, to form the Lake Cities First and Second Wards with Calvin Griffin and David McEntire, respectively, as bishops. After about five years, leadership changes were made in the two Lake Cities wards. In October 2007 Bob Foster became bishop of Lake Cities First Ward, and in December Michael Liddell became bishop of Lake Cities Second Ward.

An increase in the number of Spanish speaking members resulted in reestablishing a Spanish language unit. The Denton Sixth Branch was created for Spanish speaking members on December 14, 2003, with Abraham Benevides as Branch President.

Since the year 2000, heavy population growth has also occurred in the Justin area on the I-35W corridor between Denton and Ft. Worth. The Justin growth, along with continued growth throughout the entire Denton Stake area, resulted in the creation of a Justin Ward on January 1, 2007, with Nicholas Kruger as Bishop. Although the Justin Ward was created primarily from a division of the Denton Third Ward, the overall reorganization included a large-scale realignments of the boundaries of several other wards in the Denton Stake.

The Teasley Lane Chapel
Dedicated 2006

One of the determining factors in the stake realignments was the completion of a new chapel on Teasley Lane in the southern outskirts of Denton in 2006. Completion of this chapel not only added much needed meeting space, it also provided some special spiritual experiences for Denton Stake's Ray Beedle who served as the construction supervisor. In dealing with the various subcontractors, Ray found that some subcontractors were happy to work with the Church because of its policies of honesty and integrity. Other contractors, however, felt otherwise because of the Church's insistence of high standards and quality beyond normal expectations.

A special experience occurred for Brother Beedle one evening when he wanted to get an overview of the work in progress. Climbing onto a large mound of dirt at the rear of the property, Ray turned to look at the almost completed building. Instead of seeing just the physical building, Ray also saw the spiritual activities and teachings that would soon be taking place within the building. He saw and felt the saving principles and ordinances that would be enabled by having the building. For Ray, it was a very moving experience, and tears came to his eyes as he related it.

The Church's initial plans for the Teasley building did not call for a baptismal font. But when it was explained that for many years the Denton Stake had led the Ft. Worth Mission in convert baptisms (e.g. seventy-five in 2005), the Church's Building Department modified the plans to include a font.

Steve Petersen
Third President of the Denton Stake

On May 4, 2008, in a multi-stake conference in which the Denton, Lewisville, and Carrollton Stakes participated, a new stake, the Frisco Stake, was created. Wards were transferred from both the Lewisville and Carrollton Stakes to the new Frisco Stake. To assist in re-balancing units and population in these stakes, the Lake Cities Second Ward was transferred from the Denton Stake to the Lewisville Stake.

President
Steve Petersen

An additional change for the Denton Stake was the release of Vaughn Andrus as stake president, and the sustaining of Steve Petersen to be the third president of the Denton Stake. President Andrus had served sixteen years in the stake presidency, including seven and a half years as a counselor to President Martino beginning when the Denton Stake was created in 1992, followed by eight and a half years as stake president.

Up until this multi-stake conference the Denton Stake consisted of eleven units. The transfer of the Lake Cities Second Ward to the Lewisville Stake, however, resulted in a Denton Stake of ten units as President Petersen became stake president.

Decatur Ward	Denton Fifth Ward
Denton First Ward	Denton Sixth Branch
Denton Second Ward	Gainesville Ward
Denton Third Ward	Justin Ward
Denton Fourth Ward	Lake Cities First Ward

Steve Petersen and his wife, Annette, arrived in the Denton area in November 1981, and they purchased property in Aubrey. Steve's parents, Burke and Yvonne, came the following year. For several years they raised quarter horses and conducted an embryo transplant business.

Before being called as Stake President, President Petersen had been Second Counselor to President Andrus in the Denton Stake presidency. He had also served on the High Council and as a Bishop of Denton Fifth Ward. Serving with President Petersen are David Martino as First Counselor and Jim Barber as Second Counselor. Brother Martino was Bishop of Denton Fifth Ward at the time of this new calling, and he had also served on the High Council and as Bishop of Denton First Ward. Brother Barber was serving on the High Council and was a former Bishop of Denton Third Ward. Kurt Hansen replaced David Martino as bishop of Denton Fifth Ward. In addition, Steve Iverson was released as bishop of Denton Second Ward, and that calling went to Steve Frederickson.

President Andrus was not without a calling for very long. He is now a counselor in the Fort Worth Mission presidency.

A Stone Cut Out of the Mountain

It must be noted at this point that in the geographic area originally covered by the Denton Branch, four stakes now exist as of May 3, 2008. These are the Denton, Lewisville, Frisco, and Carrollton Stakes. In addition, some southernmost portions of the original Denton Branch are now contained in the Hurst, Colleyville, Arlington, and Dallas stakes. The stone cut out of the mountain without hands is truly rolling.

CHAPTER 27
A Sampling of
Recent Community Services

*T*hroughout its approximately fifty years of existence, the Denton Stake has sought energetically to be an integral and an accepted organization within the community. Community services of many kinds, and especially with music, have been forthcoming.

The focus of this book, however, has been on the early years of the Church in Denton. Those were the years in which many unique and exciting things of a special spiritual nature were happening. Today, although the Church is still growing and prospering in Denton just as in other areas, it is the uniqueness and the special spirit of those "start-up" years that this history has attempted to capture for our posterity.

This is not to say, however, that exciting things are no longer happening in Denton. Community contributions are being made in many areas. Church units along with church individuals

LDS Service Project
Merle Eggett lends a hand as Rick Martino paints playground equipment at North Lakes Park, September 4, 1993
(Photo courtesy of the *Denton Record-Chronicle*)

have been, and still are, making concerted efforts to be good citizens and to contribute to the betterment of the various communities in which we reside. Here are a few examples.

Family of the Year Program

Started in 1997 by Betty and Frank Martino and continued by Billie Hubbard as stake Public Affairs Directors, the Family of the Year program has grown and prospered in Denton. Under the guidance of Kevin Dartt, current Public Affairs Director, and with special support from Trey Martino and David Passey, Denton's Family of the Year program is now under a three-way sponsorship consisting of the Denton Stake, the Denton Kiwanis Club, and the City of Denton Parks and Recreation Department. This has become a grand example of Church and community cooperation.

Sen. Gramm to announce Family of the Year winners
16 Nov 1997

By H. Janet McDaniel
Staff Writer

Texas Sen. Phil Gramm will announce the northern Denton County Family of the Year winners Dec. 2 at a buffet luncheon in the Southwest Dining Room of Hubbard Hall at Texas Woman's University.

Two winners representing outstanding traditional and single-parent families were chosen by a panel of judges selected by the Public Affairs Council of the Church of Jesus Christ of Latter-day Saints in Denton, sponsor of the competition.

Nominees were judged on quality of family life, family spirituality, community service and citizenship.

The purpose of this event is to recognize and promote measures designed to maintain and strengthen the family.

The awards luncheon is open to the public. Cost for the lunch is $6 and reservations are required. Lunch is at 11:30 a.m.

Reservations may be made by sending a $6 check, payable to Mrs. Billie Hubbard, 3011 Santa Monica Drive, Denton 76205.

Tickets are not required — paid reservations will be confirmed at the door the day of the luncheon.

Deadline for reservations is Nov. 25. Kiwanians and their guests should R.S.V.P. to Joyce George at the Kiwanis office at (940) 387-6323.

Family of the Year Program
Billie Hubbard and Betty Martino, Stake Public Affairs Directors, initiateed Denton's annual Family of the Year program in 1997.
(Photos courtesy of the *Denton Record-Chronicle*)

Family History Center

As has already been mentioned, the Denton Family History Center, established in 1978 by Dayonne Work and Vic Nielsen, has been a major source of genealogical research for members and non-members alike. Similar, but smaller, centers have also been established in Decatur and Gainesville. Over a large number of years, until the advent of so many genealogical resources via the Internet, non-member patronage significantly exceeded member patronage at these centers.

In 1993 the Denton Family History Center undertook a large-scale project intended to make the general public more aware of the Family History Center and its services that are available to the public. The project was one of compiling the genealogies of Bob Castleberry, Mayor of Denton, and of Fred Patterson, publisher of the *Denton Record-Chronicle*. Holly Hervey performed the bulk of the research for the Castleberry ancestry, and Marge Abbey, a non-member staff worker in the Family History Center, did the major research for the Patterson lines. The recipients expressed sincere appreciation for the compilations, and the Center sign-in sheets showed an increased patronage following the public presentations.

Family History Fair

April 23-24, 2004

Sponsored by
The Church of Jesus Christ of Latter-day Saints
300 Old North Road
Denton, Texas

Learning Who I Am!

Documenting Who I Am!

**GENEALOGY WORKSHOPS FOR
NOVICE TO EXPERT!**

Family History Fair
Sample Program

Another example of special activity in recent years is the Family History Fairs sponsored by the Denton Family History Center in 2003 and 2004. Designed to benefit community genealogists as well as church genealogists, these fairs had a community attendance numbered in the hundreds. Many expressions of "thank you" and appreciation were received from attendees from the community. When the fairs were discontinued, one non-member who had attended called it a "great loss."

Granny's Pantry

It is believed by many that the Granny's Pantry offerings, described in an earlier chapter, have been the most well received and appreciated of the Church's many community-orientated functions. Presented four times from 1979 to 1991, Granny's Pantry is well remembered for its ambitiously comprehensive booths, demonstrations, and skits pertaining to self-sufficiency and provident living. Many individuals in the community voiced their appreciation of the events.

Disaster Relief

The Denton Stake has responded well in a variety of relief efforts after natural disasters. Blankets, clothing, and other types of supplies have been sent to people in other nations. Several hundred sanitary kits were prepared and sent to families devastated by the Katrina hurricane.

Annual end-of-the-year clothing drives bring in huge amounts of clothing to be donated to the poor. The Public Affairs program cooperates with Carter BloodCare to sponsor frequent blood drives. The youth of the stake, at Youth Conference time, engage in significant service projects.

Work parties went to Oklahoma after its tornado in 2002 and to Gainesville following its 2007 flood to help clean up. In Oklahoma, one radio commentator gave special praise to the Church for its relief efforts. On the air, he said, "There are two churches that have been especially helpful in cleaning up the debris. One was The Church of Jesus Christ of Latter-day Saints, and the other was the Mormon Church." We'll take praise wherever we can get it.

A Continuing Tradition of Music and Drama

"An Evening of Christmas Joys," currently coordinated by Carol Harlos, is the Denton Stake's annual Christmas gift to the community. Begun by Kevin Dartt in 1987 when Denton's Festival of Carols was discontinued, "An Evening of Christmas Joys" is an outstanding performance of music and song appropriate to the Christmas season presented by the best of the musical resources in the Denton Stake. In 2005, for example, the program featured selections from *The Messiah*.

In these Expansion Years music has remained one of the outstanding strengths of the Denton Stake, and the traditions established by Margaret Porter continue. Sister Porter actually served twice as Stake Music Chairman. Kevin Dartt replaced her in 1987, and then when the Denton Stake was created in 1992, Sister Dartt received a different calling, and Sister Porter was called back to that position. In 1997 Mandy Reid followed Margaret Porter as Denton Stake Music Chairman, and in 2002 Carol Harlos succeeded Sister Reid. Under all these leaders, excellence was maintained.

When Margaret was released as Stake Music Chairman in 1997, she was presented with a gold baton as a token of appreciation of the energy, quality, and enthusiasm she had put into the creation and direction of outstanding musical performances.

The musical talent now available from the UNT School of Music, namely Steve Harlos and Brian Bowman, combined with professionals and semi-professionals such as Carol Harlos, Carol Crossley, Kevin Dartt, Patricia Diers, Susan Myatt, and Mary Poulter gives assurance of music of the highest quality in the Denton Stake. And the Stake's musical presentations are not limited to just the Christmas season.

In 2003, the Denton Stake performed *The Glory of God*, an introduction to the temple through music. Composed by Mary Poulter (Lake Cities First Ward) and Jerry Smith of New Hampshire, the presentation featured the Denton Stake Choir, a children's chorus, vocal solos, and vocal ensembles. Musical accompaniment included piano, brass, and some strings. Two performances were presented, one on October 26 for the Denton Stake and Denton community, and one on November 16 for a Dallas Temple workers' fireside.

Carol Harlos, Denton Stake music director since 2002 has provided the stake with outstanding cultural experiences including an annual chamber music fireside in addition to the Christmas programs.

Dramatic productions are also still presented, although not with the frequency of earlier years. For a 1998 production of "Barefoot to Zion," participants came from the Denton wards, the Decatur and Gainesville wards, and The Colony wards. Presented in the stake center on April 10 and 11, the play portrayed the pioneer experience to an audience of over 250 people. It is estimated that about a third of the audience were non-members.

Part Six
CUTTING ACROSS
THE TIME PERIODS

Introduction

*T*hus far, this book has been a chronological presentation, insofar as possible, of the history of the Church in Denton. However, there are topics to be included that cut across chronological boundaries, and which cannot adequately be presented within any one period of the Church's development in Denton.

In keeping with this premise, two chapters are herein included. One deals with some selected families of notable interest. The other presents some special conversion stories.

CHAPTER 28
Some Additional Notable Personalities

$\mathcal{T}$he Church of Jesus Christ of Latter-day Saints is made up of people—people from all walks of life who are seeking common goals of happiness in mortality along with eternal life with Heavenly Father and with friends and loved ones in the Celestial Kingdom.

Although a major focus of this book has been on the large collection of church members with outstanding leadership skills that the Lord brought together in Denton to nurture the Church during its early years, the Church in Denton has also been blessed with thousands of members who have served in less visible callings and who have made the Church what it is today in Denton. Many of these members have come from unique and interesting situations and backgrounds, and they have their own special stories to tell.

A selection of these "special" members must be included in this book because they are also part of the history of the Church in Denton.

Charles Mayfield

Charles Mayfield is a convert to the Church. His wife, Kathleen, who is a life-long member, is a daughter of Harvey and Judy Thompson. Harvey, in turn, is a son of Doyle Thompson, Sr., who was one of the very early Church members in Denton.

Brother Mayfield makes furniture. In his shop in Argyle, he turns out tables, chairs, and cabinets that are expertly

Charles Mayfield
at work in his furniture shop, now located in Argyle
(Photo courtesy of *Denton Record-Chronicle*)

designed and crafted. When the announcement was made of a temple to be built in Nauvoo, Charles, a member of Denton Second Ward, felt a strong desire to contribute something to the project. Perhaps the Church would accept a contribution of furniture made especially for the Temple.

By telephone, Brother Mayfield managed to make contact with the right people at Church headquarters, and they suggested that he send some photographs of his products, which he did. Several weeks passed without any further response from Salt Lake City. Phoning again, Brother Mayfield learned that the people with whom he had previously talked had been replaced by others who knew nothing about his earlier communications. They suggested he send photographs again.

This time several phone calls were exchanged between Brother Mayfield and his new contacts in the Temple Department. Shortly thereafter, the Church's Purchasing Department called Brother Mayfield and requested that he provide some items of furniture for the children's waiting room in the Nauvoo Temple. Specifically, they wanted a large TV cabinet, a round table with four matching chairs, and a drop-leaf occasional table. They followed up by sending Brother Mayfield pictures of what they had in mind.

Brother Mayfield then launched an intensive study of furniture that would be appropriate for a city on the American frontier in the 1840s. He studied styles, types of wood, and accessibility of the wood, and he developed some designs that were somewhat different from what the people in Salt Lake had in mind. After further phone conversations, Brother Mayfield decided to go to Salt Lake and meet personally with the brethren there. As a result, he convinced them that his designs would be more appropriate than what they had originally envisioned.

Next, a Brother Chugg called from the Purchasing Department, saying, "We have not received an invoice from you."

"I can't do an invoice yet," Charles responded. "I don't know what size cabinet you want, and we haven't agreed on what kind of wood to use."

Brother Mayfield recommended black walnut which is grown in the general area of Nauvoo. Mahogany, his second choice, is not native to the United States.

An hour later Brother Chugg called again saying that the cabinet should be seven feet tall and four feet wide, and black walnut was acceptable. An invoice amount was determined, and the next day Charles received by Federal Express a check for half the total amount that had been agreed upon. Although Charles had wanted to donate the furniture, the Church insisted on paying for it. They told Brother Mayfield that he could make a monetary contribution if he so chose.

Brother Mayfield states that the actual construction of the furniture should have been a smooth operation. He was already expert in wood turning and in the other needed skills. "This has to be perfect," he confidently thought.

"But everything went wrong," he reports.

First, the wood he ordered came with a few flaws, but not serious enough to be rejected. Then he made mistakes in the turning process and found himself throwing away piece after piece. He made other mistakes, and instead of its being the spiritual project it should have been, it became a contest against an opposition that seemed determined to stop the project.

Finally, however, the project was completed, and Charles crated the furniture, rented a U-Haul truck, and he and his wife, Kathleen, drove to Utah where they delivered the furniture to a Church warehouse in North Salt Lake City.

Two years later, the Church contacted Brother Mayfield and asked him to make a table with four matching chairs for the children's waiting room in the Salt Lake Temple. Brother Mayfield responded to this request with much less difficulty than before. He was also asked to submit a bid for making the furniture for the San Antonio Temple, but his was not the low bid, so he did not get that job.

Trey Martino

As a tribute to Joseph Smith's role in ushering in the Gospel in these latter days, Trey Martino has written an oratorio commemorating the life and contributions of the Prophet Joseph Smith. Consisting of eleven songs, each introduced by a brief historical narrative, the oratorio begins with the expectation of a prophet in these latter days and carries through to the martyrdom of that prophet. Included are songs and narrative focusing on the restoration, the Nauvoo period, and the prophet's love for his wife and family.

Trey Martino
entertains with music and song.

A special aspect of the oratorio is that Trey Martino composed seven of the eleven songs himself. While on his mission in 1975, he wrote the song "Eternal Brothers" about Joseph and Hyrum and their love for one another. Upon returning to BYU after his mission, Trey spent six months researching Mormon history and writing his other six compositions.

The entire oratorio was first performed in its entirety in 1977 for a ward fireside at BYU. There have been many subsequent performances, including extensive renditions throughout Utah Valley, Salt Lake City, Ogden, Idaho, and Kansas with Eric Knoeppel. In 1978, Trey and Eric recorded the oratorio as a long playing record, and it has more recently been released as a cassette tape and as a DVD.

Following Trey's graduation from BYU, the oratorio sat idle for a few years. Then Trey and Jon Ingram began performing it in the Denton area to audiences equally as enthusiastic as those in the mountain west. In 1984 they began a tradition of performing at the Dallas Mission Home on the first Sunday evening of most months. To these performances, which still continue, missionaries and members have brought countless numbers of investigators and new members to strengthen their faith in the message of the restoration.

Others who have performed with Trey include George Strasser, Bill Wawro, Kevin Dolan, Guy Stewart, and Troy Johnson.

Russell and Willie Jean Morgan

It is believed that Russell and Willie Jean Morgan were the first black members to join the Church in Denton. They were baptized on May 10, 1985, in the Malone Street building.

Russell and Willie Jean Morgan

It might be said that the Morgans were a captive audience. For years, Willie Jean had been domestically employed by Frank and Betty Martino. Russell spent a short time working directly for the Martinos. He then worked briefly for Russell-Newman before moving on to the maintenance staff at UNT. Although the Martinos had a great influence on the conversion of Russell and Willie Jean, their decision to be baptized was strictly and freely their own.

One of the great milestones in Willie Jean's life occurred on March 14, 1961, when Rick Martino was born.

"A sweet little boy," Willie Jean later wrote. Having no children of her own, she looked upon Rick as "her baby." She helped care for him all through his infancy and growing up years, and the bond between the two became unbreakable.

When Rick left on May 15, 1980, for his mission to Costa Rica, Willie Jean mourned his leaving.

"That was a hard day for me," she later wrote. "My baby was leaving! I knew by this time what doing missionary work was for, so I knew he was doing the Lord's work."

While on his mission Rick sent Willie Jean a *Book of Mormon*. "He was so sweet to put his testimony in it," Willie Jean remembers.

Following his mission, Rick enrolled in BYU and shortly thereafter he married Connie Eggett. Willie Jean attended LDS church meetings a few times during this period, but "things really started when Rick and Connie moved back to Denton after college." At that time Russell started attending church with Willie Jean, and he found himself liking it.

"I like this church a lot," he said to Rick.

"Well, would you like to see the missionaries?"

"Yes."

The Morgans began meeting with the missionaries.

"They were nice young men. We were interested, but not real sure," Willie Jean explained. "We had to pray and think about it."

Soon they were attending church every Sunday, as well as cottage meetings in the homes of various members. Russell liked the way the brothers at church treated him.

"The spirit there was good," Willie Jean said. "People treated us with respect."

"It's very nice." For Russell, a man of few words, that was the ultimate compliment.

In May of 1985 the Morgans attended a meeting in the home of Bill and Dorothy Cudd. The men all adjourned into a separate room, and after a short while, Rick came bounding out with his face beaming.

"Willie Jean," he announced, "Russell says he and you are going to get baptized."

"When?" was her only comment.

"May 10 at 7:00 pm at the Malone Street church."

Willie Jean was pleased that Russell had made up his own mind. She had wanted to join the church, but not without him. Her happiness showed.

Rick had the honor of performing the baptisms, and a large number of the Morgans's relatives and friends showed their support by attending. Willie Jean expressed her feelings succinctly, "Talk about being reborn! This began a new time in our lives."

Russell and Willie Jean quickly became active in home teaching and visiting teaching, and they loved the sociability and the service involved in these callings. They also loved welcoming home and visiting teachers into their own home. Tithing was another aspect of the gospel they quickly embraced. As a member of the stake High Council, Rick took Willie Jean with him on speaking assignments to the Gainesville Ward and to the Denton First Ward to bear her testimony of tithing.

"He chose the right person," she commented. "I love to talk about tithing."

Needless to say, Russell and Willie Jean are frequent temple attenders, and they have also been blessed by the priesthood in times of illness and serious physical afflictions.

At Rick's request, Willie Jean has written several installments of her life story. With regard to the Church, she has summed her feelings in the following words:

"The church is like one big family. When friends separate, they are welcomed by another part of the family. Even in death there's church family to welcome you on the other side. I wonder what surprises lie ahead for me. My testimony holds strong. I love my blood family, my inherited family, and my church family."

CHAPTER 29

Some Additional Special Conversions

*I*n a missionary-minded church such as The Church of Jesus Christ of Latter-day Saints, one should expect not only a large number of conversions, but also some very special conversion stories. The early Church in Denton is no exception to this expectation.

With the Porters and the Eliesons leading the way, the Denton saints exhibited a missionary spirit that was special and exciting to this growing area of Zion. Cottage meetings were occurring every other Thursday night and whenever else there was a need. It was not unusual to have six to eight investigators and ten to twenty members at any one of these meetings. The Spirit was there, and the desserts afterward were an enticement to keep the people coming back. These cottage meetings were usually in the homes of the Porters, the Martins, the Nobles, or the Steiners. Sanfred and Virginia Elieson were frequent speakers. The Denton Ward was averaging in the neighborhood of thirty baptisms annually year in those years.

Notable conversion stories of the Porters, Ragsdales, Martinos, Nobles, and Wilsons have already been presented in this history. A few more such stories, based on three themes, will here be presented. First, the conversion of Tom and Kevin Dartt presents an outstanding example of how fellowshipping and brotherhood from within the Church affected one family of investigators. Then a series of conversions will be presented illustrating the chain reaction of new converts bringing in additional new converts. Each of these experiences within the chain to be presented has unique and notable elements associated with it. Finally, the conversions of Susanne Stewart and her four children gives a unique example of five people in one family each encountering the gospel separately from the others.

An Example of Fellowshipping and Brotherhood: Tom and Kevin Dartt

The conversion of Tom and Kevin Dartt in 1977 can be considered a textbook example of combining the missionary spirit with fellowshipping and brotherhood.

Their story begins years earlier in Wisconsin when an LDS family moved in up the street from Tom. Every time the daughter's mother called for her she went directly home. This obedience was an example that left an impression that Tom never forgot. Only later was Tom able to attribute her obedience to "When my mother calls me, quickly I'll obey ... ."

Kevin went to school in Colorado and knew members there and was often asked to sing in the ward choirs. After the Dartts were married they both went to school in Stevens Point, Wisconsin, where Donald Ripplinger (a future associate director for the Mormon Tabernacle Choir) taught in the music department. Both Tom and Kevin spent time with him and thought he was a wonderful and loving man.

In 1975, Tom was accepted into graduate school at UNT. During their first year in Denton, Kevin was pregnant, and she became dissatisfied with her doctor because he could never remember her name. Switching doctors, she then began going to Doctor Robert (Bob) Nobles. She found him to be kind and loving, and he always remembered her name. To Kevin, he was just the right man for the job. The birth of Andrew came on a Sunday morning in 1976 as Dr. Nobles, who was also bishop of Denton Second Ward, ran between his hospital and his meetings at church. It was a wonderful and spiritual experience for the Dartts.

In 1976, when Tom and Kevin advertised a double-legged grand piano for sale. Bill Hatch and his wife, Jannet, came to see the piano. Bill, a faculty member in UNT's medical school, was also Elders Quorum president in the Denton Second Ward. Liking the piano, the Hatches bought it and agreed with the Dartts to pick it up the following Saturday.

On the appointed Saturday morning, Brother Hatch appeared at the Dartts's home with a pickup truck and eight helpers. Tom was flabbergasted.

"Where did you get all these guys at eight o'clock on a Saturday morning?" he wanted to know. "I hope you have a case of beer to give them."

"Oh no, we don't drink beer," Jose Fernandez responded.

After the work party left with the piano, Tom discovered that they had forgotten to take the music holder. Calling Brother Hatch, Tom said, "I'll bring it over to your house. Where do you live?"

When Tom and Kevin arrived at the Hatches's home they saw Jan Martin arrive in his Delta Airlines pilot's uniform, on his way home from a flight. Inside the Hatch home Tom recognized the piano movers who were eating cookies and enjoying the new piano. Again, Tom was amazed. "What kind of church is this," he mused, "where a fellow can find so many friends to help him on a Saturday morning to help move a piano?"

A short time later, the Hatches returned to the Dartts's home and gave them a book, *Meet the Mormons*. The Hatches also began calling and inviting the Dartts to attend church with them. It was the Christmas season, and Tom and Kevin were very "busy," but realizing that these invitations were not going to cease, the Dartts finally agreed. They attended their first LDS church meeting on the first Sunday in 1997. It was a fast and testimony meeting. Bishop Nobles made it a point to greet the Dartts warmly, as did most of the other ward members.

Gary Case bore a strong testimony about tithing. Tom and Gary had much in common. Both were master's degree students at UNT. Both were the fathers of new babies. Tom and Kevin had been searching for four years for the right church for their young family. The Spirit bore witness that their search was now over.

The Dartts accepted an invitation to go to the Hatches' home that evening for pancakes. The missionaries were also invited to the dinner, and the Dartts invited the elders to come to their home for dinner the following week, which they did. The Dartts received all six missionary lessons, and they were baptized on February 25, 1977.

Kevin received her first calling as Primary chorister that same day, even before she was confirmed a member of the church.

It should also be noted that Brother Hatch borrowed from Bishop Nobles the pickup truck used to move the piano. Bishop Nobles, who had delivered the Dartts' baby four months earlier, said that the only stipulation was, "Bring them into the church and you can use my truck!" The Hatches, and the ward, certainly did that.

A Chain of Conversions

One of the interesting phenomena in a missionary-minded church is the chain of conversions that result when one convert family, either directly or indirectly, becomes responsible for the conversion of another family, who in turn, becomes responsible for the conversion of a third family, and so on. Although this chain effect is not at all uncommon in the LDS environment, one such chain is present in Denton with some rather unique circumstances. The chain to be described begins with Terrill Wheeler, Joe McWilliams, and Joe's second wife, Jeanette. From Joe, the chain branches, and one branch includes Joe's third wife, Patricia (née Diers), and then Barbara Crandall (née Stewart). The other branch from Joe McWilliams includes David and Sue Welch, followed by Bob and Ann Hall.

In addition to the "domino effect" that will be seen, each of these families has a special story to tell. It is hoped that these families can represent the hundreds of other convert families during the Church's earlier years in Denton who also have special stories to tell.

Joe and Jeanette McWilliams

The conversion of Joe and Jeanette McWilliams begins with Terrill Wheeler, himself a convert. Terrell and his wife, Wilma, came into the Church on October 19, 1962, through the combined efforts of the Porters and the full-time missionaries. Although convinced of the truth of the gospel, Terrill nevertheless had difficulty giving up some of his earlier ways.

In the spring of 1965, Joe McWilliams owned a club called the "Cap N Kid" located at the intersection of Mayhill Road and I-35E. Catering to the teenage crowd, the club did not sell alcoholic beverages. The club also did not bring in a satisfactory profit, so Joe leased it to a businessman who opened it as a night club that did sell alcoholic beverages.

Late one afternoon, Terrill Wheeler came into the club while Joe was there, and as the two visited, the conversation got around to the Mormon Church and Joe became quite interested.

With modesty, Terrill said, "I'm not a very good example, but I would like to show you one." He then invited Joe to a cottage meeting to be held a few days later at the home of John and Margaret Porter in Argyle. Terrill took Joe and Jeanette (Joe's wife) to the meeting, and they were very impressed. The meeting was conducted by two full-time missionaries, Elder Gary Foster and Elder Roger Merrill. This was the same Elder Merrill who was so instrumental in helping to convert the Ragsdales and who is now (at the time of this writing) the General Sunday School President for the Church. Joe and Jeanette invited the missionaries to come to their home a few days later, and for the next few weeks they had several discussions with the missionaries. One evening Jeanette laid the *Book of Mormon* on the bed, and she knelt down and asked Heavenly Father if it was true. If it was not true, she didn't want to be led astray or teach something false to her children. A few days later, the missionaries took Joe and Jeanette to a cottage meeting at the mission home in Dallas where Sanfred Elieson was serving as mission president. As President Elieson read aloud from the *Book of Mormon*, the Spirit was able to bear a powerful witness to Jeanette that the things being taught were true and that this was indeed the Lord's true church. Without saying anything to anyone, she kept that feeling to herself.

A few days later the missionaries visited the McWilliams' again. On this visit they read a scripture saying that those who accepted these truths and repented of their sins would be forgiven by the Lord. Joe responded that if it was true that the Lord would forgive him of all his sins, then he should be baptized. Joe then asked Jeanette how she felt about it all, and she responded that she had already come to know that it was true.

Elders Forrester and Merrill then asked Joe to pray and ask the Lord as to the truthfulness of the *Book of Mormon* and if he (Joe) should become a member of the Church

"I went out into the country to be alone, and with a broken heart and a contrite spirit, I asked the Lord if the *Book of Mormon* is true and if I should join The Church of Jesus Christ of Latter-day Saints. As I felt the mercy, love, and warmth of the Lord descend upon me, I wept with joy and humility."

Joe and Jeanette McWilliams were both baptized on July 25, 1965, in the Malone Street building.

After joining the Church, Joe felt that he needed to dispose of his club, as it was not in keeping with the spirit and teachings of the Church. In a conversation with John Porter on that subject, John agreed that Joe should sell the business.

"But don't lose any money on it," John Porter advised.

Joe McWilliams is largely responsible for the conversion of several people to the gospel. He also was instrumental in completing the conversion processes of David and Sue Welch.

Patricia McWilliams (née Diers)

Patricia McWilliams became Joe McWilliams' third wife following his divorce from Jeanette. Although raised in a strict Catholic family in Wisconsin, Patricia had her own ideas about religion and family life. A high standard of personal integrity was important to her, and she wanted a family that would be filled with love and happiness in a Christ-centered relationship.

Blessed with musical talents, Patricia Diers came to Denton to study music at UNT. Shortly after arriving in 1971, Patricia met Joe McWilliams. At that time, Joe was working on the loading dock of Red Ball Motor Freight, having already sold his nightclub. Following his missionary inclinations, Joe introduced Patricia to the gospel. The teachings of the Church and the personal lives of the members she met fit her ideals exactly.

"They were such great role models," Patricia said when reflecting back on those years. "They were such valiant souls, not only the ones who were settled here, but also the ones who passed through. They taught me how to model the spiritual values I sought."

Joe McWilliams baptized Patricia on November 19, 1971. He married her thirteen months later.

Barbara and Wayne Crandall

As a new member of the Church, Patricia Diers wanted to share her newly-found religion with everyone who would listen. At the same time, even though she was studying to become a harpist, her music curriculum at UNT in 1971 included a class in voice to improve her vocal talents. She had a good relationship with her voice teacher, and they occasionally engaged in religious discussions, some of which were fervent and heated.

During one of these class periods, Patricia and her teacher got onto the subject of Mormonism, and with great enthusiasm, Patricia told him all she could about the LDS church and its teachings. While it is not known how well the seeds of the gospel message germinated within the teacher, they certainly were not wasted, for the piano accompanist who was also in the room, heard every word and believed what she heard. That accompanist was a young lady named Barbara Stewart, daughter of Richard and Susanne Stewart, and later the wife of Wayne Crandall.

"I knew everything she said was right for it agreed with everything I had come to believe was true," Barbara reminisced. "I was so excited!"

Barbara, a native of Denton, had searched for many years for the "true religion." At the age of thirteen, she asked for and received a Bible for Christmas. She studied it, and she prayed. She asked all her friends about their religions, and she went to church with many of them. She even considered becoming a nun, but she gave up on that idea because of a stronger desire to become a wife and a mother. Then, at age eighteen, as a voice student at UNT, Barbara's search was fulfilled. As a means of earning extra money, she became an accompanist for dance classes and for voice lessons. She was at the right place at the right time to hear about the Church from Patricia Diers. After the lesson, Barbara talked with Patricia, discussed religion with her, and confirmed the feelings she already had.

Going home that evening, Barbara got out a *Book of Mormon* and the other LDS literature which her mother (whose conversion story will also be included) had tucked away in a chest of drawers almost ten years earlier, and she stayed up all night reading by the dim light of a closet.

"By morning I knew that it was all true, that Joseph Smith was a prophet and that the *Book of Mormon* was true. I was so happy!"

The next day, after her father, an airline pilot, returned home from a trip, Barbara announced to all the family that she was going to become a Mormon. Although objections were voiced, Barbara held firm even though she had to wait a year and a half (until 1973) to be baptized. In the meantime, she attended the Denton Ward faithfully and even held callings.

"Everyone was so friendly and accepting. I felt like I was home at last!"

When Barbara learned that Sanfred and Virginia Elieson lived "just around the corner," she was thrilled. The Eliesons played a leading role in fellowshipping and in responding to questions that Barbara occasionally raised.

Barbara eventually married her high school sweetheart, Wayne Crandall, and after four years, he also joined the Church.

David and Sue Welch

Joe McWilliams, along with many others, played a significant role in the conversions of David and Sue Welch.

The Welches had moved to Denton so that David could work toward a master's and doctor's degree in psychology at UNT. After completing his degree programs, David earned his living by owning and operating two clinics for psychology services. But in addition to his school work, things were coming together from several directions for drawing the Welches into the gospel fold, and without realizing what was happening, David and Sue became virtually surrounded by Mormons in Denton.

In one of his psychology classes, David took offense at the pornographic nature of some of the films being shown, and he went to the Dean of Men to voice a complaint. The Dean of Men at that time was Ell Sorensen, who was also bishop of the Denton Ward. Wearing two hats at the same time, Brother Sorensen responded with some thoughts on the concepts of academic freedom and free agency.

On another occasion, when David and Sue needed a baby sitter, they got Judy Thompson, wife of Harvey Thompson. Sue and Judy became good friends, and Judy invited the

Welches to participate in a community garden located behind Bob Nobles' hospital. David and Sue soon realized that they were the only non-Mormons participating. The pump was being primed.

As a result of their new friendship, Sue and Judy spent a lot of time together, and they did a lot of talking. David and Sue enjoyed occasional visits in the Thompson home for Family Home Evenings. "The first time I saw you, I knew that eventually you would join the Church," Judy told Sue on a later occasion.

A highlight of the conversion process for the Welches occurred in 1974, when David and Sue Welch were driving in the Lake Dallas area. Stopping at a small Mom and Pop grocery store to make some purchases, they couldn't help noticing a large sign in the front window saying, "No Success Can Compensate for Failure in the Home." Their attention was immediately captivated. The store was located on the west side of I35E at the Highland Village overpass. It was operated by Wilma Stokes, a very missionary-minded member of what was then the Lewisville Ward.

These Denton encounters were not the first that David and Sue had experienced with the Church. On two earlier occasions, they had been contacted by LDS missionaries — once in Cedar Falls, Iowa, in 1965 and a few years later in Houston, Texas where David was in law school — and they had even had a couple of lessons, but at those times they were not ready to internalize the gospel. Sue, who grew up in Iowa, had even attended a wine festival in Nauvoo, but she heard nothing about the Church on that visit.

In Denton, however, they had become receptive. Over the years they had been looking for a meaningful religion, one in which they could get satisfying answers to their many questions.

Acceptable answers had not come from ministers of other religions they had investigated. In their current search they had established a three-fold criteria for the church they sought. First, it had to be Christ-centered. Second, it had to be family-oriented. And third, it had to require the active participation of its members. The sign in the window immediately caught their attention.

Going into the store, David walked all around just to see if there was anything else of a special nature. Then going to the check-out counter, he saw a stack of books on the counter – *The Book of Mormon* – along with a sign saying "Free!! Take one." Although he still knew nothing about the *Book of Mormon*, David took one of the free copies, and he wrote his name and address on an accompanying sign out sheet, knowing full-well that it would result in a visit from someone.

So when David walked out of the Lake Dallas store and looked again at the sign, "No Success Can Compensate for Failure in the Home," he said, "That's it! That's for us."

David and Sue didn't have to wait long for a follow-up visit by the LDS missionaries. Taking the six missionary lessons, they asked a lot of the same questions that they had asked of other religions. This time, and for the first time, they got satisfying answers. Sometimes the missionaries would have to leave, study, and then come back with the answers, but the answers always came.

The first LDS church meeting for David and Sue was a fast and testimony meeting which they attended with Harvey and Judy Thompson. It was at this meeting that the influence of Joe McWilliams made the difference. When the meeting was turned over to the congregation for testimonies, Joe was the first one on his feet. Striding up to the front of the chapel, he took the microphone, turned and faced the congregation, and bore a fervent testimony. Citing the positive effects of the gospel on his life, Joe said, "I love the Lord. I love my wife. I love my family."

David was mesmerized. He couldn't believe that a tough and rugged man, as Joe appeared to be, could express such tender feelings in public. "It blew me away," David later recalled. As a result of Joe McWilliams' testimony, David was ready for baptism.

During this investigative period, the Welches went with the Thompsons and the Biggs to Ft. Worth to dinner and had a wonderful time. David was further impressed with the solidarity of the husband-wife relationships on that occasion. David and Sue were fully converted, and they were baptized on June 14, 1974.

One of the highlights for Sue, after joining the church, was attending the genealogy classes taught by Virginia Elieson. Sister Elieson instilled in Sue a passionate love for genealogy and family history that has endured through the subsequent years.

"She set me on fire," Sue commented in retrospect.

Sometime after joining the church, David learned that there were openings for chaplains in the army, and he felt a desire to enlist for a seven-year stint. To become a chaplain, one had to be approved both by his church and by the military. After making his application, David was interviewed by Apostle Boyd K. Packer and then set apart by Apostle Joseph B. Wirthlin. He also passed his military interviews, and he was sworn in by none other than Denton's Lt. Col. Carl Guess, husband of Lucile Guess. Lucile was also a member of the Denton Ward, and her husband Carl was a former West Pointer and now a retired army Lt. Colonel.

As a new convert energized with missionary zeal, David Welch took advantage of every opportunity to share his joy and understanding of the gospel with others. One of his efforts

bore special fruit as he successfully introduced Bob and Ann
Hall to the gospel.

Bob and Ann Hall

Robert (Bob) Hall had a brilliant mind, and as a UNT
graduate student in behavioral psychology, he had a promising
future. For recreation he loved to ride his motorcycle, and he
found relaxation in so doing.

Bob's life took a dramatic change in October 1972, when
he had a motorcycle accident that almost cost his life and left
him permanently impaired. Bob had been physically exhausted
on that day, and he simply went to sleep while riding. The
resulting accident left him with severe head and body injuries
and a multitude of broken bones. He was in a coma during
most of the 31 days he spent in a hospital. Following Bob's
release from the hospital, his wife, Ann, rendered loving service
to the extreme in helping him rehabilitate and adjust to a life of
reduced mental and physical capabilities.

Bob and Ann were not members of the Church at the time
of his accident, but for most of his life he had wanted to meet a
"Mormon." This desire goes back to a very special dream he
had at the age of three years. In this dream, he saw a set of
crystal stairs going upward and people dressed in white were
climbing the stairs. Bob wanted to join them and climb the
stairs also, but a spokesman in the dream said, "You can't do
that." He then heard the spokesman say, "Send him to Earth."

The next morning, young Bob told his mother about the
dream, and mentioned that he wanted to be a Mormon also.

"Where did you learn that word," his surprised mother
asked.

"I heard it in my dream," he explained.

Bob's mother then tried to dissuade Bob from having an

interest in Mormons.

Additional dreams occurred during Bob's early life, but after the age of eight, there were no more dreams of a spiritual nature until after his accident. During his teenage years, not only was there no contact with Mormons, he gave no further thought to the Mormons.

It was while Bob was convalescing in the hospital that his dream at the age of three was brought vividly back to his memory. A new dream occurred in which Bob, while sitting in a chair, heard a knock at the door.

"What do you want," he yelled out in a gruff tone of voice.

The door opened, and a man dressed in white stood there.

"Bob, you are going to be OK," the man said. The door then closed, and the man was gone.

When Bob awoke, a nurse dressed in white was bending over him.

"Am I in heaven?" Bob asked.

"Not yet," she responded.

Shortly after this experience, contact with the Mormons came. While walking in the hallway of the rehabilitation facility one day, Bob met David Welch, a newly baptized local Church member. Eager to share the gospel with anyone who would listen, David felt impressed to approach Bob. David asked Bob if they could talk, and Bob agreed.

They visited for about a half hour and David told Bob many things about the Mormon church. Upon hearing the word "Mormon," Bob reflected immediately on the dream he had had as a three year old boy. Although Bob had retained a vivid memory of the dream in his earlier years, he had let it fade from his memory during his teenage and early adult years. Now, the dream was again a vivid reality in his mind, and he was not going to let it go again.

Determined now to locate a Mormon church and meet some of its members, Bob asked the rehabilitation secretary if she knew of anything nearby. She thought there was such a church on Malone Street just north of University Drive. Bob was stunned to realize he had been so close and yet so far away. Unbeknownst to Ann, Bob started walking. He was going to find that church. He walked from the rehabilitation center to Malone Street. He then walked north, crossing University Drive; and he came to a building. Because there was no cross on the building, he didn't know if it was a church or not, but he believed he had located the right place.

Attempting to go inside the building, Bob found that the doors were locked. After walking so far and with great difficulty, he was devastated. Dejectedly he started walking away when a voice from the rear of the church building called out, "May I help you?"

"Who are you?" Bob blurted out.

"I am the janitor. Can I help you?" It was Peter Covino, who was not at all bashful about talking about the gospel. Peter took Bob into the building and let him walk around in the chapel. Peter also got Bob's name and address, and it was not long afterward that the missionaries were calling on Bob and Ann and giving them the lessons.

Bob and Ann started attending Sunday meetings of the Denton Ward at the Malone Street building. Their first Sunday of attendance was especially meaningful to Bob, for he saw at that time several of the people he had seen almost 35 years earlier in his dream. He recognized them, and he looked at them with tears welling up in his eyes. Now he was going to become able to climb those stairs also.

Bob and Ann were baptized on February 14, 1975. David Welch had the privilege of baptizing them.

An Instance of Individual Conversions
Within One Family

Susanne Stewart and Children

Although the conversion of Susanne Stewart's daughter, Barbara, has already been cited in this chapter, there is more to be said about the rest of the family. The first to learn of the gospel was Susanne herself.

Religion and spiritual living were always important to Susanne, and she lived according to the light and knowledge she happened to possess. Each weekday morning before school, she would gather her children in the living room of their home and have Bible study and prayer. But even though conducting such sessions, Susanne knew something was missing, and answers to many of her questions were not forthcoming. So this void became the focus of personal prayer on Susanne's part, asking God to reveal to her what it was that was missing.

For three months in 1961, Susanne prayed for the understanding she sought. Then one day there was a knock on her door. It was the Mormon missionaries. But Susanne did not recognize them as bearers of the answers she sought, and she characterizes herself as having been somewhat rude to them. She did, however, accept a pamphlet describing Joseph Smith's First Vision which she read.

"This has to be a fairy tale," she thought to herself.

Shortly thereafter, Velma Brown, an LDS member who worked closely with Susanne in PTA, mentioned to Susanne that she (Velma) would be feeding the Mormon missionaries. Susanne's mind went back to her encounter with the missionaries, and she regretted having been rude to them. Her chance to redeem herself came quickly.

About a week after Susanne's conversation with Velma,

there was another knock on Susanne's door. It was the same set of Mormon missionaries. This time Velma had sent them to try again. Inviting them in, Susanne treated them cordially, but she still considered them to be from an oddball sect. When they offered her a *Book of Mormon*, she accepted it on condition.

"I'll read your book if you will read one from me." She was going to straighten out those two young men.

True to her word, Susanne read the *Book of Mormon*, and she immediately knew it was true. She never gave any reading material to the missionaries.

Susanne could hardly wait for her husband to return home from a flying trip to share with him what she had found. His reaction, however, was very negative, so she placed five copies of the *Book of Mormon*, along with some pamphlets, into a chest of drawers, and she told her children about them.

"I can't give these to you," she explained, "but if the time ever comes when you want to know about the religion I have found, you know where to look."

Learning about Susanne, Margaret Porter began visiting her, and Margaret always had the right responses to Susanne's questions. She and Margaret became close friends, and Susanne enjoyed the visits. But to keep peace in her family, Susanne ceased showing any open interest in the Mormons. Largely because of Margaret, however, the fire within Susanne continued burning.

Just as there was no stopping the stone cut out of the mountain without hands in Daniel's vision, there was no stopping the conversions in the Stewart family once they began. Quite separately from her own encounters with Mormonism, each of Susanne's children – Barbara, Laura, Allen, and Buddy – found the Church individually.

Barbara's conversion experience in 1971 has already been

related. Separately, but at the same time, Barbara's younger sister, Laura, found the Church. In high school, Laura and Debbie Brown (daughter of Kay and Myrna Brown) had become best friends. In the summer of 1971 Laura asked her parents for permission to attend girls' camp with Debbie. Not realizing it was a Mormon activity, her father gave permission. Laura then started attending early morning seminary. She had found the gospel, and she had a testimony.

Because of a peculiarity in Texas state law at that time, a person eighteen years of age was considered an adult and did not need parental permission for adult decisions. Taking advantage of that window, Barbara and Laura both joined the Church. They then prevailed upon their mother to begin attending with them and to exercise the faith and testimony she had developed ten years earlier. Susanne began attending and became fully involved, but she had to wait another five years before receiving permission to be baptized.

Susanne's younger son, Allen, was next to find the Gospel. Observing what the Gospel had done for Barbara and Laura, Allen felt that he needed something of a similar nature in his own life. Allen attended a fireside at the home of Sam and Carol Briggs, and Gregg Head's testimony given at that fireside led Allen to begin investigating and attending Church. Allen was soon baptized, and he went on a mission one year after joining the Church.

Last but not least, Susanne's older son Buddy (Richard, Jr.), and his wife, Debbie, also came into the Church. They had been living lives somewhat on the wild side, but when they found that they were expecting their first child, they resolved to make needed changes. They began investigating various religions, and Buddy approached his mother and asked if he could borrow some of the Church literature she had put away years ago in the chest of drawers. As Buddy and Debbie read, the Spirit bore witness to them. They joined the Church, and Buddy eventually became bishop of the Everman Ward in the Vancouver, Washington Stake.

Susanne considers herself to be a very blessed person. "I have four children, nineteen grandchildren, and twenty-two great-grandchildren, and they are all trying to live active lives in the Church." Her family has produced missionaries, bishops, High Council members, and temple workers. And the stone is still rolling downhill.

In thinking back on her experiences, Susanne said, "Over the years I have learned that our Heavenly Father loves us and He knows each of us and we are important to Him. One of our greatest gifts is to know our worth."

Part Seven
CHURCH GROWTH
IN DENTON'S
NEIGHBORING CITIES

Introduction

A history of The Church of Jesus Christ of Latter-day Saints in Denton, Texas, cannot be considered complete without including brief accounts of the local Church's influence on the development and growth of the Church units in Decatur, Gainesville, and Lewisville. In all three locations, the Church started with Sunday Schools organized by the Denton Branch. Members of the Church in Denton were instrumental in providing early leadership and nurturing, leading eventually to full wards in Decatur and Gainesville and a stake in Lewisville that has since mushroomed and contributed to the establishment of other stakes.

CHAPTER 30

Decatur

*I*t is believed that Latter-day Saints were living in Wise County as far back as 1908; however, there was no organized Church activity in that area until 1962. Formal activity began in 1961 when John and Margaret Porter began proselyting and searching for Church members in that area. It appears that the first baptism in Decatur was that of Thomas Lee Wright on December 31, 1961, as a result of missionary efforts started by the Porters. The Porters also found the North and Parrish families, who were already members.

A Relief Society was organized in Decatur on November 11, 1962, with Patricia Ann Wright as president. Informal Sunday School services were also begun in 1962.

Clifton and Ara North were an older couple and not in good health. Luke and Anna Parrish, although elderly also, were more mobile. To accommodate the Norths, Bill May and his family drove from Denton to Decatur each Sunday and conducted Sunday School in the Norths' home. Brother North, dressed in the bib overalls he always wore and sitting in his favorite chair, was always appreciative. In attendance at the first of these Sunday School sessions were Ara North, Anna Parrish, Esther Payne, Pat Wright, and Jo North.

A few additional church members were found in Decatur and in its surrounding communities, and a Decatur Branch was organized in 1963 as a dependent branch attached to the Denton Branch. To provide a temporary meeting place for the Branch, John Porter and President Atkerson purchased a building on old Highway 287 just east of Karl Klement Dodge, and Thomas Wright became the Branch President two years after his baptism. At its height, active membership in Decatur ranged from 30 to 50 members. Many of the members, however, moved away over the next few years, and both of the Norths died. By 1968 active membership was down to ten members, and as a result, the branch was discontinued.

Upon discontinuance of the Decatur Branch, Luke and Anna Parrish began attending church in Denton, driving an old vehicle of questionable reliability. Bill and Nina Salter drove even farther, from Bowie to Denton. The Parrishes and Salters would attend Sunday School in the morning, then go to the Eliesons' home to eat and to nap until time for Sacrament Meeting.

Known as the "Candy Man," Luke Parrish always had a pocket full of peppermint candy which he delighted in giving to the kids. Brother and Sister Ragsdale have commented about the stickiness on the upholstery in their car as their kids sucked on peppermint sticks all the way home from church, but they appreciated the love the "Candy Man" had for the kids, and the love the kids had for the "Candy Man."

In 1975 a second attempt was made to provide an organization for the saints living in the Decatur area. This second attempt began with the organization of a Relief Society in October 1975. Organized in the home of John R. and Susan Porter at 1200 North Trinity Street, the Decatur Relief Society functioned actively, and it quickly appeared that the sisters and their families had sufficient numbers for a Branch to again be considered. John R. Porter was the son of John W and Margaret Porter.

President Leithead of the Ft. Worth Stake called a special meeting to be held on January 28, 1976, and on that date he and his counselors came to Decatur to determine if the Saints there could support an active Branch. By a unanimous vote, they pledged to support the proposed branch, and on February 29, 1976, the branch was reorganized with Roy B. Robinson as Branch President. Subsequent Branch Presidents were John R. Porter, O. H. Niblett, and Jack Cannon.

Organized in the First National Bank building, the branch met in several locations before constructing its own building in 1983 on Thompson Street. The first meeting place was in the home of John R. and Susan Porter (1976), and meetings continued there for about two months. Subsequent meeting places included "Sweets" pool hall in Decatur (1976), the Presbyterian Church in Bridgeport (1977), John R. Porter's car dealership in Decatur (1979), and finally to the warehouse of a carpet store owned by Thomas and Pat Wright (1981).

Each of these meeting places left much to be desired. The pool hall was without one of its walls, so the members hung sheets to provide privacy and a measure of protection from the outside weather. At one point, while meeting in the Presbyterian Church building, the Presbyterians accused the Mormons of depleting the building's coffee supplies. When the Mormons replied that "we don't drink coffee," their hosts apologized and suggested extending their lease for another year.

The new branch carried out a full church program, and yet the saints struggled for lack of strong priesthood leadership. The widespread geographical distribution of members throughout Wise County also had a negative effect. Then, in the latter part of 1976 and the early part of 1977, the Decatur Branch got a shot in the arm as several families moved in from the Moorpark Valley of southern California. Some of the surnames in these new families were Stockwell, Pratt, Poulsen, Dietrich, Miller, and Hines. Major credit for these moves goes to David Hines, who had formerly lived in the Decatur area, for extolling the beauty, the cheap prices, and the productivity of the land to these California families.

One person, however, in Moorpark thought these moves were a bad idea. So Jack Cannon, Branch President of the Moorpark Branch, made a trip to Texas with his wife, Claudia, to convince these families to return to California.

"As I drove eastward from Ranger and Cisco," Brother Cannon reminisced, "I began to see the beautiful green countryside, and it did look productive. I fell in love with this part of Texas."

So instead of convincing the other families to return to California, the Cannons went back and prepared to make the move themselves. It took a year and a half for the Cannons to divest themselves of business and church ties, but in July 1978, they too became Texans.

While the Decatur Branch now had added priesthood leadership, it also had much disunity. Roy Robinson exhausted himself as Branch President and was released. John R. Porter

Groundbreaking for Decatur Chapel, March 2, 1982
O. H. Niblett, Branch President, Decatur Branch,
and Richard Ragsdale, Stake President, Ft. Worth North Stake

became the new branch's second Branch President in February 1977, and he served in that calling for approximately two years. Under President Porter's tenure, animosities were lessened, and a high degree of love and unity were established. President Porter was released in September 1981, and O. H. Niblett became Branch President. John G. (Jack) Cannon succeeded President Niblett in October 1982.

During these years the Branch grew, and soon the need to have their own meeting facility became recognized. Finally, on March 2, 1982, and under the direction of Richard Ragsdale, President of the Ft. Worth North Stake at that time, the Decatur saints met and broke ground for their own building. It was to be a relatively small building with one large room serving as both a chapel and a cultural hall, but it would be their permanent home. The Saints held their first meeting in the partially completed building on September 5, 1982, with 122 persons in attendance. Construction was completed the following year, and President Ragsdale dedicated the building on September 25, 1983.

Like other units of the Church in those years, members of the Decatur Branch engaged in money making projects which not only helped provide funds for ward and branch budgets and for buildings, but which also tended to coalesce the participants into a more unified whole. One such project in

Sacrament Meeting and
Dedication of Decatur Branch
March 1, 1987

Presiding: President Gordon Watts
Conducting: President Jack Cannon
Chorister: Terri Mulkey
Organist: Pat Wright

Welcome.

Opening Hymn: #2
"The Spirit of God"

Invocation: By Invitation

Branch Business:

Sacrament Hymn: #177
"Tis Sweet to Sing the Matchless Love"

Administration of the Sacrament

Speaker: Pat Wright
Speaker: Thomas Wright
Choir: "How Great Thou Art"
Speaker: John Porter
Speaker: O. H. Niblett
Speaker: George Hubbard
Choir: "O Render Thanks"

Dedication: President Gordon Watts

Closing Hymn: #152
"God Be with You Till We Meet Again"

Benediction: By Invitation

Dedication of the Second Phase of the Decatur Building
March 1, 1987

Decatur in 1963 was a potato project in which the branch raised 4,200 pounds of potatoes. They sold 2,000 pounds to the LDS cannery in Carrollton for ten cents a pound, and they sold the rest to the general public. The Branch netted $330.00 for the branch budget.

Church membership continued to grow in Decatur, and it was soon apparent that the Decatur saints needed a larger meeting facility. A second phase of construction began which would include a full size chapel and additional classrooms, and this phase was completed early in 1987. On March 1, 1987, Gordon Watts, President of the Lewisville Stake dedicated the new facility. On this same day, the Decatur Branch became the Decatur Ward with Jack Cannon as the Bishop. Subsequent bishops have been Tad Billmire, Brad Ough, and Ken Blankenfeld. A third phase was added to the building in 2005, thus expanding it to a full size meeting house in every respect.

Decatur Chapel
Dedicated September 25, 1983
Expanded and Rededicated March 1, 1987

CHAPTER 31

Gainesville

$\mathcal{C}$hurch activity in Gainesville began officially on March 3, 1963, when the Denton Branch received eighteen membership records for families having Gainesville addresses. Under the Porters' direction, contacts were made and a search began for additional members. Nothing was formally organized, however, until 1965 when missionaries were assigned to Gainesville. With the missionaries in charge, a Sunday School was organized on September 5, 1965, and it soon became a dependent branch attached to the Denton Branch. Lack of growth, along with doctrinal discord and inconsistency on the part of the members, were such that the Branch was discontinued the following year.

Missionary activity continued sporadically in Gainesville, and in February 1967, two Elders knocked on the door of Ruby Mauldin. Embracing their message, Ruby was baptized the following month on March 11, and her three children followed shortly thereafter. Because there was no church organization in Gainesville at that time, Sister Mauldin believed her family to be the only Mormons in town. Each Sunday they drove twice to Denton to attend church meetings.

For the next six months following Sister Mauldin's baptism, missionary activity in Gainesville flourished. Additional convert baptisms included Bill Mauldin, Norma Wheeler Harper, Gladys I. Ailey, Pearlie Mae Van Zandt, Paul Townsend, and Kenneth Carden. Brothers Townsend and Carden became the only priesthood holders. Edna and George Bland joined later on March 17, 1969. Because there still was no church organization in Gainesville, these new members drove to Denton on Sundays to attend meetings. Some attended both the morning Sunday School and the afternoon Sacrament Meeting while others attended only the afternoon meeting.

In 1966 Darlene Johnson (now Darlene Denton) moved from California to Denton to attend Texas Woman's University, and on February 4, 1967, she joined the Church. She was present each Sunday for Sunday School and Sacrament Meeting, and she soon was called to be the Denton Branch Librarian. Because Darlene had no car, Margaret Porter would pick up Darlene and her two children each Sunday morning and then return them to their home after Sacrament Meeting. Between meetings Darlene stayed busy with her library responsibilities, and she and her children would eat with the Gainesville members who were also staying over for the day. In August 1969, Darlene moved to LaGrange where she taught school for four years, and in 1973 she came north again and settled in Gainesville.

Norma Wheeler (now Norma Harper) has written of some of her experiences and feelings.

"I recall my first visit to the church in Denton. The missionary Elders who taught me accompanied my children and me to church. A loving Primary teacher was there to greet us. She stooped to the level of my young children with her arms outstretched and a smile on her face to welcome my little ones. I have never forgotten that image and the love she showed still touches my heart as I think of it. Her name was Linda May (now Linda Barnett). What a wonderful first impression she made on a tentative new convert."

Sister Wheeler was also impressed with Denton's Sunday School chorister, Carol Joy Cooper, who led the singing enthusiastically with "a warm smile and flashing black eyes."

Although the fledgling Gainesville group struggled, the saints who were a part of that early organization still have poignant memories of their experiences. After joining the church, Sister Wheeler was called in 1968 to conduct a Home Primary in her home.

"They handed me a box containing some Primary manuals and a song book and wished me good luck," she recalled. Sister Wheeler had an old blue station wagon with which she would pick up children from six families each week and take them to her home where they would sing, pray, have stories, play games, and have refreshments. Then she would deliver the children back to their homes.

"It certainly was the blind leading the blind," she recalled.

Sister Wheeler still chuckles about one occasion when Mrs. Carden (not yet a church member) forgot one day that her daughter would be in Primary. Fearing the worst when her daughter was not at home, Mrs. Carden called the police and reported a missing child.

In those years there were only five active sisters in Gainesville. Shirley Jean (Gerri) Sparkman, already an LDS member living between Gainesville and Whitesboro, became part of the group and was its first Relief Society president with Sister Wheeler as First Counselor. These two sisters did all the visiting teaching, and they were always one hundred percent. In addition to serving the active sisters in the Gainesville area, Sister Sparkman held a number of socials in her home in an effort to reactivate other sisters. Those who were active developed a strong spiritual bond.

In later years, Sister Wheeler (now Sister Harper) recalls, "I have never felt the Holy Spirit manifest himself as much as in those early days."

A second formal organization of the Saints in Gainesville occurred on January 4, 1972, when seventeen persons gathered in the home of Gladys Ailey and organized a branch Sunday School. Thirty-seven people were present for the first meeting of the new Sunday School on January 16.

On December 17, 1972, Denton's Ralph Davis was called to be the unit leader in Gainesville. As growth continued, the Gainesville saints were organized into a dependent branch on December 3, 1973, and then into an independent branch on September 15, 1974. Denton's John W. Porter was called to be branch president, with Ralph Davis and George Bland of Gainesville serving as counselors to President Porter. Roger Fraim also came up from Denton to lend additional support.

Art Cooper added needed strength to the new unit by accepting a call to do home teaching in Gainesville. Making frequent trips from Denton, Art teamed with Gainesville's Paul Townsend as finders and teachers. Theirs was an interesting relationship. Art, with a Ph.D. degree, was a professor

Gainesville Branch Presidency, 1972
John W. Porter, Branch President
George Bland, Second Counselor
(Not shown: Ralph Davis, First Counselor)

at the University of North Texas and had extensive prior church experience. Paul, with relatively little education, worked for the City of Gainesville as a garbage collector and had almost no prior church experience. And yet, these two worked together with mutual love and harmony, another testimony of the equalizing effect the Church has on those who love the gospel.

George Bland became Gainesville's second Branch President on December 15, 1974. After having had an auspicious beginning, the Branch began to retrogress spiritually. Severe internal contention among some of the members, coupled with a lack of LDS experience and leadership skills, prevented the Spirit from operating as it should. On at least one occasion in 1968, the missionaries had been accosted in the community, and four years later in 1974 an anti-Mormon feeling still ran high among Gainesville residents. According to Alfred H. White, III., the situation was further compounded by the fact that most of the members were not well-known members of the community. The Adversary was clearly at work.

In addition, their meeting locations left much to be desired. After meeting for a while in Sister Ailey's home, the early Sunday School met next in the Cardens' home. Then as a branch, they moved to an abandoned, rat-infested dentist's office at Pecan and Rusk Streets. The sisters of that time still comment about how the rats would jump out of the cupboards during their meetings. Next they went to an old lumber yard on Highway 82 East. Finally, in the late 1970s the branch moved into a downtown bank building owned by John Porter. The bank's vault served as the Branch President's office, and President Bland built a plywood platform for the branch leaders and the speakers. There they stayed until 1985 when their chapel was built.

In the mid-1970s it was clear that the gospel was not flourishing in Gainesville, and some kind of action was needed. And it came.

In August 1977, President Ragsdale called Brother Al White, a member of the Ft. Worth North Stake High Council, to go up to Gainesville as Branch President, replacing George Bland in that position. Brother White, a native of Salt Lake

City, was a lifelong member of the Church, as was his wife, Susanne. They were living in Sanger, only twenty miles from Gainesville, and were members of the Denton First Ward. Al and Susanne, along with their four children (Denise 11, Patricia 9, Becky 6, and Mary 2) accepted the call with enthusiasm. Two weeks later, Susanne gave birth to their first son, Chip.

The Whites proved to be the right people for the job at hand. When Brother White was sustained as Branch President, there were only 24 people in the congregation, and there was only one active Melchizedek Priesthood holder in the branch. When he was released three years later, the average Sacrament Meeting attendance was up to 65-70 members.

One of the persons especially helpful to President White, as he entered into this new assignment, was a young priest, James Johnson, a junior in high school. James, a son of Darlene Johnson, had been baptized on January 10, 1969. He was a committed young man who took President White from home to home visiting members during the week, and he also assumed much of the responsibility for the Sacrament on Sundays.

At the young age of sixteen, James was called to be a counselor in the Sunday School presidency. Sensing the congregation's surprise at such a calling for such a young person, Sanfred Elieson, who was in attendance on that occasion, rose and addressed the Branch citing the larger call given to the fourteen-year-old Joseph Smith. Brother Johnson proved to be capable of his responsibilities, for when the Sunday School president became inactive, it was James Johnson who kept things going and who handled the problems as they arose. Very quickly he was accepted and fully supported by the Branch members.

James Johnson later became the first person called from Gainesville to serve a mission for The Church of Jesus Christ of Latter-day Saints. After graduating from Gainesville High School in 1979 as an honor graduate, James was called in 1980 and assigned to the Tokyo North Mission.

Gainesville Youth enjoy a hayride

Significant help also came from three sets of older missionary couples: Elders and Sisters Shepherd, Hurst, and Glines. Elder William Hurst, a former mayor of Blanding, Utah, and a man of considerable influence in southeastern Utah, was especially helpful in many ways. For two years, these missionary Elders served as counselors in the branch presidency until local members could be called.

These were difficult days for President White, and for the first few months of his calling, he felt very much alone, receiving very little help from the local priesthood brethren. On one Saturday, discouraged to the point of tears while driving to a Stake leadership meeting in Ft. Worth, Al vocally pleaded with the Lord for almost the entire driving distance.

At the meeting, the visiting authority, Elder Richard G. Scott of the Council of the Twelve, seemed to speak directly to President White.

"Some of you may think what you have been asked to do is hard, but remember the task given to Nephi."

Elder Scott then read from I Nephi, Chapter 4 about how Nephi went forward in faith, never complaining, and never considering the possibility that he might not succeed. These remarks came to President White as the Lord's response to his earlier pleadings. He drove home that night rejoicing. He still didn't know what to do, but he had spiritual assurance that if he continued making the effort, the way would be opened. And it was.

The next day in Sacrament Meeting, President White addressed the congregation, and he minced no words in telling the members why he was there.

"President Ragsdale sent me here to do two things. He sent me to add a measure of stability to the branch which vacillates between hot and cold. He also sent me here to appraise your situation and make a recommendation as to whether or not the Branch should remain open as an independent branch, or should it be closed and made a dependent branch attached again to the Denton First Ward. I want to tell you right now that I will never (with emphasis on the "never") recommend that this branch be closed. So let's all get together and get involved, and do what we need to be doing."

President White's message had a positive effect, and the members began to function more as a unit. According to Sister Darlene Denton, "President White had the foundation in the gospel that we had lacked. He taught strict adherence to gospel principles. He was the strong leader who guided us for the next several years."

In an effort to improve the image the townspeople had of the Latter-day Saints, the Stake decided upon an all-out effort to show the citizens of Gainesville that Latter-day Saints are people of worth. The citizens would be invited to attend a series of four firesides in which the beliefs and practices of Mormonism would be explained. An additional purpose of the visits was to let the influential citizens of Gainesville see that Mormons were also desirable and upstanding citizens.

The plan was that on an appointed day, all the bishops, high counselors, and stake presidency would go to Gainesville and go out two by two to make short visits to the people of Gainesville. Each group of two would be assigned to visit three or four pre-selected families, and an effort was made to create assignments in which the visitors and visited would have some characteristics or interests in common.

February 11, 1978, was the chosen day for the visits. For spiritual preparation, February 4 was designated as a day in which all concerned would fast and pray that the people to be visited would be at home and would receive the visitors. On the appointed day, the stake leaders met together in Gainesville and received instructions on a recommended door approach. They then went out into the community. Eight sets of full-time missionaries also participated.

The tangible results of these visits were disappointing. Out of 55 contacts by stake leaders and 200 more by the missionaries, only two investigators came to an LDS meeting and one baptism occurred. But on the other hand, a distinct improvement in the perception of the Mormons was noticed in the community.

One of the visits made that day had a humorous aspect. Bishop Newell Kay Brown and President White, both Ph.D. college professors, went out together, and one of the persons they called upon was the superintendent of schools in Gainesville. His wife answered the door when they knocked.

"Is Mr. Echols in?" President White asked.

"No, he isn't," she responded.

"I'm sorry. I am Dr. White, and this is Dr. Brown, and we were hoping to have a brief visit with him."

"Oh, I thought you might be Mormons. Please come in. He's in the basement doing some work. I'll get him."

"Well, we *are* Mormons," President White had to acknowledge. "I hope that won't make a difference."

An amiable visit ensued. Brothers White and Brown left a

Book of Mormon with Mr. Echols along with an invitation to attend an open house and a fireside at the church building. Other church leaders from the stake also had amiable visits in other parts of the city; however, no one attended any of the four firesides. But leading Gainesville citizens became acquainted with a distinguished group of Latter-day Saints that day.

Branch President Al White endeavored in several ways to stimulate activity and build spirituality in Gainesville. Despite his being discouraged again on several occasions, ideas came into President White's head, and he put them into practice. Although some were more or less successful than others, the overall effect on the branch was positive.

One of President White's efforts was getting the men of the branch involved in playing basketball, as both a proselyting effort and a unifying effort. Al was an athlete, having played defensive back on the University of Utah football team, and he also loved basketball. The Gainesville brethren formed a team and even had a few non-members playing on it. Led by the McCage brothers and Rex Morris, their day of glory came in 1979 when they entered and won the Ft. Worth North Stake basketball tournament, which included beating a powerful Denton First Ward team led by Tony Wright and Wally Cochran, both former college players. The basketball experience went a long way in coalescing a diverse branch.

President White started an early morning seminary which he taught himself. Two boys and two girls attended. In an effort to combat the smoking habit that some of the members had, President White arranged to have a non-smoking clinic conducted by a professional from the metroplex area. Again, the results were disappointing.

Accolades must also be directed to Sister White, a 34-year

old-mother of five children, one of whom had serious birth defects. With her husband gone almost every night and most of the day on Sunday, Susanne not only supported him fully, she also served in up to eight callings herself. One of her experiences is especially worthy of note. While driving from her home to Gainesville with her children in an older pickup truck, the vehicle suddenly stopped running. Needing to be there to fulfill a leadership role in Primary, she was very upset and even angry with the Lord for her plight. After a few minutes of inner anger, she humbly bowed her head and asked most contritely for the Lord to help her get to her assignment. The truck responded immediately when she tried again to start it, and she made it to Gainesville and then back home without further incident.

Under President White's leadership, and aided by the senior missionary couples, the branch grew. A spiritual stability was being attained, and the branch was now ready to function under its own leadership. As a result of current conditions and future expectations, land for a chapel was acquired adjacent to Cook County Community College (now North Central Texas College).

During the Whites' tenure in Gainesville, the list of local members who rendered outstanding support included Darlene Johnson, Norma Harper, Brother and Sister Rothacher, Sharon Carlisle, and Paul Townsend. Norma Harper led the music, and young Denise White played the piano for Primary, Sunday School, and Sacrament Meeting. Sister Rothacher was Relief Society President, and Darlene Johnson seemed to teach everything as well as manage the Branch library. Paul Townsend was a dependable home teacher.

On one occasion, Kathleen Fette, who had just come back into activity, expressed concern to President White about her husband's lack of interest in the Church. President White's response surprised even himself as he said, "Sister Fette, you remain active and do your duty, and someday your husband will be the president of this Branch."

President White was released in June 1980, and replaced by Charles McCage. Ken Fette, who joined the Church in November 1980, shortly after his wife's conversation with President White, became the branch president in 1982, replacing President McCage. Brother Fette's call to become Branch President came only a half year after receiving his endowments in the Provo Temple.

"Actually my newness in the Church proved to be a plus," he later recalled. "I didn't know anything, so I wasn't bound by past tradition. I made mistakes, and it was a growing experience."

President Fette encountered many organizational problems, including instances of false doctrine, inconsistency, and lack of commitment on the parts of Branch members and leaders. Some of the leaders dropped into inactivity as a partial result of working on Sunday. There were also some excommunications. It became apparent that divine assistance was needed, and on December 18, 1982, Stake President Ragsdale went to Gainesville and re-dedicated that area for missionary work. President Fette held things together and greater unity among the Branch members began to develop. Not only did they elevate themselves spiritually under President Fette's tenure, they succeeded in attracting new converts and in getting their meeting house built and dedicated.

"I would have to say that my service as branch president was the highlight of my entire Church experience so far," Brother Fette said in retrospect.

Although there was growing momentum in Gainesville, the stake leadership still felt that the Branch needed support and participation from Denton, so a number of Denton families were called during those years to function as members of the branch and give shadow leadership. Lee and Georgia Head and Jim and Karen Simpson were the first to function in this assignment. They were followed by Ralph and Sarah Davis, Bob and Jimmie Lou Nobles, George and Billie Hubbard, and finally Frank and Betty Martino.

As the members were strengthened and additional converts and move-ins arrived, a gospel maturity began to grow in Gainesville. The branch members were a talented group, and they staged some outstanding roadshows. Additionally, the Branch made its share of contributions to the building of the Dallas Temple.

Gainesville Ward Chapel Groundbreaking, April 20, 1985
Standing: Bob Nobles, John W. Porter, Gainesville Mayor Harry M. Roark, Gordon T. Watts. *Foreground:* Emily Smith, Angela Smith, Ryan Smith

Gainesville Ward Chapel
Dedicated March 8, 1987;
Expanded and Rededicated February 21, 1999

With President Fette leading the way, ground breaking for their new chapel occurred on April 20, 1985. As an indication of how far the Church had advanced in the eyes of the community, Gainesville Mayor Harry M. Roarke attended the groundbreaking ceremony. Not only did he participate in turning a shovel full of soil, he acknowledged the Church as an integral part of the community, and he spoke to the group about the virtues of religious freedom. (Mayor Roarke was also a minister in Gainesville's First Baptist Church.) Two years later, the building was completed, and it was dedicated on March 8, 1987, by Lewisville Stake President Gordon Watts.

Now, with their own building, the enthusiasm and morale of the members in Gainesville was significantly enhanced. On March 26, 1995, the Gainesville Branch became the Gainesville Ward under the leadership of Max Chartrand, who was Branch President at that time. Growth in the Gainesville Ward was such that additions to the building were soon needed. Additional classrooms and offices were added, and the expanded building was rededicated on February 21, 1999, by Denton Stake President James Martino.

Morgan Lybbert, who followed Max Chartrand as Bishop, had a somewhat unusual start in that office. The day after he received his call in June 1997, Brother Lybbert left the country on a business trip to France and Germany. Therefore, he made his recommendations for counselors by phoning long distance from France to President Martino. Bishop Lybbert was ordained and set apart on July 20, 1997, upon his return to this country.

The Church of Jesus Christ of Latter-day Saints has now gained respect as a contributing part of the Gainesville community. One evidence of this changed feeling is evidenced by Mayor Roarke's presence and participation in the ground breaking ceremony in 1985 prior to building the LDS chapel. The saints there have been quite active in participating in community-wide events. For example, in May of 2003 the Gainesville Ward was one of fifteen organizations participating in the "Gainesville Rebuilding and Neighborhood Development" program in which general cleanup was done in several residential neighborhoods. The ward continues to participate in this twice-a-year program. On June 30, 2001, the ward furnished the noon meal for volunteers laying railroad track in Gainesville's Leonard Park. Following the devastating flood in the summer of 2007, the Gainesville Ward, along with other wards in the Denton Stake, gave significant help in cleaning up and in helping victims become reestablished.

The Gainesville saints endeavor to increase their community acceptance by contributing to the community.

CHAPTER 32
Lewisville

The Lewisville story is quite different from the stories of Decatur and Gainesville. While the saints in the latter two communities struggled for years with low membership and a lack of strong leadership, people poured into the Lewisville area because of its close proximity to Dallas and Ft. Worth. Lewisville was truly a part of the greater metroplex area. The LDS units in Decatur and Gainesville are still units in the Denton Stake; whereas, the Lewisville nucleus grew into its own stake.

The initial Church organization in Lewisville was a Home Primary organized in July 1972. Then in December 1972, Richard Ragsdale, Bishop of the Denton Ward, organized the Lewisville saints into a dependent unit with a Sunday School and a Relief Society. Howard Arrington was called to be the unit leader. Maureen Richards, Denton Ward Relief Society President, divided Lewisville into two visiting teaching districts, and in each district, she had a sister from Denton paired with a sister from Lewisville to visit the other sisters in Lewisville.

"There were very few members in Lewisville at that time, and we wanted them to be involved as much as possible," Sister Richards explained.

Sunday School meetings were held in the cafeteria of the College Street Elementary School. Classes were held in one of the school corridors because the classrooms were not made available.

As membership increased, the Lewisville unit became a dependent branch in July 1973, and then an independent branch in March 1974. S. Willard Elieson, a son of Denton's Sanfred and Virginia Elieson, was called to be the Branch President.

The Lewisville saints continued meeting in the elementary school building until the middle of 1974 when the school asked them to find some other place to meet. For about a year they arranged to meet in one of the Episcopal churches and occasionally in the First Christian Church on Fox Avenue. Then they moved into some unfinished office space at the intersection of Highway 121 and Interstate 35E. Here they remained until their own chapel on Kirkpatrick Road (on the boundary between Lewisville and Flower Mound) was completed.

The Lewisville Branch became the Lewisville Ward on March 28, 1976, and on that same day they dedicated the land on which their first chapel was to be built. Today (2008), the geographic area served by that struggling branch contains over seventeen wards spread over five stakes.

Because of the number and strength of the members moving into the Lewisville area, the Lewisville Branch did not need Denton's sustaining infusion of priesthood guidance and leadership that were necessary in Decatur and Gainesville. Therefore, an account of their progress is not included in this book. It is interesting to note, however, the ironic fact that the Lewisville Branch, started by the Denton Ward, eventually grew into the Lewisville Stake, and until the Denton Stake was organized, all the Denton wards were units within the Lewisville Stake. Thus, the child became the parent.

As growth continued in the greater Lewisville area, the Lewisville Stake was created on April 12, 1981 from a division of the Fort Worth North Stake. On December 9, 2001, the Carrollton Stake was created with wards from the Denton and Lewisville Stakes as well as from the Dallas and Plano areas. On

April 3, 2008, wards transferred from the Lewisville and Carrollton Stakes helped form the new Frisco Stake. In the original footprint of the initial Lewisville Branch, there are now (2008) at least seventeen wards distributed over five stakes. The population growth in that area continues.

APPENDICES

Appendix 1
Attendance at the Organization of the
Denton Dependent Sunday School
November 1959

Dallas Stake Sunday School Superintendency
Ronald Whiting, Superintendent
Bobby Combs, First Counselor
Don Borgalthaus, Second Counselor

Fort Worth Ward Bishopric
N. Marcus Peterson, Bishop

Denton LDS Residents	Denton LDS Students
John W. Porter	Martin Guillot (NTSC)
Margaret Porter	Bill McGinnis (NTSC)
John R. Porter	Carol Willhite (NTSC)
Ann Porter	Ann Musgrove (TSCW)
Betty Porter	Pat Thompson (TSCW)
Alvis Melchior	
Bill Pate	
Myrtle Pate	
Pamela Pate	
Karen Pate	
Trudie Swanson	
Ellen Swanson	
Margie Swanson	
Ray Swanson	

Appendix 2
Development of the Wards
and Branches in Denton

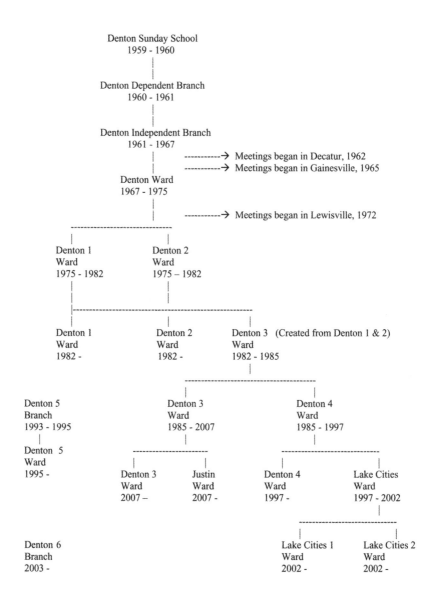

Denton Sunday School
1959 - 1960

Denton Dependent Branch
1960 - 1961

Denton Independent Branch
1961 - 1967
            -----------→ Meetings began in Decatur, 1962
            -----------→ Meetings began in Gainesville, 1965
Denton Ward
1967 - 1975
            -----------→ Meetings began in Lewisville, 1972

Denton 1   Denton 2
Ward   Ward
1975 - 1982   1975 – 1982

Denton 1   Denton 2   Denton 3   (Created from Denton 1 & 2)
Ward   Ward   Ward
1982 -   1982 -   1982 - 1985

Denton 5   Denton 3   Denton 4
Branch   Ward   Ward
1993 - 1995   1985 - 2007   1985 - 1997

Denton 5
Ward
1995 -   Denton 3   Justin   Denton 4   Lake Cities
                Ward   Ward   Ward   Ward
                2007 –   2007 -   1997 -   1997 - 2002

Denton 6   Lake Cities 1   Lake Cities 2
Branch   Ward   Ward
2003 -   2002 -   2002 -

Appendix 3
Bishops and Branch Presidents
in the Denton Area
(As of 1/1/2008)

Denton Dependent Branch
(Created 8/14/60)

John W. Porter	August 1960 – January 1961

Denton Independent Branch
(Created 1/22/61)

John W. Porter	January 1961 – February 1967

Denton Ward
(Created 2/12/67)

John W. Porter	February 1967 – September 1967
Richard W. Ragsdale	September 1967 – September 1973
Ell Sorenson	September 1973 – July 1975

Denton First Ward
(Created 7/20/75)

Newell Kay Brown	July 1975 – October 1978
John W. Porter	October 1978 – December 1979
Frank Martino	December 1979 – June 1984
John Child	June 1984 – February 1989
James Martino	February 1989 – May 1992
William Cudd	May 1992 – June 1997
David Martino	June 1997 – August 2003
Kerry Tryon	August 2003 – June 2008
Trey Martino	June 2008 –

Denton Second Ward
(Created 7/20/75)

Robert H. Nobles	July 1975 – June 1980
Lee Rasmussen	June 1980 – June 1982
Charles Bates	June 1982 – September 1984
Victor Nielsen	September 1984 – September 1988
B. James Richards	September 1988 – September 1993
Bill Brixius	September 1993 – February 1998
Bob McEwan	February 1998 – September 1998
John R. Porter	September 1998 – January 2004
Steven Iverson	January 2004 – June 2008
Steven Frederickson	June 2008 –

Denton Third Ward
(Created 11/14/82)

Alfred H. White	November 1982 – November 1987
Vaughn Andrus	November 1987 – May 1992
David Richards	May 1992 – April 1995
David Passey	April 1995 – January 2000
James Barber	January 2000 – August 2005
Jason Labrum	August 2005 –

Denton Fourth Ward
(Created 9/15/85)

Doyle Thompson	September 1985 – March 1988
Richard Blanco	March 1988 – May 1993
James Gwilliam	May 1993 – November 1997
David Harris	November 1997 – August 1999
Eric Kartchner	August 1999 – January 2004
Michael Gwilliam	January 2004 –

Denton Fifth Branch
(1/17/93)

Paul Fisher	January 1993 – February 1995

Denton Fifth Ward
(Created 1995)

Paul Fisher	February 1995 – April 1996
Steve Peterson	April 1996 – April 2001
Bryan Galloway	April 2001 – February 2005
David Martino	February 2005 – June 2008
Kurt Hansen	June 2008 –

Denton Sixth Branch
(Created 12/14/03)

Abraham Benevides	December 2003 –

Justin Ward
(Created 1/1/07)

Nicholas Kruger	January 2007 –

Lake Cities Ward
(Created 2/18/97)

Dean Garner	February 1997 – October 2002

Lake Cities First Ward
(Created 10/13/02)

Calvin Griffin	October 2002 – October 2007
Bob Foster	October 2007 –

Lake Cities Second Ward
(Created 10/13/02)

David McIntire	October 2002 – December 2007
Michael Liddell	December 2007 –

Spanish Branch
(Created 7/09/95)

Leonardo Osorio   July 1995 – 1997 (Discontinued 1997)

Bishops and Branch Presidents in Decatur
(As of 1/1/2008)

Decatur Dependent Branch
(Created 1963)

Thomas Wright   1963 - 1968   (Discontinued 1968)

Decatur Independent Branch
(Created 2/29/76)

Roy Robinson	February 1976 – February 1977
John R. Porter	February 1977 – September 1981
O. H. Niblettt	September 1981 – October 1982
Jack Cannon	October 1982 – March 1987

Decatur Ward
(Created 3/1/1987)

Jack Cannon	March 1987 – July 1991
Tad Billmire	July 1991 – February 1998
Brad Ough	February 1998 – August 2003
Ken Blankenfeld	August 2003 –

Bishops and Branch Presidents in Gainesville
(As of 1/1/2008)

Gainesville Dependent Branch
(Created 12/3/73)

John W. Porter   December 1973 – September 1974

Gainesville Independent Branch
(Created 9/15/74)

John W. Porter	September 1974 – December 1974
George Bland	December 1974 – August 1977
Al White	August 1977 – June 1980
Charles McCage	June 1980 – May 1982

Gainesville Independent Branch, continued

Ken Fette	May 1982 – March 1987
Pete Paulsen	March 1987 – April 1988
Jim McCage	April 1988 – February 1993
Max Chartrand	February 1993 – March 1995

Gainesville Ward

(Created 3/26/95)

Max Chartrand	March 1995 – July 1997
Morgan Lybbert	July 1997 – June 2003
Roger Adams	June 2003 –

Appendix 4
Stakes Having Jurisdiction Over Denton

Stake	Stake Presidents
Dallas Stake (Created 10/19/53)	Ervin Atkerson
Ft. Worth Stake (Created 9/24/67)	John Kelley Horace Leithead
Ft. Worth North Stake (Created 11/14/76)	Richard W. Ragsdale
Lewisville Stake (Created 4/12/81)	Richard Ragsdale Gordon Watts
Denton Stake (Created 5/03/92)	James Martino Vaughn Andrus Steve Peterson

Appendix 5
LDS Faculty Members at UNT and TWU

Art Cooper	UNT	Education	1966
Jim Richards	UNT	Art	1968
Vic Nielsen	UNT	Political Science	1971
Newell Kay Brown	UNT	Music	1971
Ell Sorensen	UNT	Dean of Students	1972
Don Williams	UNT	Business	1975
Al White	TWU	Communications	1975
Ben Patton	TWU	Art	1976
Jon Young	UNT	Education	1977
John Child	UNT	Religion	1979
Larry West	TWU	Drama	1980
Steve Harlos	UNT	Music	1983
Tom Richards	UNT	Business	1983
Margaret Dixon	UNT	Education	1988
Paul Fisher	UNT	Computer Science	1992
John Hubbard	TWU	Physical Therapy	1999
Brian Bowman	UNT	Music	2000
Nate Cottle	UNT	Education	2004
Angela Nievar	UNT	Education	2005

Appendix 6
Resources for this History

Persons Consulted

Ann Andrus
Vaughn Andrus
Joe Arrington
Kenneth Arrington
Jo Ann Baria
Bill Barnett
Linda Barnett
Leah Beedle
Ray Beedle
Ellen Swanson Bently
Bill Biggs
Kay Brown
Kaye Calabrese
Linda Carlson
Tom Carlson
John Child
Betty Cochran
Art Cooper
Barbara Crandall
DeLynn Decker
Darlene Denton
Patricia Diers
Bill Elieson
Dave Elieson
Ken Fette
Janice Fraim
Lucile Guess

Bob Hall
Norma Harper
Gail Head
Georgia Head
Holly Hervey
Dawn Letson
Margie Swanson Lyman
Jan Martin
David Martino
Frank Martino
Jim Martino
Rick Martino
Trey Martino
Jim Matheson
Billy Joe May
Charles Mayfield
Russell Morgan
Willie Jean Morgan
Joyce Murphy
Susan Myatt
Marlene Nielsen
Vic Nielsen
Bob Nobles
Jimmie Lou Nobles
Brad Ough
Myrtle Pate

Mabel Pennington
Steve Petersen
John R. Porter
Margaret Porter
Susan Porter
Gordon Pyper
Dick Ragsdale
Pat Ragsdale
Maureen Richards
Ell Sorensen
David Steiner
Mary Steiner
Scott Steiner
Suzanne Stewart
Carl Stocker
Doyle Thompson
Joyce Thompson
Doug Turner
Don R. Van Dever
David Welch
Sue Welch
Al White
Dayonne Work
Pete Work
Dick Yates
Pearl Yates

Church Historical and Genealogical Department

Books

Jed Arthur Cooper, *Panguitch Professor* (Freeman South Dakota: Pine Hill Press, Inc., 1990)

Brenton G. Yorgason, *Seamless Lives: The Frank & Betty Martino Story* (Provo: Lighthouse Publishers, 2004).

Margaret G. Porter, *Denton Ward Reunion: 1959-1979*
(Privately printed, 1979).

Margaret G. Porter, *Historical Notes of The Church of Jesus Christ
of Latter-day Saints in Denton, Texas: 1959-1989*
(Privately printed, 1989).

Ivan L. Hobson, *Dallas Texas Temple: An Early History*
(Privately printed, 1991).

Scrapbooks compiled by Sanfred and Virginia Elieson.

Scrapbooks of Local Church History compiled by
Betty Duncan.

Personal Testimonies compiled for the Twentieth Anniversary
Reunion of the Church in Denton.

Scrapbook of Gainesville Church History compiled by Darlene
Denton.

Index

W

Warner, Lars A. 61, 64
Warner, Mark 221, 236
Warner, Mrs. (Sister) 61
Watts, Gordon
122, 165, 168, 209, 211, 212, 213, 216,
236, 300, 313
Wawro, Bill 256
Welch, David 273
Welch, David and Sue
263, 265, 268, 270, 315
West, Larry 314
Wheeler, Terrill 263, 264
Wheeler, Wilma 263
White, Al
127, 164, 191, 291, 293, 294, 295, 296,
310, 311, 314, 315
White, Al and Susanne 292
White, Alfred H. III 291
White, Alfred Jr. 191
White, Becky 292
White, Chip 292
White, Denise 292, 297
White, Mary 292
White, Patricia 292
White, Susanne 292, 297
Whiting, Ronald 307
Wickman, Lance B. 235
Wilhite, Carol
29, 39, 46, 47, 96, 307
Williams, Don 314
Williams, Don and Mary 160
Williams, Richard S. 181
Williamson, Bill 147, 148
Williamson, Lynne 102
Wilson (family) 259
Wilson, Clara 48, 101
Wilson, Hoyt
48, 51, 52, 73, 90, 101, 120, 156
Wilson, Hoyt and
Clara 39, 50, 51

Wirthlin, Joseph B. 271
Work, Adrian 102, 179
Work, Dayonne
87, 143, 145, 158
Work, Pete 87, 145, 158
Work, Pete and Dayonne
145, 315
Wright, Ernest D. 61
Wright, Patricia Ann 281
Wright, Thomas 73, 311
Wright, Thomas and Pat 283
Wright, Thomas Lee 281, 282
Wright, Tony 93, 171, 296

Y

Yates, Dick 127
Yates, Dick and Pearl 149, 315
Yates, Pearl 52, 149, 150
Young, Jon 314